Never Trust a Sneaky Pony

Never Trust
a Sneaky Pony

And Other Things
They Didn't Teach Me in Vet School

MADISON SEAMANS MS DVM

Illustrations by
MADISON SEAMANS MS DVM

TRAFALGAR SQUARE
North Pomfret, Vermont

This paperback edition first published in 2022 by

Trafalgar Square Books
North Pomfret, Vermont 05053

A prior edition was published by the author under limited release.

Disclaimer of Liability
This book is not to be used in place of veterinary care and expertise. The author and publisher shall have neither liability nor responsibility to any person or entity with respect to any loss or damage caused or alleged to be caused directly or indirectly by the information contained in this book. While the book is as accurate as the author can make it, there may be errors, omissions, and inaccuracies.

Trafalgar Square Books encourages the use of approved safety helmets in all equestrian sports and activities.

Library of Congress Cataloging-in-Publication Data
Names: Seamans, Madison, author, illustrator.
Title: Never trust a sneaky pony : and other things they didn't teach me in
    vet school / Madison Seamans, MS, DVM.
Description: North Pomfret, Vermont : Trafalgar Square Books, 2022. |
    Summary: "Veterinarian, lecturer, radio personality, and
    Idahoan-by-way-of-Texas (and other places) Dr. Madison Seamans shares a
    wonderful collection of stories from over 30 years in an equine
    veterinary practice and a lifetime of working with horses and their
    ever-surprising barnmates. Through ready humor and with a keen eye for
    calling out the particular peculiarities of horse people and horses
    alike, Dr. Seamans aims to teach readers how to be with and care for
    horses, promoting the health and happiness of all with lessons laced in
    laughter. Entertaining and educational by turns, this unique memoir is
    for anyone who loves animals (and some who just don't know it yet)"--
    Provided by publisher.
Identifiers: LCCN 2022011176 (print) | LCCN 2022011177 (ebook) | ISBN
    9781646010417 (paperback) | ISBN 9781646010424 (epub)
Subjects: LCSH: Seamans, Madison. | Veterinarians--Southwestern
    States--Anecdotes. | Veterinary medicine--Southwestern
    States--Anecdotes. | Horses--Physiology--Anecdotes. |
    Horses--Southwestern States--Anecdotes.
Classification: LCC SF613.S38 A3 2022 (print) | LCC SF613.S38 (ebook) |
    DDC 636.089092 [B]--dc23/eng/20220322
LC record available at https://lccn.loc.gov/2022011176
LC ebook record available at https://lccn.loc.gov/2022011177

Illustrations by *Madison Seamans*
Interior design by *Katarzyna Misiukanis–Celińska (https://misiukanis-artstudio.com)*
Cover design by *RM Didier*
Typeface *Utopia Std*

Printed in the United States of America

10 9 8 7 6 5 4 3 2 1

This book is dedicated to my fellow crazed horse fanatics. We share a common passion, for reasons non-horse people can never comprehend, to spend our lives in the company of horses. I am thankful for these folks because, as much as I love a horse, I have never had one call me on the phone.

CONTENTS

① CHAPTER 1: Vet School   1

College for most people is about four years. While most veterinarians finish the entire curriculum in about eight years, I artfully squeezed mine into twelve. I wanted to specialize, so I took a little extra. The truth is they can't teach you how to be a veterinarian in just eight years. All they can do in that short amount of time is teach you how to pass the board exams so you can be real dangerous for about twenty years trying to learn how to be a veterinarian. Mom always told me I was special. That's why it took me twelve— twelve of the most difficult, challenging, maddening, delightful years of my life. I'd do it all over again in a heartbeat. This chapter will give you a taste of why.

② CHAPTER 2: Horse Feet   19

The most common orthopedic problems in horses start with feet. This chapter outlines a typical day in vet practice, along with the symptoms of hoof disease, the process of diagnosis and treatment, and the outcome of our efforts. Most of the stories I've included end with interesting twists that are the nature of equine specialty practice and the crazy people involved with horses—and the reason I wrote this all down. You can't make this stuff up!

CHAPTER 3: Foals   **63**

3

One of the most endearing aspects of working with horses is babies (aka "foals") This chapter is part medicine, part physiology/pathology, and some just plain fun stories about neonates.

CHAPTER 4: Colic   **89**

4

An acute abdominal crisis (aka "colic") is the most common cause of death in horses and is the source of much wailing and gnashing of teeth among horse people. There is a large body of misinformation about this painful, potentially fatal malady. Here I try to dispel some of the myths about equine colic and relate some interesting anecdotes that prove to be more common than you'd think.

Neurology, the study of the nervous system, is as fascinating as it is complicated. Most diseases of the equine nervous system share common symptoms, so it is not usually possible to make a quick diagnosis simply on presentation. The pages ahead give an overview of common equine neurologic diseases, as well as their diagnosis, treatment, and prevention, and what happens when things go wrong. (One of these diseases is transmissible from the horse to human!)

CHAPTER 6: Boys and Girls Will Get Together   187

⑥

Mammalian reproduction is a miracle that nobody really understands. Inject semen in the shoulder of a mare and you get a nasty abscess. Put the same sample in her uterus and you get a foal...with a little luck and three hundred and forty-five days, or so. The pages ahead address the reason we call castration "brain surgery," what happens when it goes wrong, and why it's always a good idea to wait a while before you make rash decisions.

7

The "C word" is terrible in general, but thankfully, serious cancer is not common in horses. Most of this type of disease involves skin, and some of 'em, while not fatal, can be a real challenge to manage. Here I discuss the cause and treatment of some common neoplasia, and one real uncommon one.

8

I kinda got a late start in horses—I did not develop a true love for 'em until I was about seven years old. But I can't really separate my private life on my horses from my professional life under (or in) those of my clients. This is a group of stories that didn't fit anywhere else, but I find so intriguing that they should be included. They illustrate how horses have become an integral part of my life: how I treat them, handle them, and relate to the folks that love them…some of them better than others.

The term "horse trader" conjures up characters that are often associated with some of God's less-than-noble children. While most people are basically honest, some horse traders are a little bipolar in the integrity department. And, amazingly, some buyers sorta fall into the mindset: "A lie is not a lie if the truth is not expected." So "buyer beware" applies to the purchase of just about anything with four feet—especially horses.

FOREWORD

by Michael Sheffield DVM

Madison Seamans is a remarkable veterinarian, horseman, artist, philosopher, poet, writer, musician, friend, and teacher. This book is a compilation of life experiences, cases, patients, acquaintances, and events recounted in a way that invites the reader into one of our vet school study sessions—a description of the presentation, a close evaluation of the situation, and then a clear, concise, no-frills discussion of what is really going on in the horse and how it needs to be addressed, all in a matter-of-fact delivery, often humorous, sometimes painful, but always touching. Reading this book gave me a rich feeling of good fortune—I am fortunate that Dr. Seamans is my friend, and how fortunate are those horses who have had him as their doctor and advocate.

"I bet you're a 'dogger'!" These were the first words spoken to me by my future friend Dr. Seamans. I was sitting on the tailgate of a pickup at a vet school "Howdy Party" in College Station, Texas, at the end of our first week of school in late August of 1981. It was hot out there, but not as sweltering as it was inside the dance hall, so some of us had stepped out for some air. I looked over at the seemingly friendly, smiling, glinty-eyed individual with a bushy mustache and cowboy hat sharing the tailgate with me and wondered, *What brought that up?* I replied that although I had indeed been on the slobbery end of a few bull-calves-soon-to-be-steers, I had, in fact, never been a bulldogger (where it is required that one launches himself from a running horse onto a running steer). "Oh, well, I thought maybe you were, you just kinda looked like you had," was his reply, and at the time I wasn't entirely sure whether or not that was a compliment. I suppose physical appearances (I had played college football at a small University in South Texas) can lead to some assumptions.

Our professional curriculum had just begun on Monday of that first week of a four-year odyssey, and none of the one hundred thirty-five of us really knew each other yet, hence the official reason for the party. There were several acquaintances made all week during the short ten-minute breaks between classes, but not really enough time to get to know one's classmates. But it's amazing what several years of elbow-to-elbow time can do for collegiality.

Veterinary school started out with heavy emphasis on didactic lectures, books, and labs, our only contact with animals limited to color plates and diagrams in the texts. Lots and lots of classroom hours followed by many more hours of studying, poring over text and notes. Soon the information all seemed to run together and I found it hard to get my head around some of the concepts, but if I could talk them out, it seemed to make better sense to me.

I found that the most effective study pattern for me was in small groups, where three or four of us would get together at the end of the day, sitting around in a loose circle on dilapidated couches or wobbly chairs in someone's swanky student hovel or surrounded by the glamour that was married student housing, poring over the volumes of notes and textbooks. The usual group included me, Madison, Ed Hager, and Eddie Heath, but many others were in and out of the scene as well. As the bottomless percolator simmered on the stove, we would sit, engrossed in our studies, someone would throw out: "So, how does this..." and each of us in turn would throw in our two cents worth of how we understood something to work. And the remarkable thing was, hearing a concept filtered through several different perspectives was actually the cement that solidified the understanding, and it frequently came down to simplifying the overwhelming. This was where Madison really shone, taking the point at hand and recalling some aspect of anatomy or physiology or pharmacology and explaining how it had created a basis, and how *that* would lead to the next level of understanding.

In this way we developed a continuous thread of steps that led to the solution, such as how a case of colic could end up as laminitis. The enthusiasm to not only answer the question at hand but to make sure there is true understanding of the answer is what makes Madison such a superb teacher.

We would take study breaks occasionally, just to step outside and get some fresh air, and most of the time they involved throwing a lasso at a wobbly saw-horse with stubby two by fours nailed on to imitate makeshift horns. Madison was pretty good at throwing a rope, somewhat due to the fact that he had some previous experience working with rank horses, but mostly because the sawhorse wasn't moving too fast. (This was where I honed the not-so-impressive roping skills that I still use to this day.)

Our 1985 graduating class worked incredibly hard over those four years, but we balanced it with enthusiastic recreation as well. It wasn't all study all the time—there were a number of epic class parties celebrating the end of a rugged series of exams or maybe the end of a term, and more-often-than-not several members of the faculty would grace us with their presence, and then we would get to see how well *they* could throw a lasso! These events almost always sprung up in some patch of woods or someone's pasture, a bonfire would be lit and a keg or two of Shiner Bock beer would show up, and at some point there were remarks about the lack of "facilities." Portapotties were expensive, and besides, we had no money left after BBQ, so Eddie and I built a two-seater outhouse that could be moved around from venue to venue. It fit into the back of a pickup, and many times it made its way down Texas Avenue or University Drive on the way to the next gala.

Madison had an old flatbed pickup that he used for a firewood business he ran on the side, and I vividly remember Madison, Hager, and I prepping for the weekend shindig, delivering the outhouse, starting and tending the cooking fire all Thursday night, and all three of us sitting in the cab of that pickup with the heater blowing as the sun came up on Friday, studying for a poultry medicine exam scheduled for later that morning. All made a passing grade! Hager didn't seem to mind hanging out in the cab of that warm pickup. We were nearing the end of our four years and he had funds enough to only get through about three and a half, so he had taken to living in his VW van, parking it in a different spot in the vet school parking lot every night to avoid the campus police, and showering in the locker room at school.

After we graduated and were granted our licenses to practice, everybody went their separate ways, but Madison and I crossed paths again when we ended up working together for a short time at the same clinic in the upper Rio Grande Valley near the southern tip of Texas, on the border with Mexico. This was a unique experience, as it was a true frontier, with the rest of the United States several hours north of us, separated by vast miles of grapefruit orchards and ranchland, including the King Ranch and their famous Santa Gertrudis breed of cattle. At this practice, we saw and treated almost anything that moved—from dogs and cats to horses and cattle, and even some fairly exotic animals.

Sometimes being isolated causes folks to feel like they don't have to really worry about anybody watching what they do. Madison was called out to see some sick cows. When he showed up at the farm, he saw they were a fairly uncommon breed, known as Pinzgauers, which have a very distinct coloration, a burnished red body with a white rump and tail. After some close scrutiny, examinations, a look around the property, and discussion with the owner, Madison felt that the cause of the problem with the Pinzgauers was not something infectious that could be easily treated, but was in fact due to poor management and exposure to unhealthy substances, and management changes would have to be implemented to avoid future problems. Unfortunately, this particular group of animals he had been called out to see was beyond help and had a very poor prognosis for return to health. The owner of the animals was not overly enthusiastic with either the news or the solution and told Madison that he didn't need any more of his "help." (This is one of the difficulties of being a veterinarian—owners who are not open to hearing the facts.) Madison, as always, handled the situation with kindness and diplomacy.

Not long afterward, for a variety of reasons, our lives again took divergent paths. I moved on to a practice near Dallas, and then started a mixed animal practice in the Texas Hill Country between Austin and San Antonio. Madison headed west, first to a practice in New Mexico, later to California. During one of his first calls in California, he went to see a group of ill cows and was told they had recently been purchased and had never really looked all that healthy to begin with. When Madison rolled up to the farm, there were the cows, all bunched up in a corral being sick, and he couldn't help but notice they were a unique looking bunch of Pinzgauers. The new owners were really impressed when Madison asked them if they had been purchased from the Valley. Now they faced dealing with a charlatan whom had sold them a bill of goods.

While in California, Madison became a teaching resident in equine reproduction at UC Davis Veterinary School. He was then invited to deliver a scientific paper at an international equine conference in France. He later left UC Davis to start a private equine practice and became a lecturer at a local college for the students of veterinary technology. He continued in private practice in California and Idaho concentrating on horses, but, as he says, he is willing to also work on donkeys and the occasional goat.

Throughout my professional career, I have called Madison countless times to discuss a tough case and get his opinion. It is such a relief to have some other head to scratch rather than your own. His perception of problems and thoughtful insight—and willingness to answer the phone—have been so helpful to me. We have kept each other company via phone on long road trips on the way to or coming home from a case, talking it out as the miles roll by. Many of my years in practice have been solo, which makes it tough when you need to consider a case as we did in vet school. Knowing he is there for support has been a lifesaver, literally. That one little thing that I may have overlooked was gently brought back to my awareness by Madison on more than one occasion. Every time I talk to him on the phone is like a throwback to those vet-school study-group sessions. I can't count the numerous cases we have discussed, nor can I relate how grateful I am for his companionship, both professionally and personally. I hope you, too, enjoy the pleasure of getting to know Dr. Seamans through the adventures in this book.

Michael Sheffield DVM
Wimberley, Texas

PREFACE

God has blessed me in so many ways, but I think that His gift of horses has to be the best part of life this side of heaven. I have been looking at the world framed in a set of horse ears since 1958. A guy with a pony and a camera came up our street offering "free" pony rides for little kids and "not free" photographs of them for their moms. Of course, this was a big hit with the kids who cared a lot more about the pony than the picture. Apparently, my mom saw the value of both, as I still have the evidence of that day, forever captured in a chemical, and the thrill I got from being near that pony has not faded in almost sixty years.

Medical professionals have two names: *physician* and *doctor*. Both of these words have ancient Latin origins. A *physician* is literally a "giver of laxatives," where a *doctor* is actually a teacher. I have done both, but I prefer teaching—it has a more lasting effect and does not require any protective clothing while I am doing it.

It has always been easier for me to teach a horse to side-pass by opening a gate while I am in the saddle. In this way, the action means something to the horse. Similarly, I find it easier to learn things when there is a story attached to the concept. During the course of my veterinary practice over the last thirty years, I have collected a few stories that graphically illustrate the cause, diagnosis, and treatment of common diseases found in the horse. And so, teaching by anecdote is what I hope to achieve in this book.

That said, it should be mentioned that the medicine and surgical procedures cited in these pages was—emphasis on WAS—once considered the "standard of practice." This means it may not have been the right thing to do, but most everybody thought it was at the time. Some of this stuff is still valid, while some has gone the way of black-and-white televisions and full-service gas stations. For example, we no longer think it's possible to turn lead into gold, there's no such thing as a "temporary tax," and stuff on the internet is not always real. Some medical advances over the recent twenty years or so have dramatically changed the way we practice equine medicine. SO...don't hold me responsible if you try something you read here as being a "good idea" and it turns into a train wreck. Oh, you'll know. (Call your vet first—let your vet share the blame.)

In some cases the actual names of the players involved have been used. However, if the story involves something the character would later regret (a kind way of saying they did something really stupid), pseudonyms have been assigned. You'll probably be able to figure out who they are, though, without much difficulty.

Madison Seamans MS DVM
Capitan, New Mexico

'Sarah'

~Madison Simmons MSBFA 2007

Vet School

College for most people is about four years.
While most veterinarians finish the entire curriculum
in about eight years, I artfully squeezed mine into twelve.
I wanted to specialize, so I took a little extra. The truth is they
can't teach you how to be a veterinarian in just eight years.
All they can do in that short amount of time is teach you how
to pass the board exams so you can be real dangerous for
about twenty years trying to learn how to be a veterinarian.
Mom always told me I was special. That's why it took
me twelve—twelve of the most difficult, challenging,
maddening, delightful years of my life. I'd do it all over again
in a heartbeat. This chapter will give you a taste of why.

CHAPTER
1

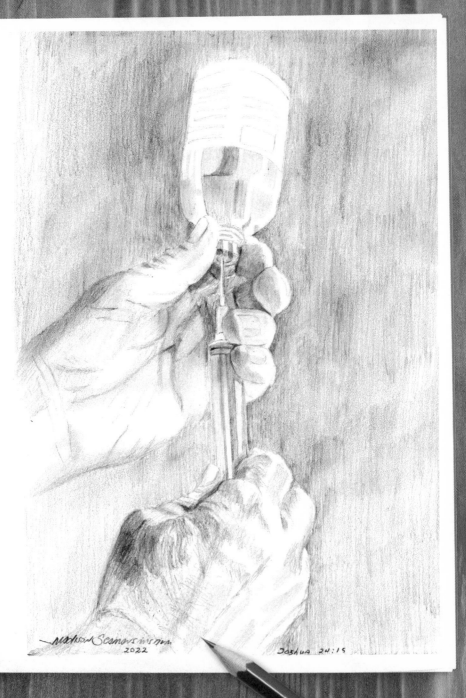

Madison Seamons
2022

Joshua 24:15

_ The First Day

Summer in College Station, Texas, is hot and humid, and the mosquitoes are about the size of small chickens and more like flying piranhas than insects. September doesn't bring much difference, but at least there's football. (That doesn't improve the climate any, but it holds the promise that cooler fall weather is near.) So, wearing a stiff new shirt *and a tie* under an equally stiff new white smock was not the most comfortable attire on that muggy September morning in 1981. But it *was* the first day of vet school, so some compromise was in order.

Room 5 was a large classroom with a stadium-like atmosphere, seating about two hundred. The lower doors opened directly to the parking lot, which was the site of many first introductions among my classmates. The first day was...a bit strained. The atmosphere was a complicated mixture of camaraderie and competition, confidence and complete panic—like the car-chasing dog that finally does catch one: *Now what*? It was tougher than you'd think. We had two or three of our fellow students drop out during the first year, and one at the end of the third. Later though, most of the faculty and staff would admit that our group was special. The class of 1985 had an intangible "something" that set us apart from others. We were close. We were friendly. We were a team. The four years we spent together forged friendships and a few marriages that would last a lifetime (and some that didn't). I remember the first day, not because of some inspiring professorial oration about the joy of academic achievements and saving lives, but because of a motorcycle—or rather, because of the guy riding it.

Several of us were standing in the parking lot outside Room 5, stiff from the combination of new shirts and attitudes that bordered on smug. (There was a dress code at A&M then, ties for boys and dresses for girls. Students who failed to comply would be excused from class.) Into this rather rigid scene, a most implausible member was about to loosen things up a bit. His first name was one of those that the bearer doesn't like so goes by a middle name. In this case, he wanted to be called "Eddie." The mere mention of his first name? Well, nobody did that more than just the one time.

So as we stood outside Room 5 in our acceptable apparel, waiting with guarded anxiety for the eight o'clock bell to mark the start of a new adventure, the relative stillness of the morning was broken by the roar of a large Harley "chopper." It was ridden by an equally large, almost mythic character who was to become a most unlikely, though truly loved, leader of our class. The sight of this Conan-the-Barbarian-clone clad in a new white smock, flapping irreverently in the wake of his Harley, tie loosely knotted in a flippant, half-mast style, certainly broke the ice. The giant stepped off his bike with easy grace and introduced himself. He was not cocky or rough, he just grinned and stuck out his hand irresistibly. Eddie would be elected class president not once, but twice. An NFL prospect, he left training camp with the Atlanta Falcons to spend an amazing four years with us at the Texas A&M College of Veterinary Medicine. He was just one of many friends I made during my time there.

Mike was another one.

Mike was another larger-than-life character—all six foot six inches of him. There's more fat on an oak tree than there was on him. Like Eddie, he played football and was on a national championship team. However, he wasn't just muscle, bone, and hide—he was, and still is, brilliant. He was generous and kind and did a lot of things for our class that further endeared him to us.

One such event required the use of a Santa Claus costume.

Many of our classmates had small children. The rigors of study for finals conflicted with a trip to the mall to see Santa, which many of the kids looked forward to each year. By the midway point through our first year, our class had grown pretty close. Since study took up so much time, our scholastic and personal lives had become somewhat intermingled. Mike, being naturally gregarious and about half-kid himself, knew most of the children of our classmates. He thought it would be fun to dress up and play Santa for an evening.

Room 5 was close to the library, where many of us were spending our "spare time" in the evenings, so it was a logical place for "Mikey Claus" to hold court. The scene was completed by two of our classmates attired in some fetching green elf costumes.

Among his first customers that night was a six-year-old boy named Nells. Mike had spent some time with this little guy, but the red suit and large fake beard had successfully camouflaged him as the legendary figure.

Mike opened the conversation: "You look like you have grown a lot since I saw you last year, but aren't you Nells?"

This got the boy's attention.

"How's your new baby sister? Did you like the black jet airplane I brought you last year? How did it hold up?"

This carried Nells way beyond attention, approaching stunned.

And then, "Have you been a good boy this year?"

A resounding "Yes!" was half-choked off and a more reserved "Mostly..." ended the sentence because, at this point, young Nells could see that any dancing around the truth was not gonna fly.

On the way home, Nells' parents asked about his experience with the Jolly Old Elf. When quizzed about how Santa knew all those things about him, the boy replied, "Dad, Santa knows *everything*!"

Most of my teachers in vet school were very good, and a few were simply outstanding. One I still remember as exceptional, although not in a positive sense. He had a DVM and *two* PhDs. From a book-knowledge standpoint, he was brilliant, and he really wanted to be a good instructor, but he never actually practiced veterinary medicine for a single day.

This teacher's philosophy was that *things are not always as they seem*. He wanted his students to learn to cut through the confusing, sometimes distracting details of diagnostic challenges. This was ironic, since, as mentioned, he never practiced, he never *had* a diagnostic challenge, and the courses he taught were basic, not "clinical."

This fellow's approach to teaching was in the use of word problems. The real challenge to these word problems could be found in the details. It was the ability to discern the relevant from nonrelevant details that would make us great diagnosticians—or so he thought. This puzzle included spelling. For example, he would give us a true/false question regarding the importance of the "jugu<u>er</u>" vein. Since there is no "juguler" vein, only a "jugu<u>ar</u>" vein, any part of the question, however you answered it, would be false. Multiple choice questions were formulated the same way. If one of the choices had a misspelled word, even an adjective, it was disqualified—or maybe not, depending upon the level of double negatives. The same "logic" was employed in relation to questions concerning the potential complications of surgical repair of the "equine gall bladder." Since a horse does not have a gall bladder, there are no surgeries for the structure.

This process of examination was completely baffling. After a few such questions, I could see many potential answers—depending on spelling and punctuation.

Midway through the semester, I was in serious danger of failing this professor's class. I knew the material; I just couldn't beat my way through his #$%&*! exams. I went to him for some help, but he was about as helpful as his exams were. The prospect of failing his course was unsettling; the thought of having to suffer through another year with him was unpleasant. In those days at Texas

A&M University, if you failed one course, you had to repeat the *entire year*! Since this course was only offered in the spring, a failing grade would land me repeating the whole year, starting the next fall.

The day of the final exam found me in near panic. I had done the math, and I needed to score sixty-five percent to pass the course and move on to the next year with my class. The exam consisted of fifty multiple choice questions, each with five parts. This basically came down to two hundred and fifty true/false questions due to the added complications inherent in the spelling. And it only got better: On the chalkboard at the head of Room 5, our teacher had listed seventeen typographical errors his secretary made before the exam was printed. These needed to be corrected before we started the two-hour exam!

The scores were posted later that afternoon. As I walked away from learning how I did, the professor saw me in the hall.

"Well, are you happy? I saw you earned a passing grade," he said with what appeared to be genuine concern.

I usually try to be polite, but with this gentleman, I just couldn't help myself.

"No, I'm pretty upset," I replied.

"Why? You passed, didn't you?"

"Yeah, but I scored a sixty-seven. All I needed was a sixty-five, so I figure I wasted time somewhere!"

_ **Smokeless Tobacco**

Everybody knows tobacco is bad for your health. There was a time, however, when chewing it was considered just about harmless. The fact that it could be used indoors added to its appeal, and thus it was the drug of choice for diehard smokers who couldn't wait between classes for their fix. The "smokeless" tobacco obviously produces no smoke, but it does generate an equally repulsive biproduct: saliva. The pinch of snuff would produce gallons of dark, smelly, absolutely disgusting tobacco juice. For smokers, a cigarette and a cup of coffee are a pretty good combination, as the caffeine and nicotine must have a synergistic effect. This was a perfect arrangement for chewers because, after their coffee was finished, the cup provided a reservoir for the unsavory salivary biproduct. (As for the caffeine biproducts, there were restrooms right outside Room 5.) The real downside for the non-chewers were the snuff juice cups, frequently left on the floor of the classroom by careless depositors.

I had a classmate we'll call "Mullen." He was a real character then, and he has since become an outstanding veterinarian. To say he thought "out of the box" is not even close—*out of the time zone* would be a better metaphor. For example, in our class yearbook, everyone had a color portrait taken in the same studio so there was some continuity. Mullen, conversely, was forever memorialized in his natural habitat: In black and white, he poses in a sleeveless sweatshirt, cutoff jeans, and sunglasses. The ensemble was completed with essential accessories—a cigarette in one hand and a beer in the other!

Many of us had complained about the spit cups left behind by our less thoughtful classmates, but things never changed. That is until the day somebody accidentally kicked over one of these "juice boxes," spilling its revolting contents all over Mullen's pathology book. That did it, no more Mr. Nice Guy. Mullen wrote out his grievances on a piece of notebook paper and signed his name. Then, like Martin Luther's complaints nailed to the cathedral door, Mullen placed his notation along with a full spit cup *in the middle of the Dean's desk*!

That very afternoon, a notice was posted on just about every bulletin board found in the College of Veterinary Medicine: You could still "chew" in class, you just couldn't spit. I doubt those rules will ever be revoked.

_ The Last Great Snowball Fight in College Station, Texas

Lots of places have been the scene of a great snowball fight, but these events generally occur in locations where there is a lot of snow—but that is not what makes this a story. The fact that the post-oak savannah of south Texas is rarely even lightly dusted with snow, much less enough to make a respectable snowball, is no more than a misplaced note in the weathered song of history. However, when an Iranian protester, three vet students, *and* snow in south Texas come together, well, *that's* a story.

To understand the unique nature of these events, you'd have to go back forty years or more. The site of this drama was in the street in front of one of the more notorious "watering holes" in the region. This bar is more than just a bar—it's an institution. For most of half a century it has been a landmark in College Station, Texas, and has the dubious distinction of being the site of more than one marriage (and I suspect more than one divorce).

The little town of Bryan, Texas, would have remained no more than a wide spot in the road had not the politics of nineteenth century Texas and something called the Land Grant College Act come into existence. Why Bryan, Texas, was chosen as the recipient of the funds to construct such a college instead of more prosperous communities like Dallas, Houston, or San Antonio is an illustration of serious political clout, but the details of such negotiations have long been forgotten. The college—now Texas A&M University—opened its first few doors in 1876, and because of the "agriculture" in "A&M," it was located several miles outside of town, where it would have "room to grow." Later, when prosperity and the railroad came to the region, a train station was built out by the new college. It's no mystery how some Texas towns were named (Plainview is not in the mountains), so the train station out by the college was called the "College Station," and soon everything that was built around it just kept the name. The vet school was built in 1909, and of course it's all a bit more than just a cow college and a train station now—it is a large university with all the houses and retail establishments associated with a medium-sized city.

Anyway, one of these businesses is a bar. It is housed in an old store front that has been on University Avenue since the 1920s, so it wasn't always a bar. In earlier lives it was a dress shop, a hardware store, and a pharmacy. In the early 1970s an enterprising young man rented the old store front and decorated it with ancient barn wood, rusty metal signs, and dry, cracked harness leather. A Plexiglas cage recessed in the wall of one room housed a pet rattlesnake. An aged, wooden barrel filled with saltine crackers sat on the end of the bar, its contents free for all patrons. Even when the washtub of potluck chili went dry for the last time (I suspect some county health officials had something to do with that), the crackers remained. Pool tables and dominoes provided diversion, and music played on an old phonograph. This was the ambience that would become the model for the classic Texas college-town bar: The Dixie Chicken.

"The Chicken" was an instant success and quickly became a popular place for vet students to decompress in the midst of significant academic stress. In fact, we considered it "our bar," as evidenced by the sea of white smocks that would fill its dark, smoky confines on any given afternoon. The vet school had a dress code; The Chicken did not. However, this uniform was sort of a status symbol, as we considered ourselves the academic cream and the pinnacle of collegiate society. We saw no reason to hide the fact from the local townspeople. Our presence in this nonacademic setting became so prevalent that Dr. George Shelton, Dean of the College of Veterinary Medicine at the time, found it necessary to send a letter to all students and faculty reminding us that The Chicken was not an annex of the college, and therefore, the dress code would not be enforced there. In fact, those of us who failed to recognize the boundaries of our campus would be summarily disciplined. I was never sure exactly what "summarily disciplined" would entail, but since my academic status was always a little precarious, I decided not to press that envelope, opting to leave my smock in the truck.

The late seventies was an interesting time in America. We had survived the sixties and were adjusting to the Middle East's significant influence on our economy. The first what at the time I identified as "Middle Easterners" I ever saw were a couple of exchange students, protesting outside the Memorial Students Center on campus. They were upset about somebody called the "Shah of Iran," but I never saw them after that day in 1977—or anybody else bearing the remotest resemblance to them—that is, until December of 1983. The day of the snow.

And this is where The Chicken comes in.

It snowed. A bunch. We had survived finals and three of us were having "breakfast" on the front porch of The Chicken, marveling at the fact that for once in our lives we were in a place where our long-necked, cylindrical "breakfasts" wouldn't get warm. A snowbank was a perfect place to them. We were glad for the break and wondering what kind of job we would be forced to take once our parents got our grades.

I was with my two best friends and study partners: Hagar and Mike (yes, "Mikey Claus," sans the red suit). Hagar, after deciding that his departure from the US Navy would be in their best interest, became a very good student of veterinary medicine. Mike had been over six feet tall since his twelfth birthday, but as imposing as his stature was, I never met a more kind, or more brilliant man. I also never met someone I would rather have next to me in a bar fight—even if it only involved snowballs.

The street in front of The Chicken is paved and fairly wide. Some cities would call it a "boulevard," with curbs and concrete or grass and trees or something else to separate cars going in opposite directions. However, the highway department had learned that cows wouldn't cross stripes painted on the pavement any faster than they would cross a traditional steel "cattle guard." I suppose they thought that "Aggies" (the nickname for students at Texas A&M) weren't any smarter than cows, so instead of a concrete median, they just painted yellow lines with hopes of achieving the same effect at a lower cost.

After a few rounds of breakfast cylinders, the conversation waned a bit, and looking for some other diversion, Hagar chucked the first snowball at a passing car. Due to the novelty and depth of snow on the street, the traffic was light. The folks who braved the weather were driving pretty slowly, as Texas drivers were unaccustomed to such precipitation. With ample ammunition close at hand, Mike and I soon joined in the fun. Although it was like shooting ducks in a horse trough, our breakfast cuisine had diminished some of our eye-hand coordination. Most of our shots went awry and thus unnoticed by the passing motorists.

Strengthened with more "breakfast," our resolve improved, if not our aim. Hagar decided to change our tactical advantage with a clever ruse. He stood in the painted median, which because of the snow cover, was invisible to the drivers. So he bravely assumed that most of the locals would remember the lines and thus keep their cars in the appropriate space. With clever pantomime, Hagar moved his hand and forearm in a circular motion. (This was long before the days of electric windows in anything other than Lincolns or Cadillacs—most folks had to crank car windows up or down. It was no great feat to mimic the motion universally understood to mean "roll down your window.")

Mike and I took the cue. Hagar gave the signal and some of the drivers took the bait, only to be ambushed by two of the most inept snowball hurlers that ever lived. We actually hit a few of the cars, and the drivers would proceed with good humor, sharing the playful spirit of the moment. Occasionally one of us would get lucky and lob one directly through the open window. This was generally met with a startled shriek and a smile or a good-natured cussing—directed at *us* for our assault or at *themselves* for being dumb enough to fall for the trick.

One victim, however, who was just unfortunate enough to be on the icy business end of a rare direct hit, was unhappy. Maybe a little more than un-happy...maybe upset. It was one of the exchange students. I don't know if he had left town or gone underground, as I hadn't seen him for a few years. But his reemergence in Texas society was a memorable occasion.

The fellow demonstrated his displeasure by ignoring some basic laws of physics. He accelerated his car at an alarming rate while turning the steering wheel. Of course, this resulted in his car skidding on the ice in an uncontrolled arc. Although this should have resulted in a crash, it ended in a perfect parallel parking maneuver that would have been the envy of the best Hollywood stunt driver. The second set of physical laws he ignored were those of range, trajectory, and windage. By getting closer to his assailants and leaving the relative safety of his car, he exposed himself to further frosty assault. At close range, our only disadvantage was our dwindling supply of ammunition. As he was being pummeled, he began to curse us in at least two languages, never repeating himself once. In English, he angrily informed us of his intention to return with his friends and teach us a lesson. I didn't understand everything he said, but the *way* he said it transcended any language barrier...we figured it was bad.

By now Hagar was back on the porch where Mike was seated, laughing un-controllably. The exchange student approached Mike, who then stood to his normal height, which looked to be about ten or twelve feet as it was augment-ed by the elevation of his perch in front of The Chicken. You could see wheels turning inside the snowball victim's head. He assessed this David and Goliath tactical dilemma with nary a slingshot or rock in sight. Hagar, never missing an opportunity to help someone make the right decision regardless of the risk of offence said, "Does the name 'General Custer' mean anything to you?"

The formerly fearless, now nearly frozen exchange student got back in his car and drove away, slipping and sliding in front of The Dixie Chicken, not knowing he had been an unwilling combatant in the last great snowball fight in College Station, Texas.

_ Toxic Fire Alarm

When I think back on those times during my "formal" education over thirty years ago now, my memory plays a little trick on me. I don't much remember the "bad stuff"—not that there was that much bad stuff, but the years have tempered the challenges a bit so they seem more like lessons than trials. There were some hard courses—heck, they were *all* hard—but some of them were nearly fatal. Toxicology was one of those.

The course itself started out easy enough. All you had to do was memorize a few nasty chemicals and what they could do to animals. Then you had to memorize a few poisonous plants, and their toxic compounds…and which animals were most likely to ingest them…and where the plants commonly grew…and which organ systems were likely to be altered…clinical symptoms, treatments, reporting agencies….

You get the picture?

During this time, the fire alarm in Room 5 had developed a mind of its own. Sometime between ten and eleven in the morning, it would decide we needed a fire drill and blast its opinion in an incredibly loud voice. This thing was *incredibly* loud and annoying, and I'm pretty sure there were folks in Nebraska that were wondering if the whole state of Texas was on fire. This was a pulsing, claxon sound—*and* there were *two* speakers in Room 5. (Like one wasn't going to be enough!)

This interruption actually brought a welcome break to the tedium of toxicology. Of course, everybody knew there wasn't a fire, so we strolled leisurely out the bottom door that led to the parking lot. There we would relax until the opinionated fire alarm stopped its incessant, useless announcement and we were given the "all clear" from the instructors. It became a regular gig for this particular alarm, but we took it all in stride—until the midterm exam. For some reason, our illustrious instructors decided that if you didn't pass this midterm, you could not complete the second half of the course. This in turn would put you back an entire year. This added just a touch of extra stress to this little quiz.

The exam was handed out precisely at ten in the morning on an unseasonably warm day and we dug in. It was hard to think, even in the relative silence of Room 5. In that environment, you could actually hear people sweat! At a quarter after ten, the alarm added its loud, joyful noise: *clang-clang-clang*! Nobody moved. It was as if there was a secret ballot taken and we voted unanimously that we'd rather burn up than have to come back and do this again. So we sat there. It was almost a test of wills as the alarm continued to scream its rhythmic distraction for twenty-two minutes. *Twenty-two minutes*! Somehow, nobody ran out of the room screaming, and at 10:37 a.m., it finally gave up.

After the vulgar clanging of the alarm, the silence was almost palpable. It was a relief to hear little else but one hundred and forty-three of my best friends sweating again. Those of us who survived agreed that if we could pass that test, we could do anything.

Amazingly, we all passed the test!

_ Prison and the Belligerent Cow

As fun as the first three years of vet school were, they saved the best for last. The "clinical year" was truly amazing. This was where we started to apply the knowledge we had stored up. Our cases around the vet school did have some limitations, as there were residents and graduate students who had seniority and were first in line. But there were still many opportunities to hone our skills and learn new things.

The most fun, I thought, was prison. Yeah, some senior vet students at Texas A&M went to prison.

Some of you might be saying, "Yeah, I figured as much," but it is not like you think.

Thirty years ago, there were still "prison farms" in Texas. A prison farm was a penal facility where prisoners did manual labor related to agriculture. And where there were prison farms, there were also prison farm animals— although the animals weren't being sentenced. Texas A&M School of Veterinary Medicine had some kind of arrangement with the TDC (Texas Department of Corrections) to have students tend to the prison farm animals. This gave the TDC cheap vet care and the students a place to "practice." The school provided an experienced clinician, usually somebody about to retire, and all the equipment of a typical mobile veterinary practice. For two weeks the students were housed just outside the prison gates in trailers and ate with the guards and other prison staff.

At the prison farm in the early eighties, the clinician was Dr. Charley Page. He was great! He had been a food animal practitioner (cattle and hogs) in the Midwest and was finishing out his career teaching us. And teach he did! He was a treasure trove of practical skills and eager to share them with us.

In cows there are a couple of metabolic diseases that can render them unable to stand. One of these problems is called "milk fever." It is a calcium deficiency that occurs just after giving birth. Once the diagnosis is made, this disease is easily corrected by a calcium-rich medication given directly into the vein of the "down cow." There is another disease called "grass tetany." This is due to a magnesium deficiency that can produce the same symptoms but not necessarily after giving birth. Since the problems look similar, most of the intravenous calcium preparations contain magnesium so all bases are covered.

Dr. Page and a truck full of us students drove out to a down cow in a fairly large pasture. I still don't know why we parked so far away—it must have been about a hundred yards and there must have been a good reason. We students gathered up all the stuff we thought we would need to treat this cow and headed across the pasture. Ever the teacher, Dr. Page gave us a "short course" about down cows in the form of half lecture and half questions to get us thinking—which is what all good teachers do. This particular cow was one of those semi-exotic breeds not known for a friendly disposition, so we approached with due caution. We then placed a large bore needle in the very large jugular vein of our patient.

The bottle of medication was just about empty when Dr. Page asked the group if we knew the difference between grass tetany and milk fever. We answered in precise, clinical terms about the finer points of metabolic pathology inherent in both diseases. He agreed with our assessment but had some practical observations to enhance our education.

"Everything you've said is right," he began, "but the grass tetany cows can become pretty belligerent when they start to respond to treat—"

He hadn't finish the word "treatment" when the not-too-friendly cow jumped up and started cleaning house on the local veterinary population. With murder in her eyes and no calf to worry about, she spent a calculating moment trying to decide who to kill first. I guess she finally figured on mounting a general charge and working out the details later. This hesitation gave us the head start we needed, and the first TDC Veterinary Hundred Yard Dash was on! The cow provided a vivid illustration of the old joke about the mad mama bear chasing the boy scouts: *I don't have to outrun her, I just have to outrun you!* The needle was still stuck in her jugular vein and the rubber hose and empty plastic bag that had delivered her medication were flailing like a racehorse jockey's whip. It was amazing how the old girl could go from paralysis to a dead run like a sprint champion.

Fear is a great motivator. I have never before or since been able to summon the athletic abilities I demonstrated that day. One student got to the truck ahead of me. He did not take the time to open the door, he just simply dove through the open window like Superman flying. I went around to the other door, losing track of my competition in the confusion.

The plastic IV set had momentarily distracted the cow, and that's all it took to save Dr. Page that day. He had forty years and forty pounds on the rest of us, but he somehow arrived safely and jumped into the driver's seat. The cow circled like she was half-shark, and you could almost hear the *Jaws* music ominously humming through the not *real* safe confines of the truck.

"Now do we know the *clinical* differences between grass tetany and milk fever?" Dr. Page breathlessly queried.

We did.

_ In a Heartbeat

When I think of my fairly long tenure in college, I cannot think of too much I would have done differently, other than steal something from Charles Dickens: *It was the best of times and the worst of times.* The undergraduate years, those needed to complete the prerequisite courses, were five years of just plain *hard.* They included history, chemistry, physics, and the ever-popular *calculus.* (To this day I still don't understand the need for *calculus.* I have never once, in thirty years of practice, needed to know the area under a curve!)

It took me seven years to get into vet school. Once I heard some guy in a movie say, "In the end, it will be okay, and if it is not okay, then it is not the end." Perseverance is a virtue, but *seven years* is rapidly approaching stupid. I learned a lot during that time. For example, after applying to veterinary college there are only two things that can happen—both of them come in the US Mail. One of them is bad. A skinny letter is a basic, boiler-plate form letter that has all the compassion of an IRS audit. It starts out: "blah, blah, blah, there were many qualified applicants…" and ends, "BUT YOU AIN'T ONE OF THEM!" Or something to that effect. (I have several of them.) The fat letter is the one you're looking for. It is fat because it has the registration packet enclosed. (It took a long time to get mine.)

Eventually, I got accepted. Vet school was unbelievably difficult, but it was also fun—real fun. A normal course load was considered fifteen or sixteen semester hours. Vet school was *twenty-two.* That gave you just enough extra time to eat, but sleep was to be rationed out in small increments. I guess they figured we could sleep after graduation.

I'd do it all again in a heartbeat.

Horse Feet

*The most common orthopedic problems in horses
start with feet. This chapter outlines a typical day
in vet practice, along with the symptoms of hoof disease,
the process of diagnosis and treatment,
and the outcome of our efforts. Most of the stories
I've included end with interesting twists
that are the nature of equine specialty practice
and the crazy people involved with horses—and the reason
I wrote this all down. You can't make this stuff up!*

CHAPTER

2

A lot like work!

Marian Saunders moovin
2014

A Good Vet Could Fix This

I had just settled down for a long winter's night, seeing the last of my patients and tending to my own horses. My wife fed me a good supper and I was ready to call it a day. I looked forward to the short days of the cool season, as we tended to go to bed earlier and sleep longer. But when the phone rang at nine at night, it generally meant the to-bed scenario would be delayed for a while.

"Is this Dr. Seamans?" a female voice queried.

"Yes," I responded. I usually answered the phone the same way, identifying myself first because I often wondered if callers didn't hear me, or if, depending on just how late it was, they were expecting some type of machine instead of a (semi-) live person to actually answer the phone.

"My neighbor's boyfriend has a horse that got badly injured up in the high country, and no other vets will return my calls."

This was not the resounding endorsement most vets want to hear at nine o'clock at night. I often wondered why people didn't

start with: "Thanks for taking my call so late, I have heard you are a good vet"...
or something along those lines.

Setting my pride aside, I said, "Thanks for calling. Who am I talking to and how can I help?"

"This is Cindy," the caller began. "You saw a horse for me a few weeks ago. I have a pet-sitting business here locally, and my friend Bob really needs your help. He's coming off the mountain after a hunting trip and in a bad area for cell phone reception right now. He can bring the horse to your clinic tonight, and he says he'll call me back when he gets in cell range."

I told her I'd be glad to see the horse, so she told me she'd have Bob call me when he got closer. I always appreciated referrals, as word-of-mouth advertising was how my practice had grown over the years. Some people that had been kind enough to refer me had actually come to the clinic with the owners they'd referred, but I'd never had one offer "help" like Cindy did.

Hunting horses.... This is a whole 'nuther class of livestock that can succumb to a whole 'nuther class of injury that I categorize as "hunting horse disease." While many hunters use their horses year-round for other purposes, and most of 'em take real good care of these trusted partners, some hunting horses are basically pasture pets until opening day of "the season" for whatever game their rider is after.

This constitutes a challenge for the horse. He's gonna get freshly shod, loaded into a trailer, hauled a few hours to a higher elevation than he's used to, and ridden a good ways to the hunting camp. This would be fairly rigorous for a horse that works for a living most of the year, but for one who stays parked in the back yard for three hundred and sixty days and then gets asked to pack a hunter and some gear in to the high mountain camp, and (if the hunter is both talented and lucky) one hundred and fifty pounds of elk meat, antlers, and cape back out of the wilderness...well let's just say that is a testimony to the hardiness of the species. And we can be thankful that the adventure usually ends with no major wrecks. However, these expeditions occasionally end with some interesting stories that won't be funny for a few months or years. And sadly, some stories that will never be funny at all.

So I was not terribly surprised to see what awaited me in front of my clinic that cool fall night.

About ten-thirty, I heard Bob's truck and trailer pull into my driveway. I walked back to the clinic to see just what kind of wreck we had. Bob and his girlfriend Gail got out of the truck and unloaded "Sparkle," a nice-looking young mare. Sparkle took one step out of the trailer, and it didn't take long to see something was terribly wrong. Her right hind foot was positioned at a ninety-degree angle from her lower cannon bone. This is bad. It usually means one or more of the bones is broken, or in rare cases, the soft tissue structures called ligaments that hold the joint together are ruptured.

"I was riding her back to camp, and I noticed she was limping a little, but I didn't think too much about it," explained Bob. "She was eating okay and drank from a bucket like she normally does. After supper, I looked over at her and saw something was wrong."

Although a fracture is very bad, there can be a chance that the bones can heal. But vets don't typically just "throw a cast on the 'arm' and keep the horse home from school for a few days." Fixing a break can take fairly extensive surgery, and not all cases respond well. With bone, at least there is a chance for recovery and soundness. But with ligament rupture, there's no bone to heal and reattaching the structures to the bones is just about impossible.

I was telling Bob and Gail this when my phone buzzed in my pocket. As bad news comes in threes, I was wondering what other type of train wreck was gonna brighten my evening.

"Hey Doc, it's Cindy. I've been trying to reach Gail, but she won't answer her phone."

"Well, she's standing right here, you should be able to reach her now," I responded.

"She won't answer, could you just please hand your phone to her? It's real important that I talk to her right now, please."

I handed my phone to Gail. She looked at me with a combination of shock and concern and quickly walked away, almost out of earshot from me and Bob, but I just barely heard something coming through the speaker:

"Don't let him..." and then Gail disappeared around the dark side of the truck and trailer.

I continued to talk with Bob. An X-ray confirmed my suspicion that the fetlock was luxated (out of joint), and the annular ligament as well as the lateral collateral ligament were completely ruptured. These structures resemble an ace bandage, like you'd wrap around your knee or other joint you strained skiing or getting bucked off your horse. They are thick, fibrous, and very tough, so a complete rupture is rare. *Very* rare. I've seen it happen only twice in over thirty-five years of practice.

Although the mare's bones weren't broken, the nature of her injury made recovery highly unlikely. So I gave Bob the bad news and offered treatment options to a referral facility about an hour away. He then agreed that now was the time to do the kind thing for Sparkle.

After I finished the injection that humanely ended the life of the lovely mare, Gail tearfully brought my phone back to me. Suddenly, another truck and trailer came roaring way too fast down my driveway and skidded to a stop. The driver and a large cloud of dust arrived simultaneously beside the recently deceased mare. It was Cindy.

The old adage "if looks could kill" was at work as she stared daggers at me. Then it finally dawned on my little walnut-sized brain the missing piece of the urgent call to Gail on *my* phone a few minutes earlier: *"Don't let him..."* Now I could fill in the blanks: *"... put her to sleep. A good vet could fix this."*

Hmmmm...this ain't something I see every day, I thought.

I have had a few people disagree with my diagnosis and treatment over the years. I've had a very few people more than just a little mad at me about how things ended with a patient. But I never had one come to *my* place, late at night, in an attempt to stop me or an owner from doing the only right thing for a horse.

I was baffled and speechless, and neither one of those things happen very often. I was on the verge of getting a little perturbed, but in a rare moment of both clarity and diplomacy (two more things that rarely happen for me, and never at the same time), I said, "Thanks for coming by to support us tonight.

I know it means a lot to Bob and Gail, and thanks for the referral. This wasn't easy for any of us."

The daggers got dulled. A little. It looked like Cindy was trying to say something, but I guess she wasn't ready for kindness and sympathy, so nothing came out. I finished my clinical report and said good night. We made arrangements for the body to be removed the following morning, and the hunter, his girlfriend, and the speechless pet-sitter friend drove away in the dusty night.

_ "Blocking"

It was late spring and business was picking up as folks were getting their horses out of "cold storage" and gearing up for trail riding, barrel racing, and other warm weather activities. And there was a small group of horses I saw occasionally that were used for racing. Not the type of racing we see on television. No, this type was... a bit less refined.

"Match racing," as it was called, usually involved only two or three horses in somebody's pasture, or occasionally, at a local fairgrounds. (In the West there are still a few old-timey fairgrounds with racetracks that host some races during annual fairs.) The purses were generally pretty small and put up by the owners of the horses, and I suspect there were more than a few side bets. There was little or no regulation of the monetary transactions—or the care of the horses. Although over the years I have seen some really nice horses in this part of my practice, they often have their own set of challenges—mostly manmade.

Many horse people are subject to something I call "Horseman's Mythology." Some respected person told them something the person learned from old Mr. Paterson, who learned it from Dr. Jones, whose granddaddy's step-uncle's sister-in-law's cousin worked for a guy who trained a Kentucky Derby winner. *Bingo!* That "something" is set in stone! *Don't let a sweaty horse drink too much. Don't let him cool off too fast. Don't let a mare pee after she is bred. (She'll evacuate all the semen, you know!)* But nowhere is Horseman's Mythology more pervasive than at the racetrack. It can be Churchill Downs or the Podunk County Fairgrounds; Belmont Park or the flat out in front of the old Raymond General

Store—wherever two or more racetrackers are gathered, science goes to the back of the bus.

So I was ready when Paul unloaded a real fancy two-year-old filly in front of my clinic, hoping I could "fix her" so she could run the next week. He told me he took her to a big vet hospital a few towns over, but, "They don't know what they doin'. That guy said her toes were too long and suggested different shoes, but I *know* that ain't right. He also said she had some problems in her back hock."

I always wondered about the "back hock," just like the "front shoulder." Was this a redundancy, or were there really "front hocks and back shoulders" that I missed in anatomy classes?

Paul's assessment of the clinical expertise of my colleagues sent up a smoke signal right away. Any time a client trashes another vet, trainer, breeder—anyone—I tread cautiously. There's no doubt I will be next. It's just a matter of time. My next move is to try to help the horse without giving the client a bunch of reasons to throw me in the same woodchipper.

This beautiful filly was obviously lame: What I'd rate "Grade 2 of 5" on the right forelimb. This meant I could detect the lameness from the office window. (Grade 1 is barely detectable, Grade 5 is non-weight-bearing—what I call "student lame" because even a vet student knows *something* is wrong!) From watching her move at the trot, it was obvious the horse had pain in the right front. When she stood still, she wouldn't relax the foot, like she didn't want to bear full weight on the limb, trembling a little.

The horse can't tell you where he hurts, so we use something called a "diagnostic nerve block" to try to localize the pain. "Try" being the operative term here, as this ain't exactly easy or precise for a couple of reasons. Firstly, it involves sharp objects injecting anesthetic agents into an area that already hurts. Secondly, the drug moves around a bit. This is the same product the dentist uses in your jaw so procedures can be done with relative comfort. But you have probably noticed that they can't block just one tooth. Within a few minutes of the injection, half your face is numb. The same thing happens with nerve blocks in horses, so this is an inexact science.

When I was in school, we had to memorize regional maps of horses, which outlined the areas served by various sensory nerves. We were taught that we could block equine heels, or even one side of the heel. Apparently, this is not actually possible. Now, in these modern times, we are pretty sure the earth is round and not the center of the universe, and the equine "heel block" is a major misnomer. So, while we can get close to the source of pain, "close" is as good as we can get. Therefore, identifying the cause often spills over into the land of educated guesses.

I tried to explain this to my new client, Paul, but it appeared that I did a better job of telling this to the horse than to him. We got her blocked, so I was pretty sure we had some pain coming from the foot.

Then, he asked, "How long does the block last before a race?"

I paused for a moment, thinking maybe I didn't hear right. My Texan ears have difficulty translating English sometimes.

"After a couple of days, it should be cleared from her system, so she won't test positive for drugs," I finally said. Most racetracks had vets on site to test horses for forbidden substances. The fact that they are needed becomes self-evident, like the warning labels on cans of insecticide: "Don't spray into your eyes!" (Obviously, somebody did that once, so later, probably *after* the company bought the guy a seeing-eye dog and a house in The Hamptons, they hired a bunch of lawyers to help with the disclaimers they had to print on every can going forward.)

"No, I mean what is the best time to block the horse before the race?"

This was a first for me. He wanted me to block her so she wouldn't feel the pain and thus run faster.

"No," I said immediately. "That is not a good idea. Do you want to be on a horse that can't feel her foot at forty miles an hour? It could result in a terrible injury. The pain is there for a reason, and it tells her not to put much pressure on the injured leg. Removing the pain and then running could cause a major wreck. It wouldn't be fair to the jockey *or* the horse."

I thought I explained it fairly well.

I X-rayed the foot but couldn't find much wrong other than the horse's shoes. We must remember that a radiograph, aka "X-ray," is just a shadow of the bone.

(In the old days, this was a shadow cast on a piece of photographic film, but now it's a bit more high tech, using computers and digital imaging processors I can't even begin to understand.) So there can be a lot of soft tissue injuries or bad stuff *inside* bones that cannot show up on radiographs. The absence of lesions visible radiographically does not mean the absence of pathology. It just means we can't see it. Many of these cases need MRI or CT to find the exact nature of the problem. These images are expensive and beyond the reach of many horse people.

This filly's toes really were way too long. She also had the "toe grabs" apparently required on all racehorse shoes and was overdue for a trim and re-shoe by several weeks. I mentioned this to Paul.

"No, Doc. She's gotta have the toe grabs for traction," was his reply. "And the long toe makes the stride longer and she can run faster. You don't work on many racehorses, do you? And, if you can't teach me how to block her before the next race, I'm gonna go someplace else."

Toe grabs have been a part of racetrack mythology for a long time. However, modern, high-speed photography demonstrated the wrongness of this theory a long time ago. The thought was the toe grab—a little piece of steel embedded in the toe of an aluminum or steel shoe—would "grab" the track. Theoretically, this was supposed to increase traction, thus increasing speed. In reality, the foot normally slides after it hits the ground in a "ski-like" motion. Toe grabs may improve traction for the first two or three strides, but once the horse is up to speed, they cause the foot to stop abruptly, sorta sticking in the ground. These things don't increase speed, but they sure increase the risk of injury.

I explained this to Paul's back as he was loading his filly, apparently off to find the "real vet" who could help him win the next race. I don't know for sure what happened, but I'm guessing he's still looking.

_ Delbert, the Cow Shoes, and the King Ranch

One evening I was talking with a friend about the anatomy and function of the equine foot. This fellow had a horse with navicular disease that had failed to respond to several attempts at treatment.

"Nothin' short of a foot transplant is gonna help 'im, Doc," my friend said with a discouraged tone. "How come a horse don't have a split foot like a cow? That way, if he went lame on one side it would only hurt 'im half as much!"

This sounded pretty good to me because I had been frustrated by chronic lameness before. Actually "curing" many such patients is unrealistic. Sometimes the best we can hope for is the ability to manage the problem and keep the horse comfortable enough to do his job. I had thought that it would sure be handy to be able to transplant feet, but I had not thought about the possible advantage that cattle had with split feet to spread the load out over a larger surface area.

The bovine foot is cloven, or split, from the fetlock (ankle) down. Instead of having just one digit, like the horse, the cow has duplicates of all three phalanges, along with the associated tendons and other soft tissue structures. The analogous structures in humans are found in the hand. The fingernail is our hoof. The underlying bone, the third or distal phalanx, is like the horse's coffin bone. The middle knuckle is equivalent to the short pastern bone, and the next one toward the main part of the hand is like the long pastern bone or first phalanx.

The horse stands on his "middle finger" (or "freeway finger" as my friends in town call it). But the cow stands on his "middle" *and* "ring finger." This provides a fairly efficient way to distribute the weight of the cow over a wide surface. I would guess, however, that it is not the best design for sustained speed, seeing as given enough space, even a slow horse can outrun most cows.

Every time I think of the cloven-footed construction of cattle, I think of my Uncle Delbert. Not because he was a brilliant anatomist or gifted bovine surgeon, but because he had a real novel use for a set of bovine feet.

Delbert is a retired chemist, school teacher, and real estate broker, and one-time mayor of a small town in South Texas. It's not that Delbert can't keep a job, it's just that he is a man of many interests (or maybe just a short attention span... nobody in the family is quite sure). Many families have a metaphoric "crazy aunt with three hundred cats." Delbert was ours—without the cats.

To know my favorite uncle, you'd have to go way back. I guess he was a favorite from the time he was born. He was the youngest of four children, thus, "the baby"—a position he used well for most of his life. As a young man, he wasn't really a "bad guy" and he surely believed in rules—he just believed they applied to everybody else, not him. As a teenager, he loved hot-rod cars and had no trouble keeping them full of gas at the expense of the local oil refinery. He apparently had developed a useful, if nefarious, skill of picking locks, and this provided an almost unlimited source of gasoline from a place he called "Midnight Gas." But he loved his kids, his nieces and his nephews—and he loved to hunt deer.

Entertainment in Delbert's part of the world did not include ballet or opera. A big night out in South Texas would involve high school football (which is more like a religion than entertainment) or two-stepping to the local country music band. While these were popular pastimes for most folks, the one thing that could truly get Delbert fired up was deer hunting. For seven weeks every fall for fifty years or more, Delbert, like thousands of other Texans, pursued his one great passion in life: a shot at a big buck.

Most Texans do not own large tracts of land on which to pursue the wily white-tailed deer. Hunting from public roadways, even in a primitive place like Texas, is against the rules (more about "the rules" later). Instead, a hunter may obtain permission to stalk private land by purchasing a legal instrument that has become a mainstay of South Texas agriculture: a hunting lease. Even if the price of cattle drops below profitability, many ranchers manage to remain solvent, though often at the cost of their sanity, by temporarily selling the hunting rights to their land on a seasonal or yearly basis. The ranchers get additional income and an *interesting* combination of alcohol and high-powered rifles. The hunters get many joyful hours in the freezing rain awaiting their chance at a true trophy buck. The delightful humidity of South Texas winters also provides ample time to compose stories about "the one that got away."

The fees for this privilege can be as much as several thousand dollars per person for a season, or even for a single day, depending on the ranch. Regardless of the price of the lease, there are seldom any frills included. The type of hunting lease most Texans can afford do not include fancy lodges with hot tubs and mints on the pillows. No, if you want any shelter on your hunting grounds, you either have to build it or haul it in. I have seen a wide variety of architectural interpretations of the legendary "hunting cabin," ranging from blue-tarp and plywood creations to luxurious motor homes with satellite TV and microwave ovens.

Although the comforts of home may be important to some hunters, to the ever pragmatic Delbert, the location was the key.

A landmark that many folks associate with South Texas is The King Ranch. For many years, it was the largest ranch in the world. It is the home of some famous cattle, pure-blooded horses and perhaps the finest population of white-tailed deer in the Western Hemisphere. While the cattle and horses are raised with careful husbandry, the deer have needed little or no cultivation. They have been well adapted to the brushy, coastal plains of South Texas for thousands of years, and even in the face of competition for grazing land, the deer still flourish.

Over the past hundred and fifty years, The King Ranch has become more than just a large agricultural endeavor. It is an institution. There are generations of people who were born, educated, employed, and buried in what is almost a sovereign state. In 1950s, the only way you could hunt on The King Ranch was to be a governor or somebody equally important. There were no public hunting leases available. In fact, the residents considered outlaw hunters as the thieves that they were and treated them as such. If caught, poachers could expect stiff fines and maybe even a little jail time. Of all the dangerous avocations we Texans enjoy, poaching The King Ranch would be among the most perilous. Like spitting on The Alamo, it is simply not done.

However, Delbert always loved a challenge, and as I mentioned earlier, the concept of rules was often a little fuzzy for him.

In Zapata County, Texas, there was another ranch that *was* available for lease to would-be hunters. This ranch was not ideal in its vegetation, watering holes, or deer population, but it had one attribute that was of interest to Delbert: It bordered The King Ranch.

Delbert saw this as an opportunity to share in the harvest of the bountiful King Ranch deer. Of course, other hunters had similar thoughts, and the owner of the Zapata ranch explicitly warned them against caving to the temptation of bagging one of Captain King's finest. The landowner informed each hunter to expect to see extra fence riders on The King Ranch side that would point out the presence of the property line to hunters who "may not have seen it."

One chilly fall night, shortly after Delbert had arrived at the Zapata ranch, one of The King Ranch vaqueros "haloed the camp" and rode into the amber circle of campfire light. In broken English, he explained to the hunters that he had seen tracks on his side of the fence made by a man wearing tennis shoes. Since none of the vaqueros or their horses wore tennis shoes, he assumed that somebody may have *mistakenly* crossed the fence. The vaquero casually touched the rifle he carried under the fender of his right stirrup—a clear warning to the hunters. Then, like a wisp of wood smoke, he vanished.

Delbert thoughtfully looked at the soles of his almost new sneakers and decided to spend the rest of the weekend on his side of the fence, but still with the resolve to somehow hunt the mighty King Ranch undetected.

Over the next few days, Delbert devised a plan. Since The King Ranch was a cow outfit, the easiest way to move around on their land would be to turn into a cow...*or leave a track like a cow*. He knew the foreman at the local slaughter-house and decided to pay him a visit over his lunch hour. Although the foreman had often been approached for dog bones or a deal on a side of beef, nobody had ever asked him for a whole set of bovine feet.

"What the heck do you want feet for?" the foreman asked.

"Oh, just a little science project for my son, little Delbert Jr." Uncle Delbert was nothing if not quick on his feet.

Soon Delbert was at work in his garage. With some effort, he managed to screw, nail, and glue the cow feet to the bottom of some old soccer shoes. Although they were somewhat bulky to get around in at first, they left a track that looked a bunch more like a cow than that of an out-of-work chemist. With practice, Delbert could walk around in his custom shoes with comfort and a fair degree of stealth.

Armed with an accurate rifle and the cow shoes, Delbert poached the forbidden pastures undetected for almost ten years. He killed many large bucks and was so used to the cow shoes that he doubted he could shoot without them.

(He shot one that could have been a record, and I asked him once why he didn't submit it to the Boone and Crockett Club—the "who's who" of trophy hunters—for documentation. He replied, "I couldn't tell 'em it was off the King Ranch! It wouldn't be ethical.")

Many times Delbert returned to camp carrying a trophy-sized deer, much to the dismay of his less fortunate *compadres.*

"How come you're always so lucky?" they would ask.

"Ain't luck," Delbert would reply smugly.

Every year, the same group of hunters returned to the Zapata ranch determined to out-hunt Delbert, but they never did.

Finally, figuring that his luck at dodging fence riders was bound to run out sooner or later, my uncle decided to retire a successful, anonymous poacher. After "one last hunt," that is. (Just "one last" is the fatal flaw in many a tale.)

Leaving camp long before sunrise, Delbert walked along the road that roughly paralleled the fence for about a mile, slipped on the cow shoes, and vanished into the vast, mesquite-thicketed pastures of the legendary King Ranch. He did get a shot at a nice buck later that morning, but his aim was off, the bullet fell harmlessly in the brush, and the deer escaped with a good story to tell his friends about the silly man with a bad aim and feet like a cow. Although he hated to quit, Delbert decided to head back over the fence, hoping that the shot had not attracted the attention of one of the fence riders.

As he carefully rounded a clump of brush, Delbert almost ran under a half-wild mustang and an equally wild vaquero astride him. It's hard to say who was more surprised. There was no escape. With the extra appendages attached to his feet, Delbert knew he couldn't outrun a slow horse, much less the range-bred, cat-like brute that stood on the trail before him.

The vaquero looked at the character clad in army surplus camo fatigues and flaps-over-the-ears Elmer Fudd cap, carrying a Bowie knife and a sporterized "06" rifle and knew the answer before he asked the question, *"Que paso?"*

As he continued to size up Delbert, his gaze fell upon the bovine-hoof-adorned soccer shoes worn by the now very pale gringo poacher. The vaquero asked to see one of the shoes. Delbert, thinking that the trade might save his life, instantly removed both of the treasured shoes and handed them over.

At this point, Delbert didn't know what to expect. He knew that some poachers had received harsh treatment from fence riders. He watched as slowly a curious look appeared on the vaquero's face, as if he had just got the answer to a long-hunted question.

Just about the time Delbert thought he was going to get shot, the vaquero burst out in laughter. Delbert swears to this day that the vaquero's laughter was so infectious that even his horse slipped a reserved chuckle.

Once he regained his composure, the vaquero explained that the feet on Delbert's shoes were from a *bull*. The toes of a bull's foot are blunt and broad. The toes of a *steer* (a young neutered male), however, are pointed and more narrow, similar to those of a *cow*. With both hands the vaquero expressively pointed to the ground and said through his laughter that he'd been looking for ten years for the mysterious bull who occasionally appeared in the cow pasture. He was so tickled with the situation, and apparently impressed by Delbert's ingenuity, that he let him go with a stern warning not to return. He even let Delbert keep the shoes, saying nobody would believe him, anyway.

Still shaking, Delbert returned to his camp and, later that day, home. He never went back to the Zapata ranch. I suppose his hunting buddies are still wondering why such a successful hunter up and quit. For almost fifty years, Delbert and the vaquero with a sense of humor were the only ones who knew the secret. Now, you do, too.

_ Dove

One blustery evening during a storm I was called out to a boarding barn to see a big, nice Appaloosa gelding cleverly named "Spot." Ole' Spot had a tendency to remodel various parts of his anatomy, using fence posts, wire, or unknown foreign objects to initiate the process that I got to finish with some fancy stitching. Someone once described a fish net as being just a bunch of little holes tied together. Well, Spot looked like a bunch of horsehide that was stitched together, patchwork-style. Over the years I had installed several miles of suture material to hold it all in place.

As a testament to his good nature, Spot stood quietly, stoic in the high wind and spattering cold rain as I quilted his hide to keep any more Appaloosa from leaking out of him. Right in the middle of the procedure, a young man elbowed his way through the gathered spectators.

"I need you to look at my horse," he said without introduction.

I looked up with instruments in my gloved hands and peered over my rain-spattered glasses. "I'm a little busy right now," I replied.

"Okay, I'll wait."

After I finished the paint-and-body work on Mr. Spot, I gave instructions not to apply any topical medications to the wound and to keep it clean and dry. The word "dry" had not completely escaped my bearded face when the heavens opened and poured all over me and Spot. Though the rain started out clean enough, it got pretty muddy on its way down Spot's body to my nice, clean sutures. (I know, most rainwater is considered sterile, but this *was* in California.)

"Oh, well." I shrugged. "Do what you can."

I paddled over to the barn with the waiting young man to where my next patient was standing in the cross-ties. Just as my new client Harold approached the big, nice-looking warmblood-type mare, she bent almost in half trying to kick the fellow's head over the fence.

After observing the performance, I was a little apprehensive about examining this beast. Harold, noticing my hesitation, said, "Don't worry, she won't hurt you," as if I had not been standing there while the mare tried to widow his wife.

"Yeah," I said as my sense of humor faded with the fatigue of a sixteen-hour day, "I can see she's a real pet! What's her name?"

"Dove."

Some replies are better left unsaid. With unprecedented restraint, I paused pointedly.

"How can I be of assistance tonight?"

"She has an abscess in her left foot and it's making her lame. I need to know how to treat it."

I looked at this mare's front wheels and notice a bowed tendon the size of a small pig.

"Which leg appears to be lame?" I asked.

"The left."

"Do you think that the bow above her right ankle is causing a problem?"

"No, that's an old injury from two months ago. She's all healed up from that. I'm sure that her lameness is from an abscess."

I cautiously picked up her left foot and examined it. Both front feet had a dished appearance to the dorsal, or front, hoof wall that just screamed *FOUND-ER!* This poor mare was so foundered that the diagnosis could be made from the front seat of a pickup truck on the freeway. Unlike the abscesses seen during the legendary California mud season, this mare had them as a sequel to laminitis.

Laminitis, like the suffix "itis" denotes, is an inflammatory disease of the soft tissue that supports and suspends the coffin bone within the hoof. Severe inflammation of this structure can cause it to break down and allow the bone to shift or "rotate" in a condition called "founder." Although many people use the terms interchangeably, laminitis is the disease; founder is a shift of the bone away from the normal position. The shift can pull the hoof wall so that it has a concave, dished appearance. Dove presented a textbook case of this.

Once the laminae have been damaged, the blood flow to this sensitive structure is altered. Among other problems, abscesses are often seen in the aftermath of the acute disease.

I explained this to Harold, Dove's proud owner. However, he was convinced that her foot abscess was only a minor problem. He was also sure that Dove could not be foundered because, in the two months he had known her, she had not been lame until now.

With all the tact of a Mack Truck with a bad muffler I said, "We can treat Dove's laminitis and make her much more comfortable. We should X-ray her feet to determine the position of her coffin bones and also examine the tendon with ultrasound."

Harold must have thought I was talking to the mare because he didn't answer.

Merriam-Webster defines "soliloquy" as "the act of talking as if alone; a literary vehicle used by Shakespeare..." And, I would add, veterinarians. It surely seemed like I was talking to myself!

Finally, after a long silence, Harold mentioned that Dove may be lame in a hind leg, also. "She does limp behind, a little," he said. "I think she may have a bad hip."

He led the mare down the shed row of the barn, and she did, indeed, have a significant short stride in her right rear limb. In addition, as if she didn't have enough problems, she had "disuse atrophy," indicating a chronic lameness. This is commonly called "knocked-down hip" by horsemen. When viewed from behind, a horse with this problem will have one hip that slopes downward to one side so that it is not symmetrical with the top line of the other hip. This *can* mean that there is a primary problem with the muscle, bone, or nerve of the hip. However, it can also be due to a chronic lameness in the lower leg on the same side. Because of the pain, the affected limb is used less and the gluteal (hip) muscles atrophy, or waste away.

By now I was truly amazed that one horse could have so many problems. Dove was a walking laboratory for the study of equine lameness, and she was lucky to be in Harold's company; plenty of folks would have hauled her to the auction. Although I had thus far failed to make any progress in convincing Harold to recognize Dove's problems, I tried to reintroduce the topic of the bowed tendon.

"I'm sure concerned about that tendon," I began.

Silence.

"You know, some folks would think that a bowed tendon was still pretty fresh after only a couple of months. I think it would be a good idea to ultrasound that leg and see how much damage is present. With proper treatment, she might be sound as a broodmare, or even, with luck, some light riding after a year or so."

Silence.

I went on to explain that a tendon has a very delicate structure and healing damaged areas is a slow, tedious process that usually takes up to a year to complete. Even then, the incidence of repeated injury is very high. That is why nursing care and adequate time is so important in these cases.

That woke him up.

"I read about tendonitis in a book. I'm sure I'll be able to ride her in a couple of weeks as soon as her abscess clears up," he said emphatically.

I could see that Harold was in denial, so I stopped talking, which is nearly impossible for me, and started placing poultices on Dove's front feet. I gave further instructions that both feet should be soaked in hot Epsom salts twice daily, but I stopped short of "until she stops limping," which is my usual end to that sentence. I didn't think that either one of them was going to live *that* long.

_ First Call

"Doc, I need for you to come out and see my horse Cody as soon as you can," an unfamiliar voice greeted me early one morning. "He's lying down a lot and when he stands, he seems to be straining his belly muscles," the caller added. The new client, named Sharon, gave me directions to her house, and because the symptoms sounded like a potential colic, I decided to go out right away. I was always glad to, if I could, help a horse.

As I drove through the thick, early morning fog of the California coast, the ghostly haze and damp smell of a new day reminded me of another foggy morning on the Gulf Coast of Texas, some ten years previous. On *that* day, just like the present one, I had been driving to meet another new client with a similar complaint. Of course, in those days, I was a bright, young, and green-as-a-gourd graduate of Texas A&M College of Veterinary Medicine, and *all* my clients were new. I had an almost new Ford pickup, a box of disposable syringes, a veterinary license, and not much else. I was dangerously armed with a vast store of medical knowledge and not short on confidence—a hazard of youth. Somehow, I had managed to pass the veterinary licensing exams and had been unleashed, syringes and ego in hand, upon the unsuspecting horse population of North America—well, Texas, anyway, and that was dangerous enough!

Some of my early forays in veterinary medicine remain vivid in my mind, and this is one of those. During that drive to one of my first cases as a *real horse doctor*, I was confidently considering my treatment plan based upon the brilliant diagnosis I had made from the client's description of the symptoms over the phone. *That* was Mistake Number Two. The first was thinking I knew what was going on.

"He's straining his belly and keeps lying down," my first client had exclaimed. "I think he's got the colic. Can you come out right away?"

"You bet!" I'd said, trying to control my enthusiasm. I wasn't glad that the horse was sick, but I was elated that I was finally going to get to be a veterinarian.

On the drive to the farm, I carefully went over the procedures that I had learned in school regarding the correct diagnosis and treatment of an acute abdominal crisis, or colic, in a horse. Of course, formulating a treatment plan *before* seeing the patient was not exactly the textbook way of doing things, but at that stage of my career, "logical" and "thought processes" were mutually exclusive terms.

I arrived at the residence of my first victim at the appointed time because, number one, I always like to be punctual, and number two, in those days I sure didn't have anything else to do that would have caused me to be late. After a quick exam and some convincing conversation from the owner—also named Sharon, but a different lady, ten years before the one I was seeing now—I began treating "Buster" for colic. I expertly passed a stomach tube and checked for "gastric reflux." Reflux is when you get more water (a lot more) out of the stomach than you put in with the pump. This indicates two things, one good, one...not: you're in the stomach, and there's probably a twist in the small bowel. So *no reflux* is good. Then I pumped a gallon of mineral oil into the horse's stomach and checked for gut sounds. With impressive professional efficiency I administered an intravenous injection of "flunixin meglamine (Banamine®)," an analgesic drug that is good for cases of colic. I fed Buster a carrot, patted his head and left the barn feeling pretty good about myself, my chosen profession, and the future health of much of the equine species in general.

During the drive back home, I began to ponder the treatment I had just expertly administered. Just as backward as I had formulated my therapeutic plan on my way *to* the patient, I was considering my diagnostic plan as I drove *away* from him! Something didn't seem quite right. As I continued to drive, my euphoria faded a bit.

Later that afternoon, I placed a call to Buster's owner to check on the progress of my patient.

"Is this the *alleged* veterinarian that quacked on my horse this mornin'?" I was asked by my first *ex*-client. "Don't bother comin' back out here," she said. "I had another vet'nary out and Buster ain't colicked, he's foundered!"

Whoops. Right about then I was wondering if it wasn't too late to sign up to "earn big bucks and work your own schedule as a professional truck driver" like the ads on late-night television promised. This was the first mistake I had made in veterinary practice, and the fact that it was just about my very first call did little to inflate my confidence. There would be other disappointments, but I remember one of my professors with a unique approach to encouragement told me, "Don't worry, Seamans, no matter what you do, you can't kill 'em all!"

It's amazing how ten years later I was called out to see a horse with a similar presentation. Of course, during the previous decade, I had seen a lot of sick horses, and I knew I probably wouldn't make another mistake like that first one again (there was plenty of new mistakes just waiting for a place to happen). I also thought that, although I would sure like to be ten years younger, I didn't think I could stand to be ten years dumber!

I arrived at present-day Sharon's barn with my usual punctuality. I introduced myself to Sharon and her big, stout, *pleasantly plump* Quarter Horse gelding Cody. All of Cody's vital signs were normal: pulse forty beats per minute, respiration fourteen, temperature one hundred point four. The mucous membrane color (his gums and inner eye lids) were pink, and he had good gut sounds. Sharon said he had not eaten much for the last twelve hours and he seemed to be "straining."

Cody was extremely reluctant to move. I tried to lead him out of his stall and he rocked way back on his rear legs and tried to land on the heels of his front feet, like he was walking on egg shells. This is why he appeared to be straining his abdominal muscles and was lying down so much—he was trying to keep as much weight as possible off his front feet.

I could feel a strong digital pulse in the blood vessels that run just under the skin on the inside and outside of a horse's fetlock joints. This is usually not easily detected, but when it is present, it is a good indicator of inflammation in the foot. With some effort and considerable patience on Cody's part, I examined the horse's feet and applied pressure to the soles with a "hoof tester"— a barbaric-looking instrument that resembles a giant pair of pliers. (I use it to help locate a source of pain.) Cody was very sensitive to the hoof testers over the toes of both front feet, but not very sensitive in his heels or over the frogs.

"What do you think is going on, here?" Sharon asked, the concern apparent in her wrinkled brow.

"Cody has laminitis," I said.

"I was afraid of that," she acknowledged. "Does that mean we will have to put him to sleep?"

"Well," I began, "it's serious, but I don't think we're *there*, yet."

"What causes this to happen? He's always been healthy, and you can see that I feed him well." She chuckled and added, "A little too well!" and scratched Cody under his jaw.

"Laminitis is a complicated disease process that is not well understood," I began. "We know a lot about the pathology, the damage caused at the microscopic level, but most of the time, the definite, inciting cause is unknown. It is really a disease that involves the whole body, but the symptoms show up in the feet." My explanation was an oversimplification, but the disease was overcomplicated.

"How are we going to treat him and what can we do to keep him from getting worse?" she asked. "Should we X-ray his feet to see if the bone has shifted?"

"Good idea," I agreed. "An X-ray will sure tell us where we are right now, and we will probably need to get several radiographs over the next few days. Sometimes, early in the disease, the bone hasn't had time to shift yet, so additional X-rays are a good way to be sure that he hasn't gotten worse than we thought at first," I explained.

As Sharon had been talking, I had started my initial treatment of Cody. I usually start with an injection of an anti-inflammatory compound—Banamine® is my personal favorite. Next, I place a roll of gauze under the frog of each foot and secure it with good ole' duct tape. These "frog supports" are a bit controversial, but I have used them with consistent success. They don't cost much, and I don't think I have ever hurt a horse with them. I am always careful not to stick duct tape to unprotected skin, especially over the coronet, so I place a thick layer of brown gauze around the entire foot first. Duct tape, while being excellent foot-wrapping material, can also make a tourniquet, especially when you don't want it to.

"Why are you putting that roll of gauze under his feet like that?" Sharon asked. "It seems like that would just add to the pressure and make things worse."

"I've thought about that myself," I said, "and I'm not exactly sure how it works, but it sure seems to help. My theory is that it helps return the bloodflow up the leg. You know, the ancient Arabians—the folks, not the horses—called the frog 'the second heart.' They must have had some serious intuition about horse physiology, because that's pretty much what it is. There's a fair amount of blood in the feet of a horse and gravity wants to keep it there. On the other hand, the body would like for it to go back up to the heart and lungs, where it can pick up another load of oxygen and nutrients.

"Anyway, the frog and digital cushion are under the coffin bone, and when the hoof strikes the ground, they act like a soft, elastic wedge to squeeze the blood out of the hoof and back up the leg. Walking tends to help the process." Laminitis treatment has always been fascinating to me, and I can't help but get a little carried away in explaining it.

"So, the gauze frog support helps the frog push the blood out of the foot," Sharon mused out loud. "But I still don't understand why that wouldn't make it hurt more, at least for a little while," she added.

"Me neither, but it doesn't seem to."

I finished placing the frog supports on Cody, and he looked like he had aluminum socks on his feet. The supports really helped ease some of the pain because he was ready to leave the stall and steal a bite off a bale of alfalfa that was near the barn.

"Whoa, Cody!" I chuckled. "That may be what got you into this trouble in the first place."

"Do you really think so?" Sharon asked. "I have heard that overeating could cause a horse to founder, but I didn't think that hay could."

"Well, there's a fair amount of argument about that," I said. "Excessive grain is more commonly a factor, but there is some thought that alfalfa can cause it too. There are other elements, like overworking ('road founder'), colic, or retained placenta after birthing. The disease is multi-faceted, but one common thread is sugar. Horses on green, lush pasture in the early spring can have problems, and the process is similar to grain overload. Horses with 'metabolic syndrome' or insulin resistance, are also susceptible..... Just one other thing to think about with Cody, since he is in such good flesh..."

"I know, he is a little overweight," Sharon conceded.

"Well," I said, "maybe not overweight, just under-tall!"

We finished up by taking radiographs of Cody's feet. I dispensed a week's worth of anti-inflammatory solution that Sharon could inject twice daily. In addition, I wanted her to leave him turned out so that he could walk around if he wanted to. Turnout in acute cases (sudden onset) of laminitis is also controversial, but I am convinced that if we allow the horse to move when he wants to, he will benefit because of stimulating normal blood flow. I choose these cases very carefully and usually don't turn a horse out with other horses so they don't have "extra encouragement" to move. Too much movement in an overly comfortable patient (or one that is running out of fear) can cause more damage to some already compromised hoof capsule tissue, so it is important to be careful with herd dynamic and pain management.

By the time I left, Cody was much more comfortable than he had been just a couple of hours earlier. The radiographs of both front feet were normal, but it was going to take some time to see how Cody would respond to treatment.

I talked to Sharon two days after I had first treated Cody, and she said that one of the frog supports had come off. I made an appointment for later in the day.

This time, Cody was moving around a lot better. The anti-inflammatory drug, frog supports, and moving around on his schedule had really helped.

"I can't believe the difference in him," Sharon said optimistically. "He sure feels better."

I replaced both frog supports and showed Sharon how to do it herself because, as good as Cody was moving around, there was the distinct possibility that he would lose another one soon. As long as he had a digital pulse and was still fairly lame, I wanted him to wear those supports. Within another week, the digital pulse had subsided to barely detectable, and Cody was moving around almost normally. He was still a little slow on the turns, but he was comfortable enough to stand some shoes.

"I think ole' Cody could do with some new shoes, now, Sharon," I said one morning after I had examined the horse.

"Anything special, or can we just put his old shoes back on him?"

"I generally recommend a special, corrective shoe for a few months after a bout of laminitis," I said. "They look sorta' strange, but I've had good luck with them," I added.

I called Mr. Hugh Bishop next. He was a gentleman of the "Old School," a good horseman, and a gifted farrier. He was the one who introduced me to the open-toed egg bar, or "backward" shoe.

"You just spin that shoe around backward so that the toe of the shoe acts like an egg bar," he told me in the spring of '93, "and place the heels of the shoe just past the tip of the frog. That gives the heels some support and allows an easier break over when the horse walks. The downside," Hugh said with mock seriousness, "is that with the front shoes on backward you can't track 'em anywhere!" He added, "The toe of the foot will wear off a little short, and straight between what are the heels of the shoe, but I haven't known it to cause any harm to the horse, though it tends to make the owners a little nervous."

"I thought he was crazy," Sharon admitted about Hugh, two weeks after he'd come to install the special shoes on her horse. "But I can't believe it. Cody seems fine now," she said. "I've been riding him twice a week, and I think I might take him to the team-penning on Saturday."

Sharon was one happy lady. That is, until I told her about convalescence— putting laminitis patients back to work too soon can have devastating, lasting consequences.

"Four months!" She wasn't hollering, but her voice was elevated an octave or two. "By then I'll be out of the runnin' for high point this year!"

I explained to her that it took a long time for the diseased tissues to heal, and if we put Cody back to work too soon, he could relapse, or worse. I really like to see a horse rested for a full four months *after* he is completely sound without medication before slowly bringing him back into work. This often means the loss of a year of competition, sometimes more...sometimes forever.

Although Cody recovered from his initial episode of laminitis, he had several bouts of mild laminitis afterward. He typically pulled out of it after a few days of anti-inflammatory therapy. Unfortunately, horses that have had laminitis are prone to relapse since the laminae are damaged and may not return to their original strength and structure. Many cases can be managed, and some patients return to full work without recurrence, although some never do.

_ If It Ain't Broke...

I have always admired the work of Gary Larson, the creator of the internationally syndicated *The Far Side* cartoons. We share a similar sense of humor, an attribute that prompted some folks to call me a "sick puppy"—and that was from my friends!

In one of my favorite comics, Larson depicts a vet student breezing through equine medicine as she reads the textbook. On one side of the page there is list of various equine maladies: lame, bad breath, ornery.... The other side lists the treatments—all of which are the same, regardless of the disease: "Shoot."

Advances in equine surgery have rendered the traditional "high velocity lead therapy" a much less common option than in years past. Modern imaging techniques can help us see things inside our patients that we could only guess at a few years ago, and this helps direct our treatment efforts. Forty years ago, X-ray was all we had. It was great for seeing bones, but very limited in imaging soft tissue structures. Then they invented ultrasound, which is kind of like the sonar the Navy uses to find "bad guys" in the ocean. This opened up a whole new world in diagnostic imaging because now we can see soft tissue (internal organs, tendons, ligaments, and the surface of joints) previously hidden to us. When I was first learning ultrasound from Dr. Carol Gillis, a true pioneer in the field, I asked her the name of a structure I was seeing on the screen of one of the first primitive machines. She said I could call it anything I wanted, as some of the things we could see with ultrasound had never been seen before!

As fantastic as this technology was, medical imaging has advanced to an even more amazing level. Magnetic resonance imaging (MRI) and computer aided tomography (CAT scan), once considered almost "science fiction," are now common in some veterinary practices. While, as I've mentioned before, the conventional X-ray basically reveals the shadow of bones, MRI and CAT actually show the *inside* of bones and soft tissue structures. Other truly astounding diagnostic techniques are being developed. One uses a combination of infrared light and ultrasound that can illustrate anatomy that was previously seen only under a microscope!

But, as exciting as diagnostic technology is, we have to ask ourselves some questions before employing it. First, do we know, generally, where the problem is (foot, knee, or shoulder)? Do we need some type of imaging to accurately diagnose the problem? (If the leg bone goes *crunch* and only bends in the places that normally do so, do we really need an X-ray?) Once the images are obtained, do they indicate pathology? Is this the source of pain? Will this knowledge change our treatment plan? In other words, if we knew *exactly* what was wrong via the diagnostic technology, would our treatment be better than if we just had a pretty good guess?

These questions are the nexus, the connection inherent between the *art* of medicine and the *science* of medicine. The science changes every day with new technology. The art has not changed since Adam put the first mud poultice on a sore-footed T-Rex. And it is this *art* that makes practice simultaneously challenging, maddening, and (usually) fun.

Those of us who have been in veterinary practice a long time are frequently reminded why they call it "practice." (This didn't happen to me when I was fresh out of school because then I already knew everything....) One of these "teachable moments" occurred in my practice not so long ago. I saw a nice eighteen-year-old Warmblood with a chronic lameness. He had been seen by two other vets and the diagnosis was "arthritis."

I was both flattered and apprehensive because providing a *third* opinion on any case can easily become a veterinary minefield. An "arthritis" diagnosis is pretty generic, and I wondered why something more specific was not offered. Was this horse difficult to work with? Was the problem too vague to detect? All this was running through my mind when I started my initial exam on the rather magnificent gelding named Ridley. He was a Fourth Level dressage horse, which is kind of like having a black belt *and* a PhD—this guy had been in school about as long as I had. He was a beautiful mover, but pretty lame on the right fore. Ridley had nothing obviously wrong on the outside— no swelling, bumps, or lumps where there shouldn't be bumps or lumps, so I knew a closer look was warranted.

Ridley stood patiently for the diagnostic nerve block, an injection under the skin of his pastern that removed most of the sensation from his right fore foot. We watched him trot in the round pen and he was almost completely sound. This knowledge indicated the source of pain was in the right front foot, and an X-ray would hopefully give us a diagnosis.

When dealing with front feet, I sometimes will take an X-ray of both of them for comparison. Imagine my surprise when the radiograph of the *left* foot revealed a large chip fracture near the extensor process. The radiograph of the right fore indicated some arthritic changes that were probably causing most of the lameness and might respond to some joint injections. The owner decided to wait a few weeks, but promised to bring Ridley back, as she was planning on showing him early fall and wanted him to be ready for the event. I put him on a low dose of an anti-inflammatory drug to keep him comfortable, and we made an appointment for the next month.

Ridley was a fastidiously punctual horse, so he showed up at my clinic right on time. We watched him go in the round pen to make sure he was still lame on the right side and indeed in need of the joint injections. The chip on the left side was still in the back of my mind, and I wanted to be sure it was not presenting a problem we hadn't seen earlier.

This time, everyone was surprised, as Ridley was completely sound! At my age, I am amazed at how many lessons I keep learning and Ridley had become a valuable resource. A little time can be our friend...sometimes. A few weeks in a pasture and a little "horse Tylenol" was just what he needed. The large chip, even though clearly pathologic, didn't cause Ridley any problems. In a classic "win/win," the more conservative approach worked out being best for the horse—no needles—and saved money best spent on more important things, like alfalfa, carrots, and horse cookies. You know, *essentials*.

If it ain't broke...

_ Nails—Some Hot, and Some "Not"

(You'll understand this in a minute.)

"Dr. Seamans," a young female voice flowed out of my phone early one evening. "I need to come by your clinic and get some 'Ace,' please."

This was a fairly unusual request, as "Ace," short for "Acepromazine," is an old drug—one of the first tranquilizers used in horses. So you gotta have some gray hair to even know what it is. It is not a real good sedative, and it doesn't do much for pain relief, so I had some questions for this client.

"I'd sure like to help you," I said. "Have I seen your horse before? Why do you need 'Ace'?"

The woman identified herself and reminded me that I had seen a horse for her a year or so before and said, "My husband shod her yesterday, and now she's real lame and we need to pull the shoes...I think she may have a 'hot nail.'"

The term "hot nail" refers to a relatively common problem when a shoeing nail gets placed too close to sensitive tissue, causing fairly severe pain within a few hours after shoeing. This can happen even to the best of farriers, so I don't consider it to be due to bad shoeing, just bad luck. Several of my clients shoed their own horses, so it was no surprise to me to hear the term.

"Was she lame before he put shoes on?" I asked.

"Yeah, she's been a little off—that's why we thought shoes would help. Now she's *really* off, so can I come by your office today and pick up some Ace?" The tone of her response revealed frustration, fear, with maybe an inkling of irritation.

Although I could empathize with this lady, I was limited in what I could do to help. A good veterinary work-up is usually better than just throwing drugs at a horse. Some people want to avoid this step. (I can't blame them. I have to be just two breaths short of an autopsy before I will seek medical attention for myself.) Occasionally, I'll get a call like this from clients requesting drugs—some Bute or Banamine (common pain relievers and anti-inflammatories), or something else they think will help their horses. However, the Veterinary Practice Acts in all fifty states prohibit veterinarians from prescribing any medication for a patient that has not been examined for a specific case. (Try calling your doctor and asking for medication based on *your* diagnosis. Once he stops laughing, he'll tell you to come to his office.)

I tried explaining this to my client, adding that Ace was probably not our first choice, anyway. I concluded by saying I'd be glad to see the horse, but I couldn't dispense drugs without an examination that deemed them necessary, as I didn't want to do the wrong thing for her horse, besides breaking the law. This did not elevate her mood very much.

"No problem," she remarked, just a few decibels shy of a shout and quickly enough to suggest that, yes, my response was indeed a problem. "I'll call Dr. Smith's office, I'm sure *he will* help me." Emphasis on *he will*.

I wasn't trying to be difficult, but as many have said before me, good judgement comes from experience, which comes from bad judgement. I was thinking of a case I had seen many years before that had been a powerful lesson in why we should not diagnose a case or make treatment suggestions over the phone.

I had been in practice in the foothills of the Sierra Nevadas near Yosemite National Park for a few years. Back then, there were many companies called "outfitters" that would rent you a horse, or at least help you pack your gear into the back country where the roads were made by elk and deer. The only way to get to some of these places was on foot—yours or those of a horse or mule. One thing all the outfitters had in common was this: by the time they called a vet, it was a wreck with a capital "R." Most of these outfits were run by real experienced horsemen, so they doctored most of what they could and relied on the hardiness of the breed and the hand of God to do the rest.

Knowing this, a call late Sunday night from one of the chief packers in the region got my attention.

"Doc, I think I need your help. One of our best horses stepped on a sixteen-penny nail earlier today, and I'm pretty worried about her cause it looks like it went all the way through her foot—it's sticking out the top of it. I called another vet, and she wouldn't even look at the mare but said just put her down, there's no hope. We're a ways back in the hills; in fact, I had to drive a half-hour just to get a cell signal. Is there any way I can meet you somewhere to look at this mare? We'd sure like to save her if we can."

Although I had seen many horse feet with nails in them, this sounded pretty bad. But we arranged to meet at a wide spot in the road about halfway between my place and Mount Everest—or somewhere in the Sierra—so I could look at the horse.

One of the most influential professors I ever had was Dr. Mike Martin at Texas A&M. He taught me lots of things, but one that has really stuck over the years is about diagnostics. "Most of this stuff is really simple," he told me almost forty years ago. "It's not what you don't know, it's what you don't *look* for."

So I have spent the last several decades trying to not only increase my knowledge base but my observation skills, as well. By a flashlight and the headlights of our trucks, I started examining this mare. She was "three-legged-lame," which means non-weight-bearing, rather than missing one leg. My first observation was the pyramid-shape point of what looked like large nail protruding from the coronet of her left fore foot. This was *bad*.

I grabbed a pair of nail pullers from my truck and picked up her foot. She willingly gave it to me with apparent hopes I could help her. I was looking for the head of the nail and hoping that the "shoe puller"—a large, plier-like device that looks like hoof nippers, would help me remove the nail. The idea here is to pull the nail out of the foot from the bottom, grabbing the end with the head on it. This would be much easier and less traumatic than dragging the head of the nail through the hoof.

This may sound like the obvious course of action, but sometimes, in the middle of a wreck like this, the obvious...ain't.

From the angle that the point of the nail was sticking out of the mare's coronet, I figured the head had to be about the middle of her frog. The confusing thing was the fact that there are a couple of pretty hefty bones between those two locations. I wondered how the nail got from the frog to the coronet without being shot from one of those air-driven nail guns used by construction workers. A careful examination of the bottom of the foot was not rewarding. To my shock, there was no nail head present! There was also a conspicuous absence of blood, serum, pus…nothing that would be expected from such a traumatic wound. So I put the foot back down and tried to remove the nail point first, thinking maybe the head got broke off somehow. It was *stuck*. Really stuck.

I went back to my truck to retrieve another underrated surgical instrument from my pack: vice-grips. I don't need 'em very often, but I sure did that night. Of course, by now, the mare had become a little apprehensive about my intentions for her already really sore foot. She greeted me with a snort and a three-legged dance to communicate her displeasure with the evening's events so far. It looked like this would require a little pharmacologically induced cooperation, what my nursing friends called "IDC." This is doctor-speak for "I don't care"—a technical term for human sedating drugs. (They don't really stop the "hurt" as much as they stop the "care.")

Within a few minutes the mare was much less worried about me and the vice-grips so it was easy to pull the offending object from her foot. It was about an inch long and buried deep into sensitive tissue, which was why no drainage was seen around the bottom of her foot. On closer observation, I discovered why I didn't find the nail head: it was not a nail at all. It was a piece of manzanita—a large-bush-small-tree that grows in the Sierra foothills. It has beautiful red bark (hence the name, meaning "little apple"), and the wood is hard—*very* hard. I had seen many injuries induced from this hardy, unyielding plant, but this was first time I had seen it impersonate a nail.

I wrapped the mare's foot with an Epsom salt poultice to draw out inflammatory fluids, and gave her a big shot of penicillin and a tetanus booster. Within a few days the mare was back to work in the pack string, and I learned a valuable lesson: It is seldom okay to diagnose stuff over the phone. Sometimes you just have to see the horse.

This is the reason for the rules outlined in the Veterinary Practice Acts. Though I tried to explain this to the lady with the lame, recently-shod-by-my-husband horse, I just couldn't convince her she needed my diagnostic help. And I was sure glad I took the time to look at the nail that wasn't in the outfitter's mare. She clearly benefitted from the outfitter's tenacity in getting her some help, and reinforced the lesson Dr. Martin taught me so many years ago: "It's not what you don't know, it's what you don't look for."

_ Sultan and the Abscess

I had started to clean my instruments after finishing some dental procedures on a particularly challenging patient. I was just about ready to go home when a little girl named May tapped me on the shoulder.

"Sultan has a sore shoulder. Can you look at him please?"

I had known May for several months, as she had her horse, Sultan, a really classy, old-style, senior citizen boarded on a ranch where I saw several clients. May was only about ten years old, but she was as articulate as any college professor I had ever met.

"What makes you think he's sore in his shoulder?" I asked.

"Well, he's been pretty lame for a couple of days, and the trainer said it must be in his shoulder."

Many people think that their lame horse has a shoulder problem. However, the vast majority are due to one or more problems below the knee or hock. While shoulder issues do occur, they are not common.

As May led Sultan over to me, it was obvious that he had a problem. He was so lame that he was almost not bearing weight on his left forelimb. As we had experienced recent rains, an abscess was the most likely cause of Sultan's severe lameness. He was very sensitive to hoof testers—that jumbo pair of pliers I used to try to localize the source of pain in the hoof. Every time I squeezed the hoof testers any place on his foot, poor Sultan just about jumped out of his skin. In doing so, he accidentally jumped on my foot. I hadn't really localized the problem, and now we were both lame.

Since I had assumed that the problem was an abscess, I really wanted to know exactly where in the foot he felt pain so I could establish drainage. I used a hoof knife to shave a very thin layer of sole from Sultan's hoof in search of a draining tract. Some abscesses can be detected this way, but in this case, it was early in the process of the disease, and it had not yet "come to a head." If it had, the horse wouldn't have been nearly so lame since the drainage would have taken some of the pressure, and therefore, the pain, away.

In the absence of a draining tract, I usually don't start carving dollar-sized holes in the bottom of the foot in a "search-and-destroy mission," *especially* if I can't localize the pain with a hoof tester. This type of exploration is often unsuccessful, and the owner is left with the responsibility of wrapping the foot for a couple of weeks to *prevent* abscesses from forming in the holes made by a dull-minded veterinarian with a sharp hoof knife. In acute cases like Sultan's that are during the rainy season and only a couple of days old, I usually don't suggest more aggressive diagnostics like nerve blocks or radiography. Most of these turn out to be simple abscesses, so the extra expense of further diagnostics is usually not justified. Instead, I put a poultice on the foot to draw out pus and inflammation. In addition, I usually administer one of several anti-inflammatory drugs to act systemically on the pain. Phenylbutazone ("Bute") is my favorite because it is safe, effective, and cheap.

May's mother showed up, so I left instructions with both of them to give Sultan two grams of Bute by mouth once daily and to call me if he wasn't significantly better in two days.

I got busy with my practice over the next few days and didn't think too much about Sultan, figuring that no news was good news. About three weeks later, I was back at the ranch where Sultan lived. I saw May leading Sultan across the barnyard, and he was as lame as when I first saw him.

"May, how long has he been lame this time?" I asked. "I mean, did he ever get any better?"

"Well," she began, "at first he got a *little* better, but he's been about the same for a couple of weeks."

"Why didn't you call me?" I asked. "I thought you were gonna' call me if he wasn't better in a couple of days!" I was immediately sorry that I got a little excited in my concern for the horse, as May looked at me like I had just hit her with a shovel full of stall cleanings. "I'm sorry," I said quickly. "I'm just worried about your horse."

"I *told* my mom, but we really thought he would get better."

"Okay then, let's see if we can help him some," I replied as I picked up his foot. It was a little warm and the pounding digital pulse I had detected during the initial exam was still present. This is detected by gently feeling the vascular bundle that runs just under the skin on the inside and outside of the fetlock joint, the first bendable joint above the hoof. A pulse here is normally not present, or just barely detectable. The digital pulse is not specifically diagnostic for anything, it just means that there is inflammation in the foot. This can be due to a deep bruise, an abscess, laminitis, or rarely, a fracture.

Since Sultan had been lame longer than I would expect from a simple abscess, I wanted to be sure that the pain was in the foot. I began scrubbing his ankle in preparation for a diagnostic nerve block. It can sometimes be difficult to tell just exactly where the horse is hurting, so a nerve block to numb the sensation from a specific area is a valuable part of a lameness exam. I blocked the nerves that carry sensory information from his foot by injecting a small amount of "lidocaine," a drug similar to what your dentist uses on your jaw before he assaults your bank account. I started just under the skin of his ankle, next to the nerve.

Within minutes, Sultan was walking and trotting completely sound. This confirmed my suspicion that the problem was in his foot.

"Let's call your mom," I said to May, more gently this time." I think we should X-ray Sultan's foot to try to find out why he's so sore."

We got Mom's permission and started preparing Sultan's foot for a radiographic study. The foot has to be clean of any dirt. This is important because it's possible for debris on the *outside* of the foot to look, on film, like a serious problem on the *inside* of a joint or bone that would mislead us in our diagnosis. These false problems are called "artifacts," and they can get pretty tricky. I cleaned his hoof with a wire brush and packed the sole with "Play-Doh." This stuff has the same density as hoof tissue, as far as the X-ray beam is concerned, and helps further reduce the appearance of artifacts on the film. I took four views of Sultan's hoof. While this may seem like overdoing it, a complete radiographic study of any part of the distal limb usually requires more than one view. Since we are looking at a three-dimensional structure on two-dimensional film, two views of the same object can look entirely different. For example, a truck tire is the shape of a bar of soap if viewed from the top, or it can look like a doughnut if you look at it from the side.

Later that night, I developed the films in my lab. (This was long before the days of the digital units vets have in their trucks now.) What they revealed was disturbing: For the past three weeks, Sultan had been walking around on a fractured coffin bone (the bottommost bone in the horse's leg)! The fragments were not displaced, and the coffin joint itself was not involved—and that was the good news. The bad news was that Sultan would have to wear a bar shoe (a horse shoe with a closed heel) with four clips on the sides and stay confined to a stall for eight months in order for the bone to heal. The hoof wall itself would act as a cast for the coffin bone, and the specialty shoe would protect the foot and confine the bone so that the fragments could heal together. Because the joint was not involved, Sultan had a good chance for returning to soundness within a year.

How did he fracture his coffin bone? I have seen several over the years and the cause is almost never determined. Sultan did return to soundness and was a good riding horse for the rest of his days.

_ **Wooden Leg**

"He's gone," I said, wiping an escaping tear from my face with my ever-present blue towel. "I'm sorry about your horse, but putting him to sleep under the circumstances, was the kindest thing you could do."

It is never easy to lose a patient, but some are more difficult than others, and Shadow's case was one of those that was tough for two reasons. First, I had to euthanize a magnificent animal to relieve the unrelenting pain due to chronic laminitis, which had caused his hoof walls to literally die and fall off. While many horses suffering from this disease can be managed successfully, some, like Shadow, cannot. In addition, while I love all my patients, the fact that he was a young horse with more heart than most made his loss all the more difficult.

"Why can't they invent some kind of prosthetic device for horses like they do for people that lose a hand or foot?" Jeff, Shadow's human, said through clenched teeth and tears of his own. I handed him my slightly used blue towel that had recently seen duty as a handkerchief...he didn't seem to mind.

"It's been tried," I said after taking a minute to compose myself. Glad for the momentary shift in the direction of conversation, I continued, "There have been several attempts to make false feet for horses that have been injured on the racetrack, or, in a couple of cases, those that had feet amputated by well-meaning veterinarians, trying to help horses with severe cases of laminitis. A group in Kentucky spent a million dollars designing an artificial foot for a horse that had lost one in a training injury. At first, it had some promise, but even with all that money, it eventually failed. Up to now, man hasn't had a lot of success manufacturing something that nature has so masterfully constructed," I said.

I had seen one of those horses a few years before. It was an interesting case. I got a call from a lady about a stallion she had that was having some fertility problems. I told her I'd be glad to examine him and maybe I could help.

I showed up at the barn with my typical timeliness and introduced myself to a well-dressed lady who told me in a delightfully musical Southern drawl that she was Mrs. Samuels, the owner of the "fahm." She ushered me into a fancy office lined with blue ribbons and rows of silver trophies. There were pictures on the walls of the stallion in question.

"This is owah' boy, Rebel, as a two-ye'ah-old," she said as she pointed to one of the pictures, not an "R" to be heard. "Thayat was the ye'ah he won his last championship," she mused, "befo' we changed trainahs and Rebel got foundahd."

You could tell at a glance that this was one classy colt, the kind of horse that anybody would be proud of. It was a shame that laminitis and the subsequent founder had shortened an otherwise potentially great career. It was obvious that this lady had tremendous affection for him.

"Anyway," she continued, "we have been breeding him artificially up until this ye'ah. We cain't seem to get him collected any moah. Ah don't know what the problem is, Doctah, but you have just *got* to help him, if you can. You see, he is a very populah' stallion with valuable bloodlines, and we would like to continya breeding him as long as possible."

I followed her out to a palatial barn—nicer than my current residence—complete with an indoor arena. All the stalls were lined with expensive wood paneling. The stallion barn, of course, was separate, but equally luxurious. I expected to find the sleek individual I had seen in the photographs, fat, pampered, and at stud. Instead, I found a poor, emaciated, pitiful creature lying in a deeply bedded stall. If she hadn't told me that *this* was Rebel, I never would have believed it. As we approached, he picked his head up and nickered at the sound of Mrs. Samuels' voice.

"Hello, shugah'," she purred, "how's mah Rebel today?"

At first, I thought that the horse had a cast on his right front leg. A closer look revealed a heavy, boot-like apparatus that was fixed to the cannon bone with a lot of bandage material. I realized this horse had no foot! It had been amputated at the fetlock.

"When Rebel foundahd," she explained, "the bone came through the bottom of his foot. We flew Doctah Mano in from Kantucky. You know, he's a world authority on foundahed horses. He told us that amputation was the only thing that could save ow'ah Rebel."

With a considerable effort, Rebel struggled to his feet. As bad as he looked when he was down, it was hard to imagine that he could look any worse standing. He did. The pinched nostrils and wrinkled brow of a once majestically beautiful head told a painful story at a glance. Because he had spent most of the recent two years lying down, he was about two hundred pounds underweight and had several deep, decubitus ulcers (bed sores) on his shoulders and hips. Since he only had one fore foot, he tucked his rear legs forward under himself to try to balance more of his weight behind. This "humped-up" posture made him look even more pathetic and, really, not much like a horse at all. In thirty years as a professional horseman, I had seen some incredible things, but I could not remember many sights that were more pitiful. It made my stomach ache.

I felt so sorry for this poor horse, I was beside myself. I was torn between abject pity and anger, wanting to tell this lady how cruel I thought she was for making this horse *live* this way for two years, much less expect him to breed mares. In an almost unprecedented effort on my part, I was silent. I was in an ethical quandary. It was like taking that mouth full of too hot coffee: after that, *nothing* you can do is right. You can't spit, swallow, or hold it!

"Well, it's obvious that Rebel has been through a lot," I said, using all the tact I could muster. "And it's also obvious that you have given him the best care possible." I proceeded cautiously from here. The situation was clear to me. This horse wouldn't ejaculate because he was in so much pain. He was in such poor condition that he was lucky, or unlucky, to be alive. I didn't think that this horse would ever breed another mare or be collected artificially again. The challenge to me was how to explain it to this lady. I didn't think that she was so mercenary as to keep this horse alive strictly for his monetary value. However, it seemed that she had been so close to the situation for so long that she couldn't see the hopelessness of it at all.

"I have treated other stallions with ejaculatory disorders. Most of them have pain as the underlying cause, so medication has been of help in many of these cases," I said, knowing that this horse had seen more than his share of injections, tablets, or powders over the recent two years.

"Oh, Doctah," she said, "we've given owah Rebel so much pain killuh, I don't think it affects him at all any mo'ah."

"I figured you'd tell me that," I replied. "I don't know that there is much you can do. You might try to live cover a mare, if you had a real gentle, smaller mare that would hold still for him. It could be that the artificial system is not stimulating enough for him," I added.

"Oh, we've tried thayat, Doctah, but nothing seems to make a difference. Do you think that it would be possible to freeze some semen so that we may preserve the bloodlines of ow'ah hoss?"

"That process would be dependent on his ability to ejaculate. If we can't collect him, there's nothing to freeze," I replied. "I'd be glad to help you, Mrs. Samuels, but truthfully, I think his breeding days are over. I think that you have done all you could, but you probably know that it is time to show him one last kindness. I know it won't be easy." I was trying, as gently as I could, to let her know that it was time.

"How much do I owe you fo' today, Doctah?" she said as she abruptly turned away, her dismissal indicating that the exam and consultation were over.

I told her what my fee was and she wrote me a check without another word. I felt sorry for her, but I was more sympathetic toward Rebel. I hate to lose a client, but what I hate more is to see a horse suffer unduly. I found myself wishing that we did have some workable, "wooden legs" for horses.

As painful as it was, the case was good experience for me. The image of the gallant but suffering horse will be with me as long as I live. He will remind me that many horses have an almost limitless will to live. However, sometimes we impose upon that will for our own purposes. The privilege of possessing horses has a price. Sometimes compassion is our most valuable asset.

As I drove away from Rebel's barn, I was thinking about artificial limbs for horses and the subject reminded me of a young fellow I had known back in Texas in the early seventies. I was working on a ranch about thirty miles south of Amarillo when I met Tim. I don't remember much about him. I don't even remember his last name. He just showed up one day and told the boss he wanted to learn to ride and work on a ranch. I could relate to that because that was exactly how *I* got a job there. He was a real average-looking, unremarkable guy, but he walked with a pronounced limp. A lot of cowboys in that part of the country walked with a pronounced limp, but they were usually a bit older than Tim. Unless you were really unlucky, it would take years of the bad weather, bad horses, and worse cooking to produce lameness as bad as Tim's.

Tim told the boss that he was missing his right leg from just below the knee, but he got around pretty good on the plastic one that the doctors had fixed him up with and he would do his share of the work. Well, you could tell by looking at him that he was used to hard work, and he gave you a firm shake with a callused right hand to prove it. The boss told him to put his stuff in the saddle house and be ready to work in the morning.

Tim was a hard worker and a likable enough kid, but he never did quite get the hang of riding a horse. I don't know if he was scared or what, but Tim just naturally brought out the worst in a horse. If a horse had a tendency to buck, Tim could make him buck higher and harder than anybody. If he had a tendency to run away, Tim could induce speed that would be admired on any racetrack. And he didn't seem to mind getting bucked off, as he repeated the performance several times, much to the delight of the other cowboys. During a horse's exhibition of uncontrolled speed, however, Tim occasionally lost his nerve and released an impressive display of profanity.

Early one afternoon Tim had the rare opportunity to show off some impromptu trick riding to the Ladies Aid Society. Said Society, having just finished a delightful lunch of those little bitty sandwiches with the crusts cut off, were about to head back to town. The boss's wife was saying her goodbyes to all the ladies, the cream of Amarillo, on the front porch of the house. Tim had just saddled a horse in front of the barn about fifty yards away. He put his good foot in the left stirrup and went to swing his bad foot over the horse's rump. Of course, Tim had no feeling in his plastic foot, so he didn't know that he was dragging his spur across the rump of a horse that had all of *his* sensory nerves intact. The horse responded to Tim's injudicious spurring by buck-jumping forward and breaking into a dead run in the direction of the recently adjourned Ladies Aid Society meeting. The motion threw Tim into the saddle and the show was on.

I'm sure that Tim didn't mean to be heard from several miles away as he hollered, "WHOA! YOU @#$%^&*!" but the volume and variety of expletives were impressive. At a dead run, he had no chance to place his plastic foot in the stirrup—it was a maneuver that was a challenge for him even when a horse was standing still. So here was Tim, with one foot in a stirrup and his other leg flopping uselessly on the right side of the saddle. Tim's imitation of a Comanche war cry drew the attention of the ladies on the front porch.

The runaway course was partially obstructed by a lone, corner fence post placed solidly in the ground between the house and the barn. This post was the start of a fencing project designed to prevent something that had happened several times in the past. While the boss's wife was generally an understanding woman, she became a little narrow-minded when it came to runaway broncs and her small children playing in the same yard at the same time. It now appeared this project was going to be completed a day or so too late, as the wreck that it was designed to prevent was about to happen.

The bronc missed the post. Most of Tim missed the post. He was in the middle of his second, resounding, profane appeal to the horse (or anybody in earshot) when the artificial addition to Tim's anatomy hit the post and stuck there, boot still attached, on the top of the post. Tim continued screaming at maximum volume, his empty blue jean leg flapping in the West Texas air. At this point, the Ladies Aid Society was about to stampede. From where they stood, it must have looked like they had just witnessed the first amputation in medical history performed by a bronc and a fence post.

The horse eventually stopped running. Tim retrieved his leg and immediately retired from professional, one-legged trick riding. I'm not sure if the reality of the event was ever fully explained to the Ladies Aid Society, but it surely left a lasting impression.

Foals

*One of the most endearing aspects of working
with horses is babies (aka "foals").
This chapter is part medicine, part physiology/pathology,
and some just plain fun stories about neonates.*

CHAPTER

3

Madison Seamans DVM 2015

_ Madison

"Hey, Doc, we got a new foal just now. I'm a little worried about him, it doesn't look like he can stand up because his legs are too crooked."

I could tell that Lisa, a long-time client and friend, was worried. She depended upon her horses for her living but was not usually the worrying kind, so I decided not to wait on this call. I used my cell phone to cancel my next appointment (my clients are usually very understanding in these situations, especially when a baby is involved) and headed directly for Lisa's barn.

It was early afternoon, an unusual time for foaling. Most mares give birth between ten at night and four in the morning, unless you are watching constantly for the blessed event. In that case, they will invariably wait until you leave for three minutes and have it the moment you are gone.

I took one look at this foal, and it was obvious that he had not been on the ground very long. He was still wet and struggling to stand. The mare stood by herself in the corner of the stall, showing only the kind of occasional interest to the new foal that she might to a stable fly. Although most mares are instinctively good mothers, some will be less attentive than others, and some will ignore their foals completely. These mares always amaze me. If I had something *that big* just clamber out of my abdomen and I lived through the ordeal, I'd sure pay attention to it!

I usually don't get too worried about brand-new foals not standing to nurse, but if three or four hours have passed without progress, intervention is warranted. By the time I get to see the foal, he's most likely been out a few hours, so I almost always milk the mare out a little, usually about two hundred and fifty milliliters, pass a stomach tube on the foal, and give him a good drink this way.

Historically we also used to give a foal that couldn't nurse an injection of "dexamethasone," a synthetic cortisone. This drug stimulates the foal's system to make more glucose and that will give him more strength to get up on his own. The more important use of this drug, however, is that it will reduce inflammation and swelling in the brain and spinal cord. This was thought to be the cause of so-called "neonatal maladjustment syndrome," which includes aimless wandering and the incapability to nurse. The old name for this problem was "dummy foal" due to the fact that many of these kids walk around the stall, sucking on the walls, doors, or anything else other than the *right* thing. (I guess they changed the name so it would not be so disparaging, but the old name was certainly more accurate even if it wasn't nice.)

Now, thanks to the excellent work by Dr. John Madigan at the University of California, Davis, we know that maladjusted foals have elevated blood levels of "neuroactive progestagins." These hormones are part of a group of compounds made during pregnancy that keep the foal sedated so he doesn't run around practicing flying lead changes in the confines of the uterus. This is certainly appreciated by the mare, as anyone who has survived a pregnancy with an active fetus can confirm. In normal foals, these hormones disappear shortly after birth, probably due to the squeezing they received coming through the birth canal. In "dummy foals" (and possibly humans delivered via C-section) the sedating hormones are not cleared, and the foal remains "under the influence" for several days. If proper nursing care, including IV fluids and feeding through a stomach tube, is provided, most of these foals survive.

The brilliance of Dr. Madigan's work is not only the discovery of the cause (he was able to produce the symptoms experimentally in normal test subjects) but how to reverse the effects with a very simple procedure. Using a rope to simultaneously squeeze the chest and the abdomen of the foal for about twenty minutes, all symptoms seen in maladjusted foals vanished! (There is a YouTube video online that is absolutely astounding: Check out "Madigan squeeze.")

By about four hours postpartum, or after delivery, Lisa's foal had made some serious efforts but still had not been able to get up and nurse. I tubed him again and gave another meal of milk. I wasn't too worried since he was still trying, so I figured that I would finish the rest of my afternoon rounds and return in the early evening.

I got back to the barn later. The foal was about seven hours old and still couldn't stand. It appeared as though he had several problems that were making this standing up business even more of a challenge than normal. Of course, if you ask any newborn foal, he'll tell you that his legs are *way* too long, anyway, but this little guy had some extra challenges. First, his back legs were "windswept." In this condition, they are abnormally bent in the same direction so that, seen from behind, they look like a set of quotation marks. This is a fairly common condition that may be due to the positioning of the foal in the mare's uterus in the weeks just before foaling. It is usually "self-limiting," meaning that it corrects itself, but it makes getting up a little tough until things get straightened out after a couple of weeks.

As if crooked back legs wasn't a big enough problem, the foal's front legs had a condition called "contracted tendons." It has long been argued whether the tendons are too short or the bones are too long. It doesn't really matter; the result is the same: the front legs can't extend properly, and the foal can't put his feet flat on the ground. The condition is fairly easy to correct with splints or heavy pressure wraps for a few days. The goal is to weaken the tendons and allow the legs to relax and extend. These corrective devices can make getting up and lying down pretty awkward for the first week of life, but it is usually an easy way to correct the problem in a short amount of time.

After a few more hours of trying, the colt finally managed to stand. His back legs were so bent and his front legs so abnormally extended in front of him, he looked like he was going up a steep hill—but he could stand. He still couldn't get the hang of nursing, and his mama was no help. She would turn abruptly in the stall and send him flying. Since the colt hadn't been able to nurse for so long, the mare's udder was full and sore, so every time he would get close to the target, she would squeal and move away. Pretty soon, he just quit trying on the mare and went to sucking on the walls of the stall. (Of course, twenty-five years ago nobody knew about neuroactive progestagins or the Madigan squeeze.)

By late that evening, Lisa was despairing of the colt's chances. Her "better half" Bill had joined us in the barn, and though he tended to be the optimist of the two, he was also concerned.

"I can't see keeping him if he's going to be a cripple," Lisa said. "His legs are all so crooked, and what are we going to do if he can't nurse? We can't stay out here and pass a stomach tube on him every two hours, and we can't afford to have you do it."

"Let's give him some time," I replied, trying to be optimistic. "Maybe things will be different in the morning."

Things *were* different in the morning. The colt was worse. I had sent some blood off to the lab the night before and the tests indicated he was septic. His white blood count was very low and there were immature cells in circulation. This meant, for one reason or another, there was a massive infection in his body. The white blood cells had been recruited to help fight the infection but had been used up faster than the body could make new ones. As the stores of cells became depleted, the body started sending out white blood cells before they were fully functional, mature cells in a futile attempt to keep fighting the infection. This is known as a "degenerative left shift" and is always a bad sign.

To add to a growing list of problems, the colt was now drooling a lot and grinding his teeth. These are textbook signs of a gastric ulcer. *What next?* I thought.

I explained to Lisa and Bill the complications of "septicemia" and that there needed to be a new treatment plan, including some potent, broad-spectrum antibiotics, anti-ulcer medication, and some intensive nursing care because the foal still couldn't nurse. I couldn't guarantee that the colt would survive, regardless of how much treatment I provided. Lisa and Bill were having a tough time deciding on the wisdom of gambling that, even if he survived, the colt would ever be correct enough to become a performance horse. They already had plenty of "pet" horses; they needed a horse they could sell.

After a few minutes of "frank discussion" between the two of them, it was decided that we'd try to save the colt. Of course, there was still the question of his crooked legs.

"At this point, the legs are the least of his worries," I said. "He's a real sick baby, and we have a lot of ground to cover first."

Of all the colt's problems, the septicemia, or infection, was the most critical so it was addressed first. I placed an indwelling venous catheter in the colt's jugular vein. Since treatment would involve many injections, the catheter would make it possible to give large volumes of medication and fluids into the bloodstream. The best thing about the IV catheter, however, was that the injections could be given quickly and *painlessly*. It's easy to give a foal a first injection. It may even be easy to give a foal a second shot. However, if he has any life in him at all, the third shot may make you glad that he isn't any bigger than he is.

Although blood cultures did not identify a bacteria, I started him on antibiotics because the other blood tests strongly suggested that there was a bacterial infection present. I also gave him two anti-inflammatory drugs: "DMSO," an interesting compound with potent anti-inflammatory properties, and more dexamethasone.

The injections were easy. The hard part was going to be milking out the mare that really didn't want any part of this foal business. There are commercial milk replacers available, but they can't provide the antibodies in the colostrum, which the foal needs. This milk, present during the first day of lactation, constitutes the majority of the foal's immune system for the first two months of life. We had a mare's milk factory standing right there next to us, ill-tempered as she was, we just had to find a way to enlist her cooperation. A small dose of tranquilizer improved her attitude considerably about being a dairy animal. Eventually, the mare either associated us with the relief of pressure in her mammary gland, or she just gave up fighting the process every two or three hours, because she got fairly easy to get along with after a couple of days.

We started treating the gastric ulcer with "ranitidine," once an expensive, prescription antacid for stock brokers, test pilots, and other people prone to gastric ulcers. This drug had just become available over-the-counter, so the price had become more reasonable.

Needless to say, the schedule of medication and nursing care would keep Bill and Lisa up most of every night. I placed a stomach tube in the foal and taped it to his halter so he could receive his milk every two hours. The IV catheter would make it fairly easy for them to give him the necessary injections. I had other patients to see, so I gave them complete instructions, plenty of supplies, and some words of encouragement before I drove away from the barn.

Less than four hours later, Bill called to tell me that the tube had slipped out of the colt, and he needed help replacing it. I went back to the barn and passed the stomach tube again, but before I even left, the thing had worked its way out again. This was an additional frustration to an already difficult case. Since the foal wouldn't nurse, a stomach tube was essential.

Sensing my impending despair, Bill reassured me: "I'll figure something out, Doc. We have no other choice." I didn't think I knew anybody with a more positive attitude than Bill, and I left his place wondering just how we were going to keep the tube in that colt.

I called several veterinary supply houses, thinking that there was bound to be some type of indwelling stomach tube available for sick foals. Sure enough, there was one that had been manufactured commercially. I even talked to the veterinarian that invented it. He told me that it worked really well, but it was not economically feasible to produce it commercially so they quit making it, and he didn't know any place that I could get one.

I went to a local hardware store and tried to figure out some way of inventing a tube that would stay in this foal. I gathered up a few items and headed back to Bill and Lisa's. Before I could get there, Bill had me on the phone.

"I figured out a way to get the tube to stay in, Doc. I need your help to put it back in, but I think it will work!" he said, barely able to contain his excitement.

I went directly to the barn and was impressed by Bill's ingenuity. He had rigged up a plastic tube that he placed inside a long steel spring. He warmed up the tube with a heat gun and bent one end so that it resembled a snorkel. I don't know *why* it worked, but it surely did stay put! With the tube securely in place, Bill and Lisa were able to provide the nursing care the colt needed around the clock.

The colt's condition stabilized by the third day. He could get up, with a little help, and his bloodwork was almost normal. He was still grinding his teeth (a sign of pain due to the gastric ulcer), and he still couldn't nurse, but I was encouraged with the foal's progress. One look at Bill and Lisa, however, showed that the three days of constant nursing care had taken a toll on them.

"You guys look like you've been up for three nights," I said in a lame effort at levity. "I hope you feel better than you look."

"Thanks for the kind, encouraging words, Doc."

I am often impressed by the dedication and shear endurance of the people that love horses. Bill and Lisa kept working because they had hope, a foal that needed them, and really no other choice.

On the afternoon of the eighth day, Bill called me to say that he thought the foal was nursing on his own and maybe we should pull the stomach tube. I went by the barn and sat in the stall with them. The colt was taking a little nap, but it wasn't long until he raised his head from the deep straw bedding of the stall, struggled to his feet, and began nursing the mare like it was no big deal.

Bill and I cheered at the sight.

The colt went on to make a complete recovery, thanks to the excellent nursing care of Bill and Lisa, and the kindness of the Good Lord.

About three months later I went back for one of many routine follow-up exams. Bill had been keeping the foal's back feet trimmed every couple of weeks, and the little guy was standing nearly correct. I was amazed at the overall progress that had been made, considering such a dubious beginning.

Bill was pleased, too. He said, "Doc, we finally figured out what to name this colt. Since he's kinda' homely, in a lovable sort of way, and a little bow-legged. We decided to call him Madison!"

_ Sarah

Early in my career, I moved to the little town of Gilroy in north central California and started a private practice. This may have been considered foolish by some, as there were about twenty equine practitioners in the area, but I figured that any place that had *that* many horse doctors just naturally had a bunch of horses. Since my ego was bigger than my bankroll and smaller than my ambition, I gave it a try.

One day after I had eaten all my goldfish and stolen the absolute last handful of oats from my horse, I was seriously considering getting a "real job." The ringing telephone rescued me from my hypoglycemic stupor.

"My burro has crooked back legs," the caller said. "Can you fix her?"

At the time, I didn't have much experience with donkeys, but they were almost horses and definitely qualified as equine medicine. I thumbed through my blank appointment book like I thought there was going to be a time when I *couldn't* be there and said I'd be right over.

That day I met Sarah. She was a little Sicilian Miniature Donkey, not quite a yearling, that stood about thirty inches tall at the withers and was absolutely one of the most adorable creatures I had ever met. Her petite frame was covered with a mat of thick fur and her small, jug-like head was topped with a pair of ears so large that, if she "grew into them" she'd be seventeen hands tall. Her cartoon appearance matched her personality. She was precisely aware of just *how* cute she was.

Sally, Sarah's owner, was concerned that the little burro's hind feet pointed outward more than normal. In horseman's terms, she "toed out behind." At her age, Sarah was probably a little too old to have this conformational fault corrected, but I thought that I might be able to trim her feet and make it easier for her to move around. She toed out so badly that she really had a hard time walking.

Working on my knees, I carefully rasped the outside of the hoof wall of both back feet so that the inside was higher. This may seem a little backward, but the reason that horses toe out is because they place the inside wall down first and it wears more rapidly. The correction is made by leaving the foot high on the inside, though this may cause other problems in mature animals.

With all the expertise of a true professional, I completed this rather simple task and it seemed to help. I collected my fee and drove away from Sally's ranch confident that the equine population of California could rest easier just knowing that there was a "sure-nuff" horse doctor on duty.

Three days later, Sally called to tell me that Sarah was not doing well, and she could not even get up! I arrived at Sally's house to find Sarah unable to stand. A physical examination revealed no obvious problems. Her temperature, pulse, and respiration were all within normal limits. She was conscious and alert as she searched my pockets for the carrot she had so skillfully found during our previous visit.

A neurologic exam gave me the first clue about Sarah's problem.

The "patellar reflex" is tested when the doctor thumps on your kneecap with that little red hammer. The doctor is probably not doing this just for fun, but because some important information about the health of the spinal cord can be determined by this reflex. When I tapped on Sarah's stifle (the equivalent of the human knee in a horse or a burro), the reflex was exaggerated, or "hyper-reflexic," like she was kicking at a fly on her belly. This usually means that the spinal cord at the lumbar vertebrae, about halfway between the last rib and the peak of the rump, is damaged.

Damage to the spinal cord is observed in one of three stages, depending on the severity of the problem. Initially, patients with spinal cord trauma often demonstrate *proprioceptive* deficits. The brain, among many miraculous capabilities, can tell you that your feet are flat on the ground and your hands are at your sides without you having to look at these parts to determine their location. This is called "proprioception." The neural pathways that conduct this information from the body to the brain are located near the surface of the spinal cord. When the cord is slightly damaged by a bruise or minor pressure, information about proprioception may not reach the brain. Without this function, an animal will not know where his feet are and will often lack coordination in the hind legs. This symptom can be very subtle, as was the case with Sarah. Patients with more severe spinal cord damage will have loss of motor function. This means that they cannot remain standing without help. The final phase of nerve damage is seen as the inability to perceive deep pain. This symptom conveys a grave prognosis.

Although initially Sarah looked like she had a problem with her feet, the exaggerated patellar reflex assured me that the spinal cord was involved. The nerve damage was in its earliest phase, the loss of proprioception, but I wanted to diagnose the cause so that I could attempt to arrest the progression of the symptoms. At this stage, her chances for a complete recovery were not good.

Sarah needed an X-ray. In the early days of my practice in California, my radiology department was remarkably short on equipment. I had a friend in town who operated a small animal clinic, and since Sarah *almost* qualified as a small animal, he agreed to give us some radiographic assistance.

The little burro only weighed about as much as a bag of oats (a "wriggly" bag of oats), so I gave her a low dose of a mild tranquilizer and put her on the front seat of my pickup. She laid her head on my lap and seemed to enjoy the country music on the radio. Our only problem came when her legs got tangled up in the gear shift. Apparently, fourth gear in my old-time standard transmission pickup pressed on her belly a little, and she resented that. Reverse was even worse, so after some trial and error, we agreed not to back up and that fourth gear was acceptable.

The radiograph showed that Sarah had a pathologic fracture of the third lumbar vertebra (L3). (Amazingly, this was exactly where my neurology book said it would be!) A "pathologic fracture" is one that occurs due to disease or malformation of the bone. Sarah had "scoliosis," an abnormal curvature of the spine, and a malformation of L3 that had become fractured. The broken vertebra was pressing on the outside of the spinal cord and producing the symptoms we were seeing. My concern now was that one of the fractured pieces would shift more and cause further damage. Of course, a spinal fracture in any animal is very serious, but in a horse or burro, it is almost always fatal.

By now, everybody was real attached to Sarah. The serious nature of her injury and the poor prognosis had little effect on Sally, however.

"Save her, if you can, Doc," was all Sally said.

Well, *this* was a tall order. I tried to tell Sally that Sarah's chances were less than one in a thousand.

"That's better than none in a thousand!" she replied.

And with this encouraging optimism, we started treating the little burro.

With any neurological disease or injury, the control of inflammation is essential. Although the process of inflammation is designed to be protective in nature, it can actually cause most of the symptoms of disease, if left unchecked. The little boney channels in the spine through which the nerves pass do not expand. And when the channels eventually begin to constrict the swollen nerves, like I said earlier, it is like stepping on a water hose—the flow of nervous information is interrupted.

I gave little Sarah injections of dexamethasone, a steroid, and DMSO, a potent anti-inflammatory drug. This treatment would help the soft tissue inflammation but would not address her skeletal problem. The first step in helping any fracture to heal is stabilization. That is why the doctor puts a cast on your broken arm. The ends of the broken pieces must be in good alignment before the first cells can migrate across the defect to form a "callus." This callus is composed of fibrous connective tissue that builds up around the fracture to form a natural "cast" that stabilizes the fragments. After callus formation, the cells responsible for the formation of bone will invade this soft tissue structure, and within about six weeks, bone healing will usually be completed. If the broken pieces cannot be stabilized, the first cells of the callus cannot migrate across the defect and a non-union will result. These types of fractures are a nightmare to manage. In the case of a non-union leg fracture, for example, amputation is often the result.

Once we had the soft tissue inflammation under control, the next problem was achieving stabilization of the fractured vertebra. We certainly could not put this burro in a body cast! We decided to hang little Sarah from the barn in a sling. Sally was an expert seamstress. With her help and an old horse blanket, we made a sling with holes cut in it for Sarah's legs and some straps for her chest and bottom to keep her from spilling out either end. Sally would need some time to manufacture the contraption, so we scheduled the "burro hanging" for the next day.

Bright and early the next morning, I had a phone call from Sally.

"There's something hangin' out the back of her," she said frantically. "I think you better come right away!"

When I arrived, Sarah was down, unable to rise, and she had prolapsed her rectum. She had been straining so hard to get up, the soft tissue that supports the rectum within the pelvis had given way and about ten inches of it was turned inside out. If she did not have enough problems before, she sure had some now. I had read about such an issue, but I had not yet seen an example of it.

Cases like this will test your nerve.

"How in the world are you gonna fix this?" Sally asked.

I did not say, "I *think* I know…" but I thought it loud enough to hear.

I gave Sarah an "epidural anesthesia." This is an injection of local anesthetic into the spinal canal next to the cord that will block any feeling in Sarah's southern end. (Some women receive epidural anesthesia to help control the pain of childbirth.) This type of anesthesia not only affects sensory nerves, it also affects motor nerves, as well. This will block the pain and stop the straining that makes replacing a prolapse more difficult, if not impossible.

After I had Sarah locally anesthetized, I cut two little holes in the skin above and below the anus to allow the passage of some heavy, nylon suture in a purse string fashion. The rectal tissue was very swollen due to the exposure to the air and dirt. Even though Sarah was not straining against me, the swelling made replacement of the rectum difficult. I asked Sally to bring me some table salt and applied it liberally to the exposed rectal tissue. This draws extra water out of swollen soft tissue the way soaking a sprained ankle in hot Epsom salts does, allowing me to reinsert what belonged inside the burro's body.

The purse-string suture was then placed and pulled snugly enough to keep the rectum from falling back out again, but not tight enough, hopefully, to "plug her up" completely. I was hoping that this procedure would cause enough scar tissue to hold the rectum in place without damaging the essential nerves to the anus.

Sally's sling was a masterpiece. She had measured, cut, and sewn the old horse blanket so that Sarah's legs fit perfectly through holes placed at all four corners. The sling was lined with sheep's wool to help prevent pressure sores that would likely occur due to the unnatural weight borne on her abdomen rather than her feet. We hung the sling from a couple of boards nailed across the top of the stall so that Sarah was close to the ground but could not bear enough weight or move around to an extent that might disturb her fractured vertebra. The goal was to stabilize her back for six weeks so that it would heal.

We also hung a bucket and hay bag within the burro's reach so she could have free-choice water and alfalfa hay. Although I was not real optimistic about her prognosis, Sarah was good about everything. She never tried to fight us or struggle in the sling, almost as if she understood that, despite all the silly things she had to endure, we really were trying to help.

I returned the next day unsure of what new trick Sarah would present since she had demonstrated an uncanny ability to surprise me. This time, her rectum was impacted with feces. I tried soap and water enemas and then mineral oil, but nothing would break loose the impaction. I was forced to cut the purse-string suture to relieve the impaction. Although I was fully expecting the rectum to fall out again, Sarah surprised me once more: Everything stayed in place. Apparently, since she was not straining to get up, there was no extra pressure exerted on her abdomen and pelvic canal, so the rectum stayed put. This was just the first of several miracles.

The next four weeks passed uneventfully. I checked Sarah every other day or so, to look for pressure sores and to give her a few pets and a carrot. It is not wise to become too personally involved with a patient, but I found myself more and more captivated by the floppy-eared ball of fur with an unbelievable will to live.

Everything seemed to be going better than expected—until one day about a month after Sarah had been put in the sling.

During one of my routine examinations, I found a small abrasion under her right flank. Sarah had such a thick hair coat that this sore was not obvious without close examination. It was soon apparent that this was just one edge of a large, necrotic area that had undermined the skin and was the result of the abnormal pressure the sling put on her abdomen. The "necrosis," or death of tissue, was so extensive that I was concerned about it actually invading the abdominal cavity. This would be fatal. Sarah *had* to come out of the sling two weeks early.

I gave the burro a sedative and gently lowered her from the sling. Maggots had invaded the wounds in her flank and belly, so I knew the pressure sores were at least two or three days old. I clipped the hair from the necrotic areas, then scrubbed and removed as much of the debris and maggot population as possible. I applied an antibiotic dressing that included a drug called "ivermectin" that would kill any maggots that I had missed. Maggots are simply fly larvae (an immature stage of the fly life cycle) that live on dead tissue, but do not usually cause major damage. Nonetheless, they are a disgusting sight. (Though Sarah's story is over twenty years old, I can still smell the wound to this day.)

After I had treated the new problem, I began to assess the old ones. The rectum was still where it was supposed to be. The patellar reflex was no longer exaggerated, so it appeared as though there was no longer significant inflammation in the spinal cord. Although these were good signs, Sarah could not rise, and her legs had become slightly flexed because she had not borne weight on them for over a month. Even if she could have stood up on her own, she would be unable to remain standing because the leg flexion meant her feet would not be flat on the ground.

I telephoned Sally and told her the extent of Sarah's new problems. Most people would have been ready to give up by now, but not Sally.

"Do whatever you have to do, Doc," Sally replied. "We've come too far to quit now!"

Although I would have dearly loved to have another radiograph of the fractured spine to see how much healing had taken place, I was reluctant to wrestle Sarah into my truck for the long trip to the small animal clinic for fear of "tweaking" her back in the process. I did decide to take her to my house where it would be handier for me to keep an eye on her. I got a neighbor to help me slide Sarah on a piece of plywood and gently load her into his trailer for the short ride.

I decided to attempt some physical therapy on Sarah's legs to help her straighten them out with the hope that she would soon be able to stand on her own. I applied light pressure wraps to all four legs, from below the fetlock to just above the knee and hock. Support wraps may not seem to be the right thing to do in a case where the tendons are too contracted, but this procedure will actually weaken the tendons and allow the lower legs to relax and the feet to be placed flat on the ground. Conversely, in a case where the tendons are too weak, no wraps should be applied because this will only make them weaker.

In addition to the leg wraps, I physically stretched Sarah's legs in extension for ten minutes, three times daily. She *hated* this. She would lay back her substantial ears and shake her shaggy head in a manner that was unmistakably burro cussin'. I knew it was painful, but it was essential for her survival. If she could not straighten her legs, she could not stand.

During the course of treatment, Sarah was mostly cooperative, and generally wouldn't cuss me as long as I didn't stretch her legs. She continued her struggling efforts to rise, and I feared that she would prolapse her rectum again. I considered replacing her into the sling, but the abdominal tissue was still too fragile to support her. After a week of physical therapy, she still could not stand, but I was encouraged that she had not surprised us with any new problems. Of course, thinking like that had jinxed me before.

Sure enough, the next morning I discovered that Sarah had prolapsed her rectum again. This time, I replaced it with skill and confidence in the knowledge that I was the best and *only* burro proctologist in the state. With one such case behind me I could certainly claim "clinical experience." With two such episodes, I could say, "In *case after case* the 'Seamans procedure' has been proven effective in resolving rectal prolapses!"

Within two weeks Sarah could stand if I helped her get up, and she could walk about twenty feet before falling down. It was hard not to become discouraged. After all the time that I had devoted to this case and all the effort that Sarah was giving, it seemed that we were only prolonging the inevitable and that we would eventually have to put her to sleep. After all, I had never even heard of an animal this large surviving a vertebral fracture. Despite our apparent progress, I didn't feel too optimistic about her chances.

I came home late one night after treating a horse with colic. It had become my habit to walk down to the barn, find Sarah down in her stall, and stretch her legs, even though by now I had almost given up hope that it was doing any good. She would give me her traditional burro cussin', but bray plaintively when I left her alone. After all the time we had spent together, I had maybe spoiled her a little.

I gave her a handful of oats and rubbed her large, soft ears. I had been leaving the stall door open because the neighbor's dog had taken up with Sarah and would sometimes keep her company at night. Tramp was a good old dog and since I always was a soft touch for all kinds of good old dogs, I left a small dish of dog food for him just outside the barn. I checked my other horses, turned off the barn lights, and wearily trudged back up the hill to the house.

Early the next morning, I awoke to the sound of a barking dog. I looked out the window and there was Sarah, standing over the dish of dog food. Tramp was raising a fuss because Sarah was eating *his* breakfast! I ran down to the barn, wearing nothing but a pair of boots and my long underwear. I couldn't believe my eyes: Sarah had stood up by herself, walked fifty feet to the door of the barn, and had successfully buffaloed the neighborhood mooch out of his breakfast!

This was the beginning of a steady recovery for Sarah. She was given free run of my place to encourage her to exercise. She was soon able to stand by herself almost all the time and could actually run a few steps. She became such a pest that I eventually had to start leaving her in the stall because she would otherwise "help me" in everything I did.

Three months after her initial injury, Sarah went back home as an almost normal, spoiled rotten burro. Within a year, her gait was nearly normal. Within two years she could playfully knock me down when I came to visit. She is still a delightful animal today (and hasn't held a grudge for all the silly things I did to her). Sarah took her one chance in a thousand and made it. In her own way, she had won The Kentucky Derby.

_ "Is He Ill or Just Napping?"

Few things in nature are more inspiring than new foals frolicking around their mothers on a crisp spring morning. The fact that a foal can be up and running within short hours after birth is but one in a long series of miracles. Conception, as we touched upon already, is miraculous in itself. Development "in utero," in the womb, begins with the formation of all the organ systems and is followed by the maturation of them. During the entire process, the foal is completely dependent on the mother's blood supply for eating, breathing, and eliminating metabolic waste products. Many of the organ systems function differently in utero than they do after birth. "Parturition," or birthing, initiates changes in the heart, lungs, liver, and urinary bladder that must occur almost instantly. These changes are essential for adaptation to life "on the outside."

Fortunately, things proceed normally almost all the time. Foals have survived the cold, cruel world much longer than there have been foal-watch teams to worry about them. However, how do we know when things are not right? What are the signs? What can and should be done? In order to understand how things can go wrong, it is important to review the normal physiological processes taking place around the time of birth.

When we watch horses, young or old, running free on a glorious day, we seldom think of all the processes that must take place for oxygen and energy to fuel one of God's most amazing athletes. It may not seem obvious, but when the foal is still in utero he does not breathe or eat. The blood supply flowing to the mother's "uterus," or womb, is very close to that of the foal. Oxygen and nutrients are transferred directly into the blood supply of the developing fetus through an elaborate system of membranes called the "placenta." This is attached to the foal through his belly button, the "umbilicus." In addition, there are "shunts," little detours, which direct blood away from the lungs and liver since these organs are not needed until the beginning of life on the outside of mom. Immediately after birth, these shunts must adjust to allow normal function of all body systems. Cardiovascular changes (involving the heart, lungs, and blood vessels) occur first and the blood is instantly directed to flow through the lungs so they can inflate, absorb oxygen, and expel carbon dioxide.

Other changes involving the liver, urinary bladder, intestinal lining, and immune system occur in the hours after birth and are critical to survival. The channel between the bladder and umbilicus, the "urachus," is normally closed at birth so urine starts flowing through the appropriate pathway. The intestinal lining, or "epithelium," remains very porous during the first six to eight hours of life. This allows absorption of some very large molecules called antibodies ingested in the first milk, or "colostrum." This provides immunity from bacteria, viruses, and other potentially life-threatening infectious diseases. The "passive immunity" is essential for the life of the foal until his immune system matures and he is capable of making his own antibodies through "active immunity" at about six months. For this reason, foals are not routinely vaccinated for most diseases before about six months, as they may not be capable of producing an immune response to "shots." If the mare is vaccinated about thirty days prior to her due date, she will pass the immunity on to her foal when he nurses the colostrum during the first day outside the womb.

Appreciation of the transition between "prenatal life" in utero to "neonatal life" on the outside helps us understand processes present when things go wrong. When a foal becomes ill, many of his body systems want to revert back to the warm, safe confines he had inside Mom. However, the prenatal function of most organ systems is not compatible with life on the outside. When the normal physiological role is absent, the invasion of bacteria, viruses, and fungi can cause illness in foals. The term "neonatal septicemia" (what Lisa's colt battled earlier in this book) describes foals with a serious infection in the bloodstream.

In sick foals, the metabolic retreat to prenatal life can occur rapidly, within just a few hours. The passage that allows blood to flow through the lungs begins to close, so respiratory symptoms are common in "at-risk" foals. Among the first symptoms noticed are cough, runny nose, high fever, and lethargy. The urachus opens again, urine dribbles from the umbilicus, and "my colt is peeing out his bellybutton" is the alarming report that comes to the vet. Gastric ulcers are also seen in these patients, and may cause rolling, teeth grinding, and increased salivation. Some foals with gastric ulceration may roll up next to a fence or wall so they are lying directly on their back with their feet in the air. The shunt at the liver can close again, and metabolic waste products that are normally cleared from circulation by this vital organ begin to increase in the blood. This buildup soon becomes toxic, the life-sustaining mechanisms cease functioning, and other potentially fatal events arise.

There are several things that suggest a foal is at risk for developing neonatal septicemia. Some of these can be quite subtle, so a "well baby exam" during the first day of life by a veterinarian is strongly advised, even if everything looks okay. Foals that fail to stand and nurse within two hours or have urine dribbling or swelling at the umbilicus are suspect. In addition, joint swelling, extreme lethargy, sometimes indicated by general weakness or "floppy" ears are also cause for concern. (It is interesting to note that before the foal can stand for the first time, he must have good control of his ears.) Diarrhea, cough, nasal discharge, and fever (a temperature over 101.5) suggest the presence of serious problems. Lethargy can be difficult to assess, as a normal foal will exhibit a cycle of nursing, playing and "power napping" throughout the day. However, a foal that is not easily aroused by human or maternal stimulus or has any of the other symptoms mentioned here, should be examined by a veterinarian immediately.

Normal nursing behavior is the most important indicator of good health. Failure to stand and nurse normally within two hours after birth, or wandering around the stall "nursing" foreign objects are clear indicators that the foal is in trouble. As the typical mare produces about four gallons of milk per day, a foal needs to nurse frequently to ingest this volume. The new foal should be observed closely to be certain that he actually has the teat in his mouth. Even though the foal's head may be seen under the mare's flank and sucking noises heard, sometimes he still has not "latched on." The presence of milk on the newborn's face is an indication that he may be getting close, but not actually nursing. This should be cause for concern. If the mare's udder is being nursed regularly, the teats will look clean and point downward or directed north and south. If the foal has not nursed, the teats may have crusty debris still present on the surface and they may point southeast and southwest, an indicator of a full udder. Normal nursing is repeated in episodes lasting fifteen to thirty seconds or longer. Nursing activity for three or four seconds is not adequate, and assistance is warranted.

If the foal has not latched on, directing him toward the teat and squirting milk on his nose can help him locate his breakfast. In some cases, however, a stomach tube must be passed by a veterinarian and the first colostrum delivered in this manner. This will ensure the presence of essential antibodies in his system, and provide the immediate nutrition needed until normal nursing patterns can be established. The importance for normal nursing cannot be overemphasized as it may be the most critical aspect of survival.

As the gut remains porous for the first twelve to twenty-four hours to absorb antibodies from colostrum, these holes can also allow the passage of bacteria. This is probably the beginning of sepsis, or infection in the blood, rather than the old wives' tale of it coming from the umbilicus and being traditionally called "navel ill." The presence of milk in the intestine triggers the mechanism, which closes the large pores in the lining and allows normal absorption of water and other nutrients. The closure of intestinal pores will guard against the introduction of bacteria into the blood stream, and the antibodies present afford protection against those that may have tried to sneak in uninvited.

Premature births are relatively uncommon in horses, but as is the case in humans, they present severe challenges to survival. Although the normal "gestation" (length of pregnancy) in a mare is three hundred and forty-five days (the average is three hundred and thirty-three to three hundred and fifty-seven days), some foals prefer their own calendar. Regardless of the duration of pregnancy, foals with a short, velvety hair coat, little body fat, or severe weakness are by definition "dysmature" (denoting faulty development) and at risk for septicemia. This is more common if the gestation is "too long" than if it is "too short." Although we may be tempted to induce labor in pregnancies exceeding four hundred days, this is very seldom advisable, as these foals aren't "done" yet. Forcing their delivery commonly results in a dysmature foal. Time sufficient for the maturation of all body systems is imperative for neonatal survival.

The production of "surfactant," a substance that allows the lung to inflate properly, is among the last components to mature in the prenatal horse. This miraculous compound reduces surface tension in the "alveoli," the microscopic spaces in the lung that are the location for exchange of oxygen, carbon dioxide, and other gases. When you blow up a toy balloon, you will notice that it is fairly difficult in the beginning. However, at some critical point, it gets easy. This is what surfactant does in the lungs—it makes it easy to inflate the alveoli. Once the lungs are properly inflated, they are functioning the way they do in an adult, so life without the placenta is possible. Dysmature foals often lack adequate surfactant, and therefore severe respiratory problems in addition to septicemia are common.

The amazing phenomenon of new life usually proceeds without difficulty. However, if a foal presents with any of the symptoms discussed here, veterinary attention is advised. Most such cases should be treated as an emergency, so waiting for normal office hours is seldom an option. Many at-risk foals can be saved with some simple mare-side techniques that can avoid major problems later. Above all, when in doubt, call your vet.

_ "How Old Is a Baby Horse When He First Opens His Eyes?"

I always recommend a wellness exam for mares and new foals because, as we've learned, some serious problems can be avoided with early intervention. And...I just like babies. Few things delight me more than seeing a new foal for the first time. I would work all year just to play with a new baby for fifteen minutes. And things are absolutely normal most of the time, but occasionally there are problems...and rarely, there's a real train wreck.

One of the latter began with an early morning phone call. The client was out of town so his wife posed the question straight out of the "you-can't-make-this-s**t-up file": "Doctor, how old is a baby horse when he first opens his eyes?"

Me: "They're born with their eyes open."

"No," (followed by a loud, exasperated sigh), "I mean, when do they *open* their eyes? I breed Yorkies, and I *know* they don't open their eyes for two weeks."

Me (patiently): "That is true for dogs but not horses."

"Well, that just can't be right. Our mare just had a foal, and his eyes aren't open yet. Jim is out of town, and I just don't know what to do."

After way more discussion than should have been required, I convinced my client's wife that an exam might help determine "when the foal's eyes would open." I arrived on the scene and was immediately truly baffled. The Arabian neonate had multiple birth defects: atlantoaxial subluxation, marked scoliosis—and, oh yeah...no eyes!

All of this meant her neck wasn't attached to the back of her skull (atlantoaxial subluxation), the rest of her spine was curved in a sideways "S" shape (scoliosis), and, more than likely, some other real bad things that would show up soon. Some blind horses can compensate for the loss of sight…*some*. But spinal cord defects like this filly's would eventually make it very difficult to walk toward food and water. Eventually, as she grew into a defective boney spinal column, the nerves would become pinched and it would become painful for her to move. The nerve damage would get worse over time until, finally, it would be difficult-to-impossible for her to remain standing.

Birth defects are seldom seen as single anomalies because there are only three basic tissues that start embryonic development. If one of those basic tissues has a major defect, this will be reflected in other structures from a common origin. For example, the "lethal white gene." This is found in many American Paint Horses with a "frame overo pattern"—pinto markings denoted by white spots on the horse's flanks and face, surrounded by a dark "frame" of color. The gene produces a fatal combination of birth defects, hence the "lethal" part of the name. Skin and gut come from the same embryonic tissue: "ectoderm." There's a defect in the development of skin, hence the lack of pigment, and this faulty development carries over to structures necessary for the completion of the gastrointestinal (GI) tract. Affected foals have very little areas of pigmented skin and the GI tract is incomplete. Instead of a long, continuous tube, the lethal white gut is missing a section. The back end is not connected to the front end. This ultimately leads to the death of the foal.

So discussion about equine birth defects always includes the likelihood of companion flaws that may also alter the quality of life. I spent a fair amount of time explaining this to Jim's wife, and I thought I had done a thorough, concise, and cogent discourse on a serious situation. I also thought I had made a compelling case for considering doing "the kind thing" for the foal. I thought I had made this compassionately, thoughtfully clear.

I had not.

"We can't euthanize this poor baby," said the wife. "She has such good bloodlines. I'm sure she will grow out of it. Once her eyes are open, she'll be fine."

How could I respond to that?

I ended up losing the client, as I guess I got a poor performance report once Jim got home. I later heard via the equestrian grapevine that the filly had to be euthanized as a two-year-old after she fell on somebody.

Colic

An acute abdominal crisis (aka "colic")
is the most common cause of death in horses
and is the source of much wailing and gnashing
of teeth among horse people. There is a large body
of misinformation about this painful, potentially fatal
malady. Here I try to dispel some of the myths about
equine colic and relate some interesting anecdotes
that prove to be more common than you'd think.

CHAPTER

4

_ A Belly Ache and a Trailer Ride

If you have ever "enjoyed" a long, cold night tending to a horse with colic, just the *word* colic is enough to incite unpleasant thoughts. The uninitiated horseman, however, can walk away from a horse that won't eat, blissfully ignorant that it is often the first sign of colic and not simply a matter of culinary snobbery. A horse without an appetite is *always* an emergency.

We had just had the first really cold spell of the year. Sudden weather changes can trigger small epidemics of colic, so I was not surprised when I was called out to see a horse with a sudden loss of appetite. In reality, lots of things can start a colic episode—the fact that it is Tuesday is sometimes enough. I also have found colic tends to happen in groups. I'll go a week without one, then I'll see three in one day. There are lots of theories about this problem and known "risk factors," but no one really knows why colic happens.

"My neighbor suggested I call you," said an unfamiliar, tentative voice over the phone line. "My mare won't eat, and I am afraid that she may have the colic. I called my regular vet, but he said that I shouldn't worry, and he would come out tomorrow. I *am* worried about her, though, and I wondered if you could come see her tonight."

"I'll be glad to come see your mare tonight," I replied.

I always tell new clients about the expected fees involved and that I need payment at the time of service, so there are no surprises when I present them with a bill after treating the horse. The caller gave me directions to her place. I hurried down a few more bites of my supper, not knowing when I would get another chance, filled my coffee cup, and left the house.

I pulled up the narrow, tree-lined drive and saw a small Paint mare surrounded by several people with my rather overly "experienced" flashlight dimly suggesting the white parts of the mare in an otherwise totally dark night. I introduced myself to the owner, Connie, and her mare, Splash. Splash accepted my introductory strokes on her jaw and withers, but she would not eat the carrot I offered her.

"She *never* turns down a treat like that," Connie said.

Within a few minutes, the aging flashlight had breathed its last, and I examined the nice mare by the headlights of my pickup. Her pulse and respiration were normal, but she had no gut sounds and a slightly elevated temperature. This, combined with the absence of an appetite, presents a textbook case of colic. Colicky horses aren't always down, rolling and thrashing around or looking at their sides while pawing out C-O-L-I-C in Morse code. Just the fact that this mare wouldn't eat was enough to direct me toward the diagnosis.

I passed a stomach tube and gave her some "dioctyl sodium sulfosuccinate"(DSS—an anti-gas drug that also acts as a stool softener) in a gallon of hot water. In addition, I gave her injections of two drugs that would help relieve the pain of smooth muscle cramping: Banamine˚ and Buscopan˚. Within the time it took me to clean up my instruments and record the examination data and treatments on the medical records, the mare was grazing around the yard and looking much more comfortable. I listened to her abdomen again with my stethoscope and was pleased to find her gut sounds had improved, even though they weren't back to normal. Normally, the gut makes gurgling and groaning noises in the lower left, and both upper and lower right quadrants of the abdomen. The upper left part of the belly is often silent because that is the location of the small bowel. Because the small bowel is usually full of ground up feed and water, or "ingesta," it doesn't have much gas in it, so it normally doesn't make much noise. The large bowel, conversely, has a larger volume and a fluid-gas interface that tends to make a lot of racket. A half-full canteen makes more noise when it bounces on the saddle than a full one does.

I left instructions to feed only small amounts of hay frequently over the next two days and I told Connie I would be in contact by phone the next morning. I drove out of the yard fairly confident that Splash would recover uneventfully, but I planned on calling in the morning anyway.

"She did okay during the night," Connie told me the next morning, "but she won't eat her breakfast."

"I'll be over in a few minutes." I hung up the phone, refilled my coffee cup, and went back to see Splash.

The first time I treated the mare, she was real cooperative and never offered to resist anything I tried to do to her. The second time I treated her, however, she was a little suspicious of my intentions. I hoped that this was a sign she was feeling better. I gave her some more pain injections and a gallon of mineral oil by stomach tube without too much difficulty. Because I had to come back to treat her a second time, I was now a little more concerned about her condition, and I really needed to examine her abdomen by rectum. Although this procedure would appear to be unpleasant for the horse, it usually is not painful, and since I have skinny arms (I look like the "before" pictures in those ads for muscle-building machines), most of my patients tolerate it. I pulled on the shoulder-long plastic sleeve. Splash looked at me sideways and snorted a little as if she knew something about the long glove. Although she danced around some initially, she stood still and patiently allowed me to examine her. The mare's large bowel was distended with gas, but there was no evidence of a twist or displacement, so it was probably a simple impaction that would be resolved within a couple of days.

Splash wasn't looking as bright as I would have liked when I left. But her vital signs were still okay, except for her unwillingness to eat, so I didn't feel too bad about continuing on my morning rounds.

I returned early in the afternoon. The sun was out, and it had warmed up considerably compared to the previous evening. Splash's condition had not changed at all since the morning. By this time, I was considering sending her to a hospital where she could be observed constantly, and if necessary, surgery could be performed. Abdominal surgery in the horse is a phenomenal process that requires special facilities and a very skilled surgical team.

I discussed the options with Connie, and because of financial considerations, we elected a more conservative approach.

"What else can we do for her here?" she asked.

"We can give her some intravenous fluids, but that is a little labor intensive," I replied, knowing that even the cost of this option was beyond the comfort level of Connie's bank account. "You know, sometimes when I send a colic case to the surgical center the horse gets better on the ride up there. I don't know if the trailer ride "shakes something loose' in there or what," I told her, scratching my head, "but I've known quite a few that responded to 'therapeutic trailer rides.'"

I left Splash and Connie feeling a little sad that money so often dictates the extent of the care we can provide our animals. Although we were not yet to a life-or-death situation with Splash, the fact that economics would dictate whether or not we could even consider a surgical option took some of the joy of practicing medicine from me.

I called Connie later that day.

"You should see the back of my nice, almost new, formerly clean trailer! Who do you think is gonna' clean up that mess!" she exclaimed with feigned resentment. "All that oil and other stuff you put into her plus about thirty pounds of mushy alfalfa is all over the back of the trailer, and I bet there's a lot more on the road between here and Watsonville. I didn't bother to stop."

It took another couple of days until Splash was nickering for her breakfast, but God's help, a little medicine, and a trailer ride did the trick.

_ Colic, Calcium, and Client Loyalty

Things ain't always as they seem. Just because a horse doesn't eat, doesn't mean the problem is primarily in the digestive tract. Just because he's weak or paralyzed, doesn't mean the problem is primarily in the nervous system. Just because you've known a client for years, given countless bits of free advice over the phone at all hours, and some free service, as well...just because you think he is *your* client, doesn't mean you're *his* veterinarian.

I get a call from Tommy about nine on a Saturday night: "I got a mare with colic, Doc," he began, "and I know it's late, but I really need some help, and I can't keep her up long enough for a safe trailer ride to the clinic. I'd sure like you to come to my place."

Tommy's place was at the end of my practice area, about an hour's drive away—not quite Antarctica, but the later the time, the longer the drive could seem. But he'd been a good client (I thought) for a while, and I always put clients like him first, so the prospect of the drive didn't bother me very much. I kissed my very understanding wife goodbye and jumped in the truck, headed south. The moon was full and bright, and the cool evening air offered a respite from the oppressive heat we had been suffering that summer. Emergency calls always gave me an adrenaline rush and a sort of second wind, even when I'd had a fairly long day. I have always enjoyed emergency work. I can usually help the horse, the clients are usually glad to see me, and my response in an emergency situation has often been the beginning of a lasting and rewarding relationship.

Usually.

I arrived in the barnyard lit by headlights from two pickups and a few flashlight-wielding neighbors, likely there for the entertainment in addition to some real concern for the horse. This is common for emergency calls. The illumination casts surreal shadows like that around a car wreck on the highway at night and generally confirms something I call "headlight triage": the magnitude to the wreck is directly proportional to the number of neighbors present at the scene. It also markedly decreases the likelihood of successful treatment—sort of a corollary of "Murphy's Law" and whatever *can* go wrong *will* go wrong. But that's a whole 'nuther story.

"This mare has HYPP," Tommy said after the dust settled in the yard, "and this is the medicine *my vet* gave me for her." He handed me a bottle of a common diuretic used for the management of HYPP, a genetically transferred, metabolic problem.

MY vet? I was thinking. *Who the heck am I?* After all the free advice I had helped Tommy with over the years, I had to wonder about the apparent lack of loyalty—or maybe I just hadn't heard him right.

"Dr. Smith's answering service said they'd let him know we had an emergency, but he didn't call me back for a while. When he finally did, you were already on your way, so I told him we had it covered."

Yep, I'd heard him right. I was not his vet. This is sorta like when your high school sweetheart, the girl for whom you would gladly die, tells you she "just wants to be friends." I was feeling a little like the runner-up in the bridesmaid contest, ugly dress and all.

I stuffed my pride up under my hat and focused on the horse. "How long you had her?"

"A couple of years," Tommy replied. "We got her cheap 'cause she's got that 'Impressive thing,' you know."

He was referring to "hyperkalemic periodic paralysis"—the HYPP the mare was medicated for—a genetic disorder found in many halter-type Quarter Horses that also plagued a few Paints and Appaloosas. It comes from at least one very popular "halter stallion" called Impressive, and that's why it's called by some "Impressive Syndrome." He was foaled in 1969, at the beginning of a movement toward massively muscled show horses. While many Quarter Horses tend to be a little "chunky"—a trait that suggests some draft horse influence among the founding family members—some breeders have taken this to an extreme.

"Halter horses" are a class specifically bred for their appearance. Although many breeds show horses "in hand," or unridden, they are also shown in athletic events. Conversely, halter horses in the American Quarter Horse breed are not typically ridden (there are some exceptions). They are selected for extreme muscle development and the modern version looks like some of those steroid-inflated muscle men in bodybuilder competitions. I guess some folks think that looks good, but I feel the breed has strayed a bit from its founding principles, as stated by the AQHA Executive Committee meeting minutes from April 22, 1940:

> *All Quarter Horses must be able to run a quarter mile in twenty-three seconds or show that they are capable of Quarter Horse Performance under ranch conditions.*

I doubt some of these modern "show horses" can run a quarter mile in twenty-three *minutes!* Selection for this extreme, over-muscled conformation has carried with it some unintended consequences—most notably HYPP. By the turn of the twenty-first century, there were at least fifty thousand carriers of this genetic defect—*and* there are five other known genetic diseases that plague the Quarter Horse breed.

Sorta like blue eyes, HYPP is genetic, meaning "they can't just get over it," and they *will* pass it along to their offspring. It is a very complex metabolic disorder that changes the way skeletal muscle uses potassium, an essential element in the diet. The extra potassium in carrots can send affected horses over the edge into a full-on, paralytic episode: You find 'em lying on the ground, shaking like they just saw a vet bill.

"Our vet sold us this stuff, and it's supposed to help with the seizures." Tommy motioned toward the bottle of tablets he had handed me, which helped lower blood potassium levels, the basis of the HYPP problem. However, the medication needed to be given on a daily basis to prevent episodes, not as a treatment when an episode occurred. Apparently Tommy didn't know this. I knew we were headed for a long night, and I wasn't real optimistic about the outcome.

HYPP is part of some real complicated physiology that we're just now beginning to understand. Skeletal muscle uses the movement of electrolytes—sodium, potassium, calcium, and carbonate ions—in and out of the cells to produce the mechanics required for contraction. At the cellular level, it is basically an electromagnetic function that reminds me of a mechanical fence stretcher, but if you don't know what that looks like, the analogy is lost. So think of it as simply a microscopic "zip tie" that sort of scrunches up the individual muscle cells like a hay hook on the rungs of a ladder during contraction. These tiny mechanical devices only move the muscle cells a few micrometers (that ain't far, at all!), but the combination of this in millions of cells results in some profound events. Skeletal muscle contracts to provide an amazing range of motion, from propelling a half-ton horse at almost forty miles per hour, to minute eye movements keeping the world in focus while at a dead run.

The electromagnetic part of this dynamic process is provided by "ions," or "electrolytes"—hence the "electromagnetic" part—which are actively pumped in and out of muscle cells in a very precise manner. (They don't just magically show up.) Horses with HYPP have a "leaky pipe" that moves sodium in and out of the cells. If sodium is leaking out at the wrong place and the wrong time, it triggers premature, uncontrolled muscle contractions in an HYPP attack. The elevated blood potassium level is where the "hyperkalemia" in the name comes from. The periodic table of elements symbol for potassium is "K," so "kalemia" is how much "K" is in the blood. Hyperpotassiumemia doesn't just roll off your tongue! (See, you learn something every day.)

Diagnosing this problem may appear fairly simple, as the horse is likely on the floor of the stall and unable to get up. Tommy knew this mare had the disease because there's a genetic test for it and she had the genes. But a horse with an acute bout of colic can present the same way as one with a an HYPP attack: on the stall floor, not eating, and apparently unable to get up. Or…she could have an infection due to the West Nile Virus, Equine Herpesvirus, hypocalcemia due to heavy lactation, or even rabies.

Simple, right?

It got just a bit more complicated. Lab results in the more rural parts of our country at ten o'clock on a Saturday night are slightly lacking, so in my case, you gotta go with your gut. The mare wouldn't eat. I'd treat her for colic. We knew she was HYPP positive, so I'd give her some intravenous calcium with glucose. This would help drive potassium back into the muscle cells where it wouldn't trigger premature contractions. I hated this "shotgun approach," and the old adage, "It can't hurt" did not apply. Too much calcium can cause some serious heart problems, so you must listen to the heart carefully and often. If you start to hear irregular heartbeats, you gotta stop administering calcium right away.

After a few minutes of treatment, the mare quit trying to go down and roll, she actually showed some interest in eating a little hay, and I was feeling a little better about her chances. In fact, I was cleaning up my stuff, writing records, and just about ready to go home when she started trembling and wanting to go down again. I did a rectal on her to make sure we were not dealing with a twisted gut, and the exam was unremarkable. This was where the complications just kept on coming.

"This is not good," I began. "We've treated her with several meds for pain, tried to balance out the calcium and potassium, but it looks like we are still not able to keep her comfortable. This is a problem, and now is the time to consider sending her to a referral hospital for surgery, if that becomes an option. I don't think she has twisted her gut, but we gotta remember we are real limited in how much we can feel. The bowel is about a hundred feet long, and we can only feel a small portion of that. She may have a major problem farther up the tract that I can't detect yet but may be real obvious later. We can try more calcium, but there's a real challenge in controlling the pain, so I'm not optimistic about our chances here."

Doing the "kind thing" is seldom easy, but after some tears, thought, and lengthy discussion about our options, Tommy and his wife decided referral was not possible. We gave her the drug cocktail necessary to anesthetize her and stop her heart.

It is amazing how quickly some cases like this can decline, and exactly why we lost this patient, and how I lost this client, remains a mystery.

_ Jade

"I hope you're close by, Doc." The panic-stricken voice crackled through the poor reception of my cellular phone. "I think Jade is colicking again."

The recent stormy weather made the electronic marvel that was my phone a little moody, but I got enough of the message to turn my truck around and head south.

Susan was the manager of an Arabian horse farm near Carmel Valley, at the southern end of my practice area. An excellent horseman, she had the ability to spot problems early, and her careful observations had saved the day on many occasions. She knew that when a horse refused to eat, it usually meant trouble, and there was no time to waste. Although she was always professional, I knew her normally calm demeanor was shaken because the subject of her concern, a fine mare named Jade...who was *her* horse.

I examined Jade and her condition was "ADR." That's a fancy medical term that stands for "Ain't Doin' Right." Although she was off her feed, she was not demonstrating other signs that are usually associated with colic: rolling, sweating, looking at her belly, or having a rapid pulse and respiration rate. I listened to her abdomen with my stethoscope on both her left and right sides and noticed that her gut sounds were depressed.

Jade had experienced some minor colic episodes in the recent few days, and it appeared that while my treatment was helping control the pain, the condition had not yet been resolved. I rolled up my sleeve and performed a rectal exam on the gentle mare. Jade probably thought the procedure did more harm than good, as she already had more pressure in her abdomen than she wanted. She had a good attitude about it, though, and stood well while I explored as much of her abdominal cavity as my limited arm would allow.

Most folks don't realize that the "abdominal cavity" (the belly) of a horse is as big as it is. A standard, half-ton horse has about one hundred feet of bowel that contains up to fifty gallons of ingesta at any given time. The abdominal cavity, containing both large and small bowels, extends from the pelvis to about the level of the sixth rib. In other words, much of what we consider the "chest" of a horse is actually the abdomen. The thoracic cavity contains the heart at the level of about the second through fifth ribs, and the lungs, which are above a line from the elbow to the pelvis. The "thoracic cavity," or chest, is fairly narrow when compared with the rest of the "barrel" of the horse. Therefore, the lungs occupy a thin slice of the outsides of the barrel surrounding the guts on both sides. With this in mind, it would be impossible to feel the entire contents of the abdominal cavity with one skinny, un-tall Texan's arm.

The only abnormality detected on my examination of Jade was a displacement of the spleen and left kidney. This indicated that there was probably an impaction in the large bowel somewhere in the front half of the abdominal cavity. Because of the blockage caused by the impaction, there was a buildup of gas in the bowel, which, in turn, caused the spleen and kidney to be pushed backward. Although I couldn't exactly feel the impaction, the change in the location of the spleen and kidney was good circumstantial evidence, the same way that traffic backs up on the freeway for a couple of miles behind a wreck. Even though you didn't see the accident, it's a safe bet that there was one.

Next, I passed a stomach tube through Jade's right nostril into her esophagus and down into her stomach. I injected some water in the tube once I was certain that it was in the stomach and looked for gastric reflux. This is done by attempting to siphon off water from the stomach and is something I look for but hope not to find. The presence of gastric reflux is indicated by siphoning out *more* water than was put in. This suggests the presence of either a severe blockage in the front part of the bowel, or a condition called "anterior enteritis"—either one of which is bad.

Since there was no gastric reflux, I pumped a gallon of mineral oil into the mare's stomach. This helps to lubricate the contents of the bowel and break up an impaction, which, at the time, was what I thought to be the problem. In addition, I gave her an injection of Banamine® with some smooth-muscle-relaxing capabilities to ease the cramps.

"I think she has a stubborn impaction in her dorsal colon," I said, "but it should break up soon. There is still nothing that I can feel that would indicate a twisted gut, and that's a relief. Twists usually cause lots more pain than Jade is experiencing now. The oil and analgesic should help break things loose within a couple of days. She doesn't seem dehydrated yet, so I don't think she would benefit from IV fluids," I added.

While we were standing there, Jade started nibbling at some alfalfa that was on the floor of the stall.

"That's my girl," Susan said. "She never met a bale of hay she didn't like!"

"You should keep a close eye on her throughout the rest of the day," I warned. "The analgesic I gave her will wear off in about five or six hours. If she gets painful again, we'll want to come up with a new plan."

"What do you think could be causing this? She has never had colic before, why is it happening now?" Susan was afflicted with a psychosis common to horse people: denial.

"Good question. I wish I knew the answer."

"Well, make something up!" she quipped. Susan was well aware of my tendency toward long-winded fabrications, which commonly ended with a shrug and an "I dunno."

"I have an old veterinary textbook at home that was printed in 1897," I started.

"About the time *you* graduated?" she interrupted.

"Don't start on me now," I joked. "I haven't finished figuring up your bill!"

What I started to say to Susan was that, although there has been a lot of research on colic over the past century, we still don't know too much about its actual cause. The obvious things still apply: Internal parasites (worms), sudden feed changes, too much cold water after a hard work, and moldy feed can all bring on an episode of colic. Most of the time, as luck would have it, the inciting cause is unknown.

"Another of your famous 'I dunnos'?"

"Exactly," and I shrugged. "The treatments are about the same, too. Of course, surgery is an option nowadays in some cases, but we are still mostly limited to painkillers, intestinal lubricants, and intravenous fluids. The modern drugs tend to be a little safer than the old ones, but the idea behind the treatment hasn't changed much in a long time. We won't be able to completely prevent colic until we understand the exact cause."

After a few days and several phone conversations between client and vet, Jade was back to her old, sweet self.

"She seems about as normal as she ever was," Susan said, "but she sure gave me a worry—especially after losing our stallion to colic a couple of years back. What can we do to prevent this from happening again?"

"Well," I replied, "you guys are doing about all you can. You have all your horses on a good worming schedule. We do routine dental exams and floats at least once a year, and you are careful to avoid sudden feed changes. I can't think of anything else."

"We did turn her out on the new grass for a couple of hours last week," she commented, "but not for more than a couple of hours a day."

"I don't see any problem with new grass being fed like that," I said, "as long as you introduce the change gradually like that, you should be okay."

"Why did she stay sick for so long? She wasn't right for almost a week, and most of the colics I have seen only lasted a few hours," she asked.

"Some impactions can take a while to break up," I answered, "and it is fairly common for a horse to develop a little diarrhea when it finally happens. This is the body's way of loosening the impaction and flushing it out. Another possibility is that she has an 'enterolith,' or stone, formed somewhere in her gut, which can also present mild, prolonged or recurring episodes of colic."

"I've heard of those. Do you think that may be what's going on? Maybe we should stop feeding her alfalfa. I've heard that the extra calcium in alfalfa hay can cause those stones to form."

I explained that the formation of enteroliths in the bowel of a horse is a problem that is poorly understood. It probably starts out with some source of irritation, and like a pearl forms in an oyster, the body deposits layers of minerals around it until a stone builds up over time, eventually causing a blockage and colic. The mild, prolonged colic like the one Jade had was typical of those caused by stones, but most impactions, regardless of whether the material is undigested feed, a mass of parasites, or an enterolith, will cause the same symptoms. Enteroliths can only be diagnosed by an X-ray or exploratory surgery of the abdomen, and either of those procedures would have had to be done at a referral hospital. The small, portable machine I carried could not penetrate the belly well enough to tell us what we wanted to know, and equine abdominal surgery "in the field" was too risky, for a lot of reasons.

"What about the alfalfa?" she asked.

"That's an interesting question. The problem with enteroliths in horses seems to be limited to the West Coast. Other parts of the country feed alfalfa hays but don't have the problems that we have with stones," I explained. "There's no doubt that they are caused by the minerals we have in our soil and water, but nobody is sure about what conditions are necessary for their formation. If alfalfa was the problem, there would be a lot of horses colicked with stones, and I just don't see that many."

Jade, like about eighty-five percent of the cases of colic I treat, responded to conservative medical treatment. The fact that it took so long for her problem to be resolved suggested that she had an impaction, but the exact cause will never be known. As frustrating as that is, at least she survived. Other horses, unfortunately, are not so lucky.

_ Moe

Not every case of colic is obvious, either in its symptoms or severity. With this in mind, even the suspicion of colic should be considered an emergency. When a horse doesn't eat, it generally means that something isn't right.

Early one spring I received a call to come look at a lame horse. Moe was a big, stout, good-doing Arab gelding that was definitely a favorite of mine. He was a no-nonsense type of horse that would let you know that you were sure'nuff horseback; it didn't matter if it was a hundred yards or a hundred miles, just get on and get ready.

Denise was the proud owner of this outstanding horse. She was concerned because Moe had been a little off in the right rear leg for a couple of days and wasn't getting any better. I started my exam by watching him move at the trot.

Although most horse owners commonly do not properly identify the affected leg on a lame horse, Denise was right on target.

I went through two hours of diagnostic nerve blocks, flexion tests, and even a little witchcraft, but I could not identify the source of Moe's pain.

"I don't know, Doc, but I sort of think it's in his hip," was Denise's analysis.

"Anything's possible," I started, "but that would be pretty rare. I've done everything I can think of, but I sure can't identify the source of his pain today."

"Do you think an X-ray would help?" Denise asked hopefully.

"I'm sure it would, if only I could figure out which spot hurt him. There's several likely places on the back leg, but we can't be sure until I can make him go sound by blocking the painful sensation to a specific area. We could X-ray him 'til his hair falls out, but it won't do us any good unless we know just exactly where it hurts, and he's being a little tight-lipped about that."

I left with a plan of returning in a few days when Moe's problem might be more obvious. I got real busy and didn't think too much about him until a week later when Denise called me again.

"Hey, Doc, I think you need to come see Moe again, something just isn't right. He seems to have lost his appetite and he's still lame."

"How long has he been off his feed?"

"Just today, but it isn't like him not to really scarf down the groceries."

I canceled my next appointment (thank God for cellular phones) and went to see Moe.

The gelding had a pulse of eighty, higher than the normal rate of about forty, and his respiration was sixty, about five times faster than it should have been. Increases in pulse and respiration rates are the primary indicators of abdominal pain in a horse. He had no gut sounds. He was clammy to touch and was a little dehydrated (I could tell because the skin over his neck stayed folded for a second after I pinched it). His mucous membrane color was bright red. Pink to pale pink is usually normal, while white points to anemia, low blood pressure or blood loss, and red may indicate toxicity, infection, or shock.

The combination of vital signs was not good.

"We got a pretty good case of colic going on here," I said.

"It can't be colic! He's never had it before. How could he have colicked?" Horseman's denial, once again. "I thought he was lame and wouldn't eat because of the pain."

"The two problems are unrelated," I said with authority that I would later have to disclaim. I went on to explain the classic signs of colic that Moe had exhibited and outlined the best course of treatment.

I passed a stomach tube on the willing patient and no reflux was present. I gave him the standard gallon of mineral oil and an injection of Banamine® for the pain. By the time I had cleaned up my instruments and completed my records he was a little better, but not fully recovered, as most cases like this would have been.

"I'm a little concerned," I told Denise, "because I would have expected him to have responded more readily to the treatment. Let's just give him some time and plan to check him again a little later in the day."

"I'm not leaving his side until he's okay," she replied with the resolve I had come to expect from this very dedicated lady.

I returned a few hours later and Moe's condition had deteriorated.

"Is Moe a surgical candidate?" I asked.

Denise thought for a long minute. "I'll have to ask Todd." She hesitated to make the major monetary decision without discussing it with her husband. They decided not to go to a surgical facility, but elected, instead, to give Moe IV fluids and pain medication with the hopes and prayers that he would respond.

I placed a catheter in Moe's jugular vein and started the steady stream of fluids that I hoped would speed his recovery, or at least make him feel better. Any time a horse with colic fails to respond to my initial treatment, I get worried. This was especially true in Moe's case because, although I can find something to like in all my patients, I must confess, I do have my favorites.

I performed an exam *per rectum* and found nothing abnormal about his abdominal anatomy except that the large colon was slightly distended with gas. Next, I shaved and scrubbed a spot right in the middle of his abdomen just north of his belly button. "Abdominocentesis" is a procedure performed by placing a needle through the skin into the peritoneal cavity, a rather small space between the bowel and the belly wall. This allows us to sample a few drops of the fluid that is normally present and examine it under the microscope. The type of cells and amount of protein present in this fluid may help us in diagnosing the problem. An increase in the white blood cell count (WBC) and protein indicates "peritonitis," a serious inflammation in the lining of the abdominal cavity that is usually fatal, and the presence of fecal material in the peritoneal space indicates a ruptured bowel, which is always fatal. Peritoneal fluid with a normal cell count and protein concentration is often an encouraging sign, but it can simply mean that a serious problem is in a stage too early to be detected by analysis of peritoneal fluid. Like most diagnostic tests, this one requires interpretation and must be combined with other factors, like the duration of the illness and the clinical signs of the horse, to be valid.

Although I had hoped to withdraw a sample of fluid from the abdomen, this was a "dry tap," meaning no fluid was present. This was not good or bad, it just meant that no abdominal fluid was present at the spot where I stuck the needle. I tried again but with the same results.

I instructed Denise in the care of IV catheters, and she was comfortable with giving Moe fluids until he urinated. "I'm just going to sit here with him anyway, Doc," she mused. "I may as well be doing something."

I left for a few hours to see some other patients and returned late that evening. Moe's condition had continued to decline, and Denise had given him some of the narcotic painkiller that I had left in case he needed it. By this time, his gums were still slightly reddened and his respiration was quite elevated. This suggested that his blood pH had been altered by increasing acid content. I added some sodium bicarbonate to his fluids in an attempt to balance his blood pH and his respiration rate dropped some.

We continued the fluid therapy through the rest of the night. Moe needed about thirty liters to rehydrate him, and he finally urinated at about three in the morning. This was an indication that the IV fluids had helped to restore hydration, because he had enough excess water in his bloodstream to stimulate urination. Unfortunately, he still was not interested in eating and had not passed any stool. By seven o'clock, he needed more pain relief.

I examined his abdomen rectally again and was about to pull my arm out when he shifted his back legs, and I felt a "pop" or slight crunching in his pelvis.

"What in the world?" I said out loud.

"What is it?" Denise asked.

"Did you hear that?"

"Hear what?"

"I think I finally diagnosed the source of his lameness, but I'm having a hard time believing it!" Now it was my turn to be in denial. "Moe has fractured his pelvis. Remember last week when you said you though that his lameness was in his hip?"

"Yes."

"Well, as much as I hate to admit it, you were almost right! This horse has a fractured pelvis!"

"How in the world did that happen?"

"I can't be sure, but I have seen several cases before. Sometimes I think that they may get cast in a stall or maybe up against a fence, and in a struggle to get up, the pelvic bone just gives way. The good news is that, as long as the hip joint itself is not involved, many of these heal up okay."

"Can you X-ray that to see if there is joint involvement?"

"My portable machine won't penetrate that much mass," I said, "and even if it would, we'd have to give Moe a general anesthetic to knock him out for the X-ray. That would be a little risky, and I'd be afraid that he would injure himself more when he was recovering from anesthesia."

The revelation related to Moe's lameness was a bittersweet victory. Later that day, in the face of uncontrollable pain, I was forced to put an end to the good horse's suffering. Euthanasia was the only humane thing to do, but the decision is never easy. I always wonder after if I had done something different, would the outcome have changed. Although I never put a horse to sleep if there is *anything* else that can possibly be done, I always wish I could have done something more. If a patient recovers, I generally think that it was God's hand that kept him alive. If the patient dies, I often think that I should have been there sooner, stayed longer, or tried harder.

The question of necropsy, especially in such heart-tugging cases like Moe's, is difficult. I really wanted to know the exact cause of Moe's illness, but I was reluctant to ask Denise if I could take apart one of her best friends right there in her back yard. I was relieved when she brought up the subject.

"Do you think you should do a necropsy on him, Doc?" she asked hesitantly. "I almost hate to ask, but I would like to know what happened inside of him. I mean, I know he had a bad colic, but, well, you know...."

"Yeah, I would like to know, myself," I said honestly, "but it's not going to be pretty. You probably won't want to watch. Heck, I don't even want to watch, but I know Moe's gone now to a place where there is no pain. All that is left here is his body. I don't think he'd mind us having a look inside."

I have learned to distance myself from the gruesome task of necropsy because of the astounding amount of knowledge that I gain every time I do it. This time, however, I had a little twinge inside of me as I started to open the lifeless form of a horse that, until a few minutes previously, had been a vital, living, beautiful animal that I was privileged enough to know on a professional and personal level. I wiped a tear from my eye and proceeded after a silent prayer to the Lord and an apology to Moe's spirit, wherever it was. I hoped that he could forgive me, but I had a couple of questions, and there was only one way to get the answers.

Within a minute I had the answer. There was a small hole in the top of Moe's cecum and some stringy, yellow fibrin was streaming out of the hole and adhering to the belly wall. The cecum is the part of the large bowel of the horse that is analogous to our appendix in its location. However, instead of it being a small, relatively nonfunctional remnant leftover from when we were hanging from tree limbs and eating lots of roots and berries, this organ of the horse is about six feet long and has a significant role in the digestion of roughage, absorption of water, and the production of B vitamins by the bacteria that normally live there.

When the body has experienced a source of serious inflammation, like in the puncture of an organ, it will often deposit a fibrous, protein-rich substance called "fibrin" in the area. This process may take a few days to occur, which would place it happening at about the time that Moe came up lame. The hole in the cecum was right next to the fracture in the pelvis where a sharp fragment of bone had penetrated it. Because the hole was in the top of the cecum where there is normally only gas, not ingesta, Moe got along fine for a few days without developing peritonitis. For some reason that will never be known, he did eventually develop peritonitis, and subsequently experienced a colic and died because of it.

It was a very unusual case. Of course, it was very sad, but nonetheless, somewhat comforting to know the cause of the illness. As I've noted, peritonitis in horses is almost always fatal, so it was fortunate that my friend Moe did not have to suffer long with it.

_ "She's GONE!"

Transporting horses is the source of some fear and anxiety among us, and I find it very interesting how many horses who may otherwise be pretty solid citizens become absolute maniacs when we ask 'em to get in a trailer. But I also think anyone that drags one of these scary rolling boxes down the road at sixty miles an hour ought to be required by law to ride in one first. They are loud, dusty, and hard to stand up in, even for me, so I can only imagine what horses must think during their first experiences in these contraptions. Thankfully, most horses are pretty forgiving, or we'd never be able to load 'em the second time so we could take 'em back where we started.

Dr. Bo Brock, a renowned veterinarian in Lamesa, Texas, told me a story years ago about a client who didn't want to pay for a farm call. Dr. Brock told him: "You could just bring your horse in to the clinic. That will save me some time and you some money."

"Well, I don't exactly have a horse trailer," the client said, "but I'll see what I can do."

There was no small stir in the parking lot of Dr. Brock's clinic when the client arrived with the horse standing patiently on a flatbed trailer—a *flatbed trailer*, as in one with no sides! I think of this episode occasionally when I hear someone stressing about hauling a horse: There are questions about how to feed and water a horse for a trailer ride. Should there be bedding? Straw or shavings? Air-conditioning? Video monitor? Meanwhile, this horse in Texas apparently tolerated a ten-mile ride into town—and back—on a completely open flatbed trailer.

This is a great illustration of just how basic we can get and how accommodating some horses can be if we just give 'em a chance. Maybe we overthink this whole trailering thing.

Up until about thirty years ago, every trailer was a "straight load," meaning the horses stood front to back. I noticed years ago that many cowboy horses were hauled standing loose in large stock trailers that doubled as cow trailers. (I guess ranchers in those days didn't get too worried about their prize show horses stepping in slimy poop left by careless cows—apparently those days are gone.) Anyway, horses in stock trailers seemed to prefer to stand facing the rear and diagonally. Then, back in the late seventies, some very smart, observant person recognized the horse figured out the easiest way to survive a ride in one of these rolling nightmares and changed the design to accept the horse's opinion on the matter. I'm guessing this was the origin of the "slant-load" trailer.

Fancy slant-loads with living quarters are all the rage now—some of 'em cost more than my house! But the standard, very useful four-horse stock trailer can still be found in the barnyard of just about every ranch in the western United States. These are usually built to last and can serve a variety of functions. One feature on most of these is a slider inside the back door. This allows the rancher to unload a calf (theoretically) without unloading the cow (real theoretically... this works a lot better on paper than on the ranch).

One of these things backfired on us a few years ago. I was attending to Cinnamon, a good mare with a bad colic. None of my go-to remedies were having any effect, and her colon was suspiciously displaced. I determined this with my favorite long plastic sleeve, some lube, and no small amount of nerve.

Upon removing my arm, I explained our dilemma to the client, Cathy. "I'm a little concerned we may be dealing with a displacement, or even a twist in her large bowel," I said, "and this may need another set of eyes and hands to figure out what to do. We may even need surgery to save her."

I really hate this type of case, as many of these surgical patients die on the table or have serious complications during the six-month convalescent period. Some do very well after surgery, but, in reality, there's only three things that can happen, and two of 'em are bad.

Cathy and I discussed the options, possible outcome of surgical intervention—and, oh yeah...the price. She and her husband Carl stepped away a few feet, but not so far that I couldn't hear some "frank negotiations"—meaning a discussion just short of flying fists.

"We are going to surgery!" Cathy announced.

I knew the surgeon would be short-handed that day, so I drove to his clinic just in case he needed help. Carl and Cathy arrived a few minutes later in their trusty Ford pickup and four-horse stock trailer. Cathy was out the door quickly to get Cinnamon out of the trailer to start her treatment.

From the back of the trailer, we heard a shout: "She's gone!"

Carl, the surgeon, and I stood silently for a few beats, respectfully waiting to share in the sorrow of the moment.

Carl spoke first: "I'm sorry, sweetheart. We knew she was pretty sick."

"No!" Cathy replied again. "NO! She's GONE!"

"I know." Carl was reaching deep into his empathy pocket. "Maybe this was for the best. She isn't suffering anymore."

"NO!" she fumed. "You stupid @#$%&*!...She's not in the trailer!"

Sure enough, the trailer was empty—the slider in the back gate had somehow opened during the trip. Apparently, Carl had missed the road to the clinic, and during his effort to turn around, the gate slid open...and the mare slid out. They found Cinnamon grazing in the ditch beside the road as if this happened all the time. The trailer ride apparently allowed her colon to reposition itself and surgery was not required. She spent the night at the clinic, just to be safe, and rode home the next day with the slider secured with the ubiquitous orange bailing twine...just to be safe.

_ Tiny

"Tiny looks real sick, Doc." Another panic-filled voice poured out of my cellular phone late in the day. "He wouldn't eat breakfast this mornin' and now he's sweatin' up a storm an' his front legs are shakin' like he can't stand up. Can you come out right away?"

I turned the truck around, headed to Joe Atwaters' place, and wondered why, no matter where I was headed, an emergency call always made me head back in the direction I had just come from.

I pulled into the barnyard, and Joe had Tiny, a very large Quarter Horse, reluctantly walking between attempts to lie down and roll. Without even examining him first, I grabbed a bottle, syringe, and needle from the back of the truck and began filling it as I walked toward the horse.

"Let's give him a little painkiller now," I said, administering the intravenous injection, which hopefully would stop the cramping that was causing Tiny to want to get down and roll. Within a few minutes, the acute pain had eased some, and I was able to start my examination without much fear of being squashed by the large, but usually gentle, beast. Tiny's heart rate was still sixty beats per minute (remember, the normal rate is about forty), and his respiration rate was fifty per minute, or about four times faster than it should have been. He had no gut sounds. This and the fact that he had not eaten breakfast that morning was the classic, textbook presentation for a horse with colic.

"What do ya' think's wrong with 'im, Doc?"

"Colic"

"Colic!" Joe was incredulous. "How could he have colic? He never had it before! I take good care of 'im. Are you sure?" (Horseman's denial, once again.)

"Yeah, I'm pretty sure. You said he didn't eat breakfast, and he was sure in pain when I first got here. He has pulse and respiration rates way above normal, his gums are white, instead of pink, and he has no gut sounds. That pretty much sums up the presentation of a bellyache."

I tried to pass a stomach tube through Tiny's right nostril, and he struck out at me with a forefoot, just missing my left knee cap, but landing squarely on the arch of my foot.

"I can see that Tiny is not keen on the prospect of swallowing a stomach tube today," I commented. "He might enjoy a little 'cocktail' to take the edge off... what do you think?"

I gave Tiny a little sedative and was able to pass the stomach tube without him rearranging my face. There was no gastric reflux, so I gave him a gallon of mineral oil and removed the tube. I began to clean the oil off of my tube and pump when Tiny began to buckle as if he was about to roll again. I grabbed another bottle from the back of the truck and quickly gave him another injection. This time, I used a preparation of a synthetic morphine. It is a much stronger painkiller, but its duration is only about thirty minutes. In addition to its painkilling action, it has a side effect of slowing down the gut. In a horse that has a problem with slowed gut motility, this is not a welcome side effect. Unfortunately, this drug must be used in some cases of colic because it may be the only way to control pain.

Within another twenty minutes, Tiny was in severe pain again. I gave him another shot of synthetic morphine and performed an examination per rectum. Although there were no abnormal findings from this exam, the fact that Tiny was in so much pain was alarming.

"He twist a gut, Doc?"

"I don't think so, but it may be too early to tell. How long's he been like this?"

"I fed him at five and when I came back out here again at six he was lookin' at his sides and kickin' at his belly," Joe replied, "an' he didn't finish his supper. You can tell by lookin' at 'im that *never* happens."

"It's possible that he does have a twisted gut, but this early, the gut hasn't filled up with gas behind the actual twist for me to be able to tell." Then I had to ask the hard question: "Is he a surgical candidate?"

"I dunno. What do ya' mean?"

"Well, it's possible that he will need surgery in order to survive. If that's the case, the time to make the decision is right now. That's the kind of thing that would require an experienced surgical team and a hospital facility. I could not do it here, by myself," I said. "It's a good two-hour trailer ride to the closest surgical facility that is set up to do it."

"I think Doc Jones has a surgery in his clinic," Joe interjected. "Can't we take him there?"

"Dr. Jones is a fine veterinarian," I replied, "and I will sure send him there if you would prefer. But you got to understand that belly surgery in a horse is a very complicated thing. Even with the best, highly experienced surgical team the procedure is risky. You probably wouldn't go to your family doctor for appendicitis. Joe, honestly, I wouldn't operate on him if he was *my* horse, and I'm a fair-to-middlin' surgeon, myself. It's just too specialized. The big referral hospitals will do two or three *hundred* belly surgeries a year and even their success rate is not that good, in some cases."

"If we take 'im to another surgeon, what are his chances of livin' through that?"

"It depends on exactly what the problem is and how long it takes us to get there," I said. "It's like asking how many people survive car wrecks. If we're talking about a wreck in the grocery store parking lot, then most will survive. If it's one out on the interstate at midnight, that's a whole 'nother thing. We probably won't know the answer to that until we have a look inside." I could see that my answer was not very comforting, to say the least.

"I sure love this ole' horse," Joe started, "but how much money we talkin' 'bout?"

"It usually runs three to five thousand."

He paused. "Is there anything else we can do?"

"Yeah, we can start him on IV fluids and keep giving him painkillers," I said. "That would sure be the next thing to do whether we send 'im to surgery, or not."

"Let's do that, if you think it will help. I don't think I could come up with surgery money right now…there's just too many other things I gotta think of first."

I shaved an area over Tiny's jugular vein and scrubbed it with surgical soap and rinsed it with alcohol. This is not necessary for a simple, intravenous injection, because the hole I make in the vein closes up as soon as I pull the needle out. An in-dwelling venous catheter, on the other hand, is a fairly large plastic tube that stays in the vein for up to three days. I like to be real clean when I put one of these things in a horse's neck because I don't want to introduce an infection into the bloodstream. I usually put a little drop of "super glue" on the skin around the catheter to seal up the hole, and in addition, I stitch it to the skin so that it cannot be easily pulled out by a reluctant patient.

"How we gonna keep 'im from rubbin' that thing out of his neck, Doc? I don't think he's gonna stand that very long."

"That'll be easy," I said. "Just think of a twenty-dollar bill."

"How's that gonna help?"

"'Cause that's what it's gonna cost you if I have to put another one in."

We tied ole' Tiny in his stall, hung the first bag of IV fluids from the top of the stall door, and watched as the lactated ringer's solution flowed down the clear plastic line into Tiny's jugular vein. This is a solution of sterile water and all the salts, or electrolytes, found normally in blood.

"What makes you think these IVs will help him any, Doc?"

"That's kind of hard to explain, but it has something to do with the way his body conserves water. When a horse goes into shock because of colic, the body dumps a bunch of water into the blood vessels around his gut. This takes extra blood away from the rest of his body and that was why his gums were white instead of pink when I first got here. At any given time, about a fourth of the ten gallons of blood in his body is in his kidneys. When another part of his body gets in a bind, the kidneys are shut down to conserve blood and water. For a short time, it's a lot more important for him to have blood for his brain, heart, and lungs than it is to have it in his kidneys. The kidneys have two vital functions: One is to filter out the 'exhaust' or products of normal metabolism from his blood. Although he can do without this for a little while, the lack of kidney function will catch up to him later, with potentially fatal consequences."

He seemed to be following, so I went on: "The other major function of the kidney is to conserve water when he's dehydrated, or to eliminate excess water when he's been licking the salt block like it was candy and then drinks ten gallons out of the tank. The kidney works too well, sometimes, and a dehydrated horse won't pee, so the products of normal metabolism build up in his blood. The more they build up, the more toxic they become, and the more the kidney shuts down. It becomes a vicious cycle that can be broken by IV fluids. By giving him extra fluids directly into his vein, we can expand his blood volume and help him to keep all his organ systems working. It also just seems to make them feel better."

My lengthy explanation was the beginning of what proved to be a long night. Several times during the first two hours, Tiny started pawing the stall floor and acting like he would like nothing better than to roll. I had to give him several doses of the painkilling synthetic morphine to keep his pulse and respiration down and him as comfortable as possible. With each dose of the narcotic, I became more pessimistic about Tiny's chances. The presence of uncontrollable pain is the beginning of the end for many colic patients.

"Do you think he twisted a gut 'cause he rolled earlier?" Joe asked.

I pulled on a shoulder-length, plastic sleeve, applied some lubricant, and performed another rectal exam. "I don't think he's twisted yet, and if he did, it probably didn't have anything to do with rolling," I replied.

Confronted with an old wives' tale that never seemed to die—and since it takes a long time to give IV fluids to a sick horse—I took the time to attempt to dispel it.

"Some folks think that a rolling horse will twist a gut, but my old brainless gelding, Buddy, has rolled every time I have taken a saddle off of him for the last eight years, and he hasn't twisted a gut yet," I commented.

"I never thought of it that way."

"The gut is really a fairly simple structure, even though it is capable of some amazingly complicated functions. It's just a hundred-foot-long tube made of smooth muscle, lined with a thin sponge so it can absorb water and nutrients. It even has its own automatic nervous system. You know, when you swallow something, you don't have to think about it. In fact, if you think about it, you can't really do it! When there is a little wad of feed in the gut, the pressure that it causes makes the smooth muscle squeeze back. This reflex occurs in just one direction, usually, and shoves feed down the tube toward the south end of the horse. This is the hundred-foot trail that turns alfalfa to road apples in just five or six days."

"It takes *that* long?" Even at midnight, Joe was awake enough to suspect that I was pulling his leg, as I had been guilty of that before.

"The rate of passage, or gut motility, depends on what the horse is eating," I said, "but five or six days is about average. The squeezing action of the gut is called 'peristalsis' and it's working all the time. That's why you ought to hear gut sounds in a horse all the time. Because the gut is always moving, it can get itself into a bind, sometimes. For instance, if it comes up against something that won't move, it can actually flip back on itself, sort of like stepping on a high-pressure water hose. So I think that most of the time, in the case of a horse that has a twist, or torsion of the intestine, it probably happened long before the horse started rolling. It could be that the twist started all the pain and the horse started rolling to try to untwist himself. You know, like a mare trying to have a foal. She can lie down, roll a little, and reposition the colt so he can come out easier."

"So we should have let 'im roll?"

"I wouldn't a told you that. I wouldn't want you to sue me if things didn't work out," I said, only half-kidding.

"I wouldn't do that, Doc."

"Thanks."

"Don't thank me. I just know that your truck ain't paid for and you live in a rented house!"

A little comic relief is always appreciated.

By two in the morning, after we had put about forty liters of lactated ringers solution into Tiny, he stretched out his massive back legs and eliminated a modest volume of dark, foul-smelling urine that permeated the small confines of the stall. Joe looked worried.

"That ain't too good, is it Doc," Joe stated, rather than asked.

"Actually, that's good. The fact that he peed means that we finally got him hydrated and the last six hours has not been wasted. The dark color and delightful bouquet means that his kidneys are concentrating urine and still functioning properly." I was becoming less pessimistic.

By three, Tiny started to nibble at some of the hay left in his stall from the previous night's supper. He still had not passed any manure, but the fact that he was interested in eating was a good sign. He had not required any pain medication in over three hours. I started to think I might be able to catch a couple of hours of sleep before my morning rounds, after all.

"Let's get some sleep," I suggested. "I'll be back at eight and recheck him, but I think he may pull through this."

I packed up my stuff and drove home bleary-eyed, and glad my truck knew the way. Joe called me at about six-thirty.

"I don't think you need to come back, Doc," a relieved Joe Atwater roared into my sleepy ear. "Ole' Tiny's tearin' the barn down an' hollerin' for breakfast!"

It never bothers me to have a wake-up call like that!

The Nervous System Makes Me Nervous

*Neurology, the study of the nervous system,
is as fascinating as it is complicated. Most diseases
of the equine nervous system share common symptoms,
so it is not usually possible to make a quick diagnosis
simply on presentation. The pages ahead give
an overview of common equine neurological diseases,
as well as their diagnosis, treatment, and prevention,
and what happens when things go wrong.
(One of these diseases is transmissible
from the horse to human!)*

CHAPTER

5

The young mare stood trembling and bleeding a little from a nasty cut on her hind leg. She was still tied to the trailer, which was the only winner in a recent battle of wills in an "unloading lesson." For reasons known only to Whiskey, an opinionated ten-year-old mare, she liked to scramble frantically out of the two-horse trailer that she apparently liked less than Shana did. Whiskey and Shana had achieved some local fame in team-penning competition, but the trailer behavior had been a source of aggravation for Shana and a potential danger to Whiskey.

"I just don't understand why she keeps doin' that," Shana said through her tears. "I got this new, bigger trailer so she loads okay now, but I'm always worried that she will slip and fall because she still hurries to get out. It looks like she really did it to herself, this time."

She had. Most of the skin of her left rear leg had been rolled down like a cheap sock from her hock to her ankle. The extensor tendon had been lacerated, but thankfully the flexor tendon had not been damaged. This was the best news of the evening, since flexor tendon lacerations are usually serious and can end the career of a performance horse. Extensor tendon lacerations, conversely, are much more forgiving. This is because the flexor tendons—those in the back of the lower leg—must bear a tremendous amount of weight. Scar tissue in one of these weight-bearing organs tends to be weaker than the normal structure of a tendon and is easily reinjured. Extensor tendons—those on the front part of the lower leg—don't bear any weight, so lacerations usually have little effect on the motion of the limb.

Although there was no critical injury to any joint or tendon in Whiskey's leg, the cut was about twelve inches long and deep. It went all the way to the cannon bone, involving the "periosteum"— the fibrous, rawhide-like tissue that surrounds the bone and carries about a third of its blood supply. I really wanted to try to suture this wound because of my concern for the exposed bone and the potential for infection.

"Do you think you can sew it up?" Shana sobbed.

"I think we ought to try," I replied. "Of course, sometimes these lower leg wounds don't heal as well as we would like. I'm not sure if it's due to the lack of blood supply, or exactly what it is, but we will likely have to deal with some 'proud flesh' no matter what we do now. If we stitch this wound up today, there's a good chance that the stitches will pull out in four or five days, but at least that will give us a little use of the 'biological Band-Aid' that her skin will provide in the meantime. Even if the stitches do pull out before we get good healing, I think we will have less proud flesh and less chance of infection."

"Let's try, then," she said. "Do you think I'll ever be able to ride her again?"

"You should be back in the saddle in a few weeks," I told her. "Whiskey's wound is more of a cosmetic problem than a functional one. There are no vital structures at risk right now. I don't think she'll have any permanent *functional* damage, but the cut leg will always be larger than the other one, and she'll have a scar she can brag about for the rest of her life."

I prepared a bucket with clean hot water and cotton to gently wash Whiskey's cut leg. Strong disinfectants like peroxide, iodine (even the denatured "tamed" variety), or wound dyes you get at the feed store (blue, red, pink—they're all bad) should never be used on horse wounds. These chemicals are very toxic to bacteria and that's good, but they are also toxic to the horse's cells, and that's bad. Since we hope to bring the torn edges together with suture, we want to keep the damaged tissue as healthy as possible. If we damage these delicate tissues, we may impair the healing process, and this would defeat the purpose of sewing the wound up in the first place. For example, if you want to glue two pieces of paper together, you start with clean paper. Suturing tissue with a lot of cells that have been damaged by trauma or chemicals is like trying to glue two pieces of dirty paper together.

I like to use large volumes of sterile saline or saline mixed with raw honey to clean wounds because these fluids are more gentle to skin and other tissues. In addition, I trim the edge of the wound with scissors until fresh blood appears. The presence of the blood supply means that we are starting with relatively healthy tissue.

As I approached Whiskey, she snorted like she didn't like the smell of a transplanted Texan with a stainless-steel bucket in his hand. Go figure. As she turned to face me, I could tell that she was not interested in *any* veterinary care at the moment. I talked to her and stroked her neck a little, but she would have none of my sweet talk. I injected a small amount of tranquilizer into her jugular vein, hoping that a mild sedative would instill a more cooperative nature in this good but worried mare. After a few minutes it was obvious that Whiskey would require a little more drug before she was going to be comfortable with the situation. I gave her some more, but by this time she was wise to the needle, and we had to dance around a little in a dangerous version of something like the "Cotton-Eye Joe" that used to be popular in the dance halls back home. Whiskey was pretty mad at me by the time I got the second shot in her after a few steps of our worried waltz. Finally, her head dropped a little, and she began to relax as the painkiller took her mind off her leg and the sedative took her mind off me.

I slowly began to wash and examine the cut leg. I was thankful that my initial impression was accurate and there was no serious damage to any vital structures. Despite the fairly high dose of drug circulating in Whiskey's bloodstream, she was still moving away and kicking at me a little as I tried to gently clean the wound.

Whenever possible, I try to suture cuts on horses while they are standing, as opposed to lying them down under general anesthesia. Modern drugs are usually safe and effective, but there is always an increased risk with a "general." Of course, an injection of a local anesthetic is often required for painless surgery, but most horses don't object too much to the shot. I mix lidocaine with a little "bicarb"—the same stuff you take after too much pizza—and it takes the sting out of local anesthesia. I learned this from an ER nurse many years ago, and I thank her (at least, in my mind) often.

I explained the plan to Shana and Whiskey, both of whom seemed to be listening attentively. I drew a syringe full of lidocaine and gently placed a small, very sharp needle under the skin near the top edge of the wound. This is usually the only part of the procedure that the horse feels. The lidocaine works so quickly that, once the needle is under the skin, the effect of the drug can block the pain before the needle is advanced. If you keep injecting a little anesthetic while you are advancing the needle, it is possible to block a large area with the horse feeling only the first needle stick. Whiskey was apparently not aware of this phenomenon, and she kicked the needle and syringe out of my hand with admirable accuracy. Repeated attempts brought similar results.

"It looks like Whiskey may require a little general anesthesia before we can sew up the wound," I said, knowing that a "little general anesthesia" was like a "little pregnant."

"I can see that," Shana replied. "Isn't that dangerous?" Then she added, "And how expensive is it?"

"It's usually pretty safe and easy," I said, "and I don't charge anything to knock her out, just to wake her up!" My lame attempts at humor sometimes lighten the mood in serious situations, but at the time I was blissfully ignorant of just how hard this was going to be. "But seriously, if we plan to suture this wound, it will require general anesthesia."

With all the skill of a truly gifted equine anesthesiologist I gave the injections that would provide peaceful sleep for Whiskey and give me eighteen to twenty minutes of deep, surgical anesthesia to get most of the wound sutured. The mare would stay down for another thirty to forty-five minutes for a nonpainful procedure, so this would allow me to wrap the leg before she tried to stand. The combination of drugs I use is quite safe and can be repeated, if necessary, several times.

About three minutes after the second injection, Whiskey started gently swaying like she was listening to some music that she really liked. Then she sat back on her hind legs and rolled over on the hard-packed, California summertime earth. I held on to the lead shank so she wouldn't bang her head on the ground and placed one towel under her head for a pillow and laid another over her eye. She trembled a little and took a couple of deep, relaxed breaths. She was ready.

I had already laid out my sterile instrument tray, towels, sutures, and other supplies that I would need to complete the surgery. The anesthetic time is so short that you need to be prepared so none of your time is wasted going after supplies.

About six minutes into the procedure, Whiskey started moving. She kicked over my instrument tray and sent sterile instruments and my stainless-steel bucket clattering across the barnyard.

The mare was obviously no cheap drunk, as her liver and kidneys had rapidly metabolized the anesthetic drugs and she was waking up more quickly than normal. I gave her a half-dose and waited a couple of minutes. Seeing that it wasn't enough, I gave her another half-dose. This seemed to be enough, so I placed my instruments in cold sterilization and started cleaning the surgical site again. I put some more sterile drapes around the wound and started trimming the ragged edges of skin so they could be sutured.

Four minutes later, she gave yet another demonstration of just how good her liver and kidneys were at removing anesthetic drugs from her body. This time she kicked the instrument trays and buckets even farther than she did the first time. I gave her another dose of anesthetic and repeated the cleaning and draping of the leg. I was getting pretty good at it, too, from all the practice I'd had during the recent twelve minutes.

Finally, in record time, I placed the last suture in the skin and applied a sterile dressing under a great big bandage that I hoped would protect the wound when she got up from the anesthesia. I gave her thirty ccs of penicillin to fight infection, two grams of bute for inflammation, and a little tetanus toxoid because it's cheap insurance to prevent "tetanus," or "lockjaw." I did all this so quickly, I had the urge to throw up my hands in the air like a champion calf roper at the end of a world-record time, but my stiff back and bruised knees wouldn't cooperate. I stood next to my now-cooperative patient, minus her smart-aleck theatrics.

I looked at the pile of drapes, dirty cotton, and gauze bandages scattered about the barnyard. I silently thanked God that this "simple" surgery was over. I wiped my hands on my last clean towel and thought, *It couldn't get any worse than this!*

It did.

The wreck that followed was one of the most horrifying experiences of my practice career. Although this happened a long time ago, I still think about it and shudder.

Field anesthesia almost always results in an uneventful recovery. I leave a towel over the horse's eyes and avoid unnecessary sound or touch, as any stimulation can cause the horse to attempt to stand too soon. It is important that the patient lie quietly until the drug is metabolized almost completely out of system. After the drug is cleared from the brain and spinal cord, the horse can stand without falling down again.

Unfortunately, Whiskey's efficient liver and kidneys combined with her being "mad" at me prior to the anesthesia worked against her. The reason the drugs didn't work very long in this case was probably due to her adrenal glands working overtime during our initial exam. This produced an excessive amount of adrenalin, the "fight-or-flight" hormone I've mentioned before named so for obvious reasons. Whiskey had a unique personality. She was a real survivor and a fighter. She was fighting me, she was fighting the drugs, and she couldn't wait to get up and fight some more. In a more natural habitat, her attitude would be to her advantage. In this situation, it was not.

Whiskey's will to get up and survive was much stronger than the will of her liver and kidneys was to remove the drugs from her system so she could be coordinated enough to do so. She tried to get up, only to stumble and fall almost immediately. The more she fell, the madder she got, and the more determined she became to stand up and fight. Up and down she went, flipping in thundering somersaults all over the hard ground of the barnyard. A cloud of dust rose from the frightening one-horse battle. Several times, she was completely up on her hind legs, but still down on her knees in front, like she was bowing to a crowd applauding her acrobatics. Instead of standing the rest of the way up, she scooted forward and scraped the hide off her knees and face in a terrifying manner. All I could do was helplessly hold the lead shank trying to keep her from banging her head on the ground too hard and pray that the nightmare would end soon.

I'm sure it only lasted for fifteen or twenty minutes, but it seemed like hours. Finally, she was able to stand, trembling once again. She had skinned her knees horribly, one almost to the bone. Much of the hide from all four ankles was gone, and she had abrasions from her hocks to her head. Ironically, one of the least damaged spots on her entire body was the part that I sutured, because it had a big, thick bandage on it. I looked at this poor mare thinking how much better off she would have been if I had just wrapped the leg and went home. At this point, I vowed to never again even think anything like "things couldn't get any worse."

After a few minutes I was pretty sure that she would not fall down again, and I quickly cleaned and wrapped Whiskey's newest wounds. Thankfully, none of them required stitches. I gave Shana two large bottles of penicillin because her mare would be receiving injections twice a day for at least a week. I cleaned up my instruments, packed up what was left of my supplies, and drove away wondering if it wasn't too late to apply to barber school.

I returned the next day to change the wraps and examine Whiskey for any further damage that had gone undetected. The previous day's experience had left her less than enthusiastic about the veterinary profession. I had to give her another sedative just to take off the bandages. This time, however, I gave her a fairly large dose while repeating some of the dance steps we had practiced the evening before. As tough as it was to get a needle into this mare, I didn't want to have to do it more than once, if I could help it. I changed the wraps and lived to tell about it, but it was not the exertion of lifting heavy bandage material that left my pulse slightly elevate. This mare really tested my nerve.

Shana was able to change the wraps and give the penicillin, but not without a twitch and the help of her boyfriend, Johnny. The mare was tough.

I stayed in touch with Whiskey's progress by telephone with Shana and a few follow-up visits in person. Within a few weeks, most of the wounds were well on the way toward healing. The sutures had pulled out five days after placement, but that was not unexpected. There was significant proud flesh on the rear leg and over the front of one knee, so these were wrapped for a longer period of time. Shana called me one day with a progress report and a concern.

"She's letting me wrap her legs without the twitch," she said, "but she is still in a lot of pain. She limps on that back leg something awful. Johnny says she's faking it for sympathy, but I'm worried about her. I mean, I think she's a smart mare and all that, but I don't think she's smart enough to fake anything."

I told her I agreed and that I would stop by the next day and check her out. I really didn't think that the wounds she had sustained several weeks earlier would still be painful, so I was wondered if maybe she had some new problem.

I parked in the driveway and walked around to the barn. Nobody but Whiskey was home. From where I was, I could see her, but she had not yet seen me. I really wasn't trying to sneak up on her, but I watched her walk around the paddock for a minute without her knowing I was there. She seemed to be fine. She walked from what was left of her breakfast over to the water trough. She lifted her head from a long drink of cool water, watched a horse next door for a moment and then walked back to see if the alfalfa fairy had magically left her some more breakfast while she was gone. She walked completely sound, with her bandaged legs the only hint of her injury. I opened the gate and walked toward her with a halter and lead shank in my hand. The next thing I saw absolutely amazed me. The mare turned away from me, limping on three legs!

Whiskey miraculously recovered from her "lameness." Two years later, I saw her and Shana at a team-penning. Although the one hind leg was still scarred and significantly larger than the other, both Shana and the mare were doing fine.

_ Rabies

One of the oldest known and most feared diseases is rabies. It is called a "zoonosis" because it is transmissible from animals to man. Although we like to think of veterinarians as people helping animals, the entire study of veterinary medicine was initiated for the detection, control, and eradication of zoonoses because of their effect on man. Although Lorenzo Rusio practiced veterinary medicine in Rome during the fourteenth century and wrote an extensive textbook on the subject, modern scientific study of infectious diseases didn't occur until Louis Pasteur and Robert Koch came up with the first effective vaccines.

Among a long list of these diseases are "tetanus" ("lockjaw"), "Lyme disease," "salmonellosis" ("food poisoning"), "tuberculosis," "ringworm," "equine encephalomyelitis" ("sleeping sickness"), influenza, and rabies. Although most people think of rabies as a dog or cat disease, cattle and horses are at risk because they are not often vaccinated, and they are exposed to the most common vectors, skunks and raccoons.

The rabies virus is transmitted by the bite of a rabid animal. The "incubation period," the time required to produce disease, is variable, depending on the location of the bite. Once infected saliva has been deposited into a susceptible animal, the virus migrates up peripheral nerves to the spinal cord and brain, the central nervous system (CNS). When the virus reaches the CNS, it starts to multiply, and the victim demonstrates clinical symptoms and begins to shed the virus in saliva or other excretions. The virus must reach the CNS before it can multiply. All rabies cases will develop signs of illness before they are capable of shedding the virus and transmitting disease. However, there are no "classical, textbook signs" of rabies, as it can mimic virtually *any* neurologic illness.

The course of the disease can be quite variable depending on the location the virus enters the body and the path it must follow to maintain its life cycle. A bite on the hand, for example, may take months to produce the disease. However, a bite on the face may produce the fatal illness in a matter of a few days. In one case of human rabies, a man had been bitten on the finger by a rabid dog. Six months later the man went to the hospital due to a vague illness. He died a few days later of rabies.

Although rabies is commonly transmitted through a bite, other, more unusual cases, have been documented. There are two cases of human rabies reported following corneal transplants (eye surgery). Aerosol transmission (by inhaling the virus) has been reported in a man who explored a cave inhabited by a large population of bats. Apparently, the virus was released into the air of the cave in the urine or saliva of a rabid bat. "Aerosol," or "non-bite," transmission is exceedingly rare, so just being in the same room with a known rabid animal constitutes almost no risk. The problem with "almost no risk" is that there is *some* risk. Rabies is a fatal disease, so it is important to be cautious, even to extremes. This is why when a dog or cat bites somebody, the animal must be quarantined and observed for signs of illness for a week or so, regardless of its vaccination status. Because a rabid animal will become ill before he is capable of spreading the disease, it is safe to assume that he is not infected if no illness is observed during the quarantine period. If somebody is bitten by an animal that cannot be caught and held for quarantine, it is *always* recommended that the person take the post-exposure rabies vaccinations.

As noted, the clinical symptoms of rabies can be quite vague initially. For this reason, rabies is *never* diagnosed based on clinical signs alone. Clinical cases fall into one of two categories:

"Furious rabies" is the source of the term "mad dog." This stage of the disease can be of short duration and may not be noticed. Affected individuals will viciously attack anything that moves. These animals have been known to bite metal fencing to the point of breaking their own teeth. The irrational behavior may include eating rocks or other foreign objects. Although the bite of a mad toy poodle may seem like a joke, it can be just as deadly as the formidable charge of a rabid cow. I have seen examples of both, and I am not looking forward to repeating either one.

As the course of the disease progresses, the second category of clinical symptoms, "dumb" or "paralytic rabies," is seen. Profuse salivation and paralysis of the throat and jaw muscles are common. Because of the paralysis, the animal has difficulty drinking and eating so he may look like a colic or like he is choking. Horses presented for colic or choke *usually* do not have rabies. Since there is a *possibility*, care must be taken to limit exposure to humans and other animals if the disease is suspected. I don't lie awake nights worrying about rabid horses, but the disease should always be kept in mind when a patient presents neurologic symptoms. I had just such a scare a few years ago.

Clyde was a great big, gentle, fat, slightly spoiled draft-type horse who lived his leisurely life eating carrots and apples and only occasionally having to pull a small wagon. He belonged to Henry and Edna, a retired couple who have been my friends and clients for a long time.

"I think Clyde's got the choke," Henry told me over the phone. "You better come out and unstop 'im. He's slobberin' a mile a minute and Edna's worried sick about 'im." (Henry always used this excuse when *he* was worried sick about 'im.)

I examined Clyde and found him just as Henry had described. This horse was salivating profusely and hanging his head over the water trough but not drinking or eating. I stuck my hand in his mouth to make sure he didn't have a bad tooth or a piece of wire or something else stuck in his mouth. Then I passed a tube up his nose and down his esophagus into his stomach. This is how a "choke" is relieved. When you feel the dry, "crunchy" resistance the stomach tube gives when it reaches a big plug of feed stuck somewhere in the throat, it is characteristic of a choke. But Clyde didn't have a bad tooth and the ease in which the tube was passed into his stomach ruled out the presence of a choke.

This is when I had to initiate "Plan B." This is a euphemism for, "I don't know what in the world is wrong with this horse, but I'm hoping to find out soon."

I treated Clyde with the standard colic treatment of mineral oil and an injection of my favorite painkiller, Banamine®. In addition, I treated him with injections of dexamethasone, and DMSO, two potent drugs that—as you have already learned—will work on inflammation in the CNS. Since Clyde was salivating, off feed, and wandering aimlessly, CNS involvement was a potential complication.

"We need to take some blood samples over to the lab," I said, telling Henry my concern about the neurological symptoms Clyde had.

"So you're workin' on 'Plan B,'" Henry quipped with a wry grin. I guess we knew each other pretty well by then. I knew that he blamed all his worries on his wife, and he knew "Plan B" meant I didn't have a clue!

The results of the blood tests were unremarkable. Although the labwork suggested that Clyde was normal, his condition continued to decline. He started stumbling around a little, and he still wouldn't eat or drink. Because there were neurological symptoms, sleeping sickness (the generic term for Eastern, Western, or Venezuelan encephalomyelitis), West Nile virus infection, protozoal myelitis, and rabies were all on the list of "possible" diagnoses.

Rabies. Just the thought sent a chilling fear through me. I thought about how many times I'd had my hands in this horse's mouth in the recent days, not to mention the exposure to Henry and Edna and their grandchildren. The "dumb rabies" phase of the disease is seen more often in horses than the "furious phase" associated with mad dogs.

As Clyde's condition continued to deteriorate, I had to weigh the potential for his recovery as opposed to the possibility that he had exposed several adults and children, including me, to rabies. There are no *ante mortem* (before death) tests for the disease. The only way to diagnose rabies is by removing the brain and submitting it to a state lab.

Someone once told me that the wisest men tend to make the most serious mistakes because people don't entrust critical decisions to fools. Anybody that thinks veterinarians only drive around, vaccinate cute little ponies, and get rich should have been with me the day I put Clyde to sleep. Although I knew it was the right thing to do, I couldn't help second-guessing myself, and I agonized over the decision for hours before I finally recommended euthanasia. All three of us had tears in our eyes as I injected the overdose of anesthetic that would gently put an end to a life. Then I was faced with the grizzly task of removing the brain from the thick, equine cranium.

As I sent the tissue off for rabies test, I warned Henry and Edna of the possibility that we would all have to take post-exposure rabies shots. Because of the slow progression of the virus up the peripheral nerves, rabies is the only disease that can be "treated" with a vaccine. This is not exactly a treatment, but the immune response to the vaccine is usually rapid enough to stop the virus before it reaches the CNS.

Thankfully, the results of the tests were available the next day and Clyde didn't have rabies. He did, however, have severe "encephalitis," or inflammation of the brain. Although the cause was unknown, it would have eventually been fatal. It was sad to lose such a good horse, but it was comforting that we were able to humanely end his suffering.

_ Butch and Mr. Skunk

Early in my private practice career, I lived in a large comfortable house a couple of miles outside of San Juan Bautista, California. I had a few saddle horses in a seven-acre trap in back of the house, a big red dog named Jake, and a fairly large collection of cats. Now some people refer to domestic felines as "house cats." This would only be an accurate description of our cats during certain times of the day—like prime nap time, which is just about any time, but you'd have to ask a given cat about his or her preference. The sound of a can opener, I soon discovered, could immediately turn the most stalwart "outdoor" cat into one of the aforementioned "house" varieties.

Since I lived in the country, there was an abundance of cat "game" to hunt in the woods and fields near the house: Lizards, frogs, gophers, mice, rats, and an occasional cotton-tailed rabbit were to become favored delicacies. It didn't take long for the cats to let me know that they would prefer to be house cats only on a limited basis. Of course, they didn't want to be exclusively outdoor cats either, but would prefer their choice. I rebelled at this idea and demanded that they stay mostly outdoors. This arrangement lasted about four minutes. We reached a compromise—they clawed the screen door until I cut a hole in the wall of the garage to make a cat door. (As it is said: "Dogs have owners, cats have staff.") The garage was connected to the house and my pharmacy, so they could come and go as they pleased. I learned an important lesson: Cats are easy to train—you just find out what it is they want to do, and then you let them do it!

The abundance of wild game, though naturally nutritious, was unfortunately not enough to sustain the local cat population. Several bowls of fresh, dry cat food were always available in my pharmacy for those individuals either lacking sufficient hunting luck to sustain their caloric requirements or just having tired of the day's reptilian entrees.

The "cat door" was convenient for all. Any time of the day or night, a cat could leave the confines of the house for a little hunting expedition and return at his leisure to the delightful aroma of the fresh, abundant cat food that they knew awaited them in clean bowls on a clean rug on the floor of my pharmacy. Unfortunately, word of the endless fountain of food apparently got out among the population of less-domesticated mammals in the neighborhood. This fact was made apparent to me when I was greeted by a distinctly recognizable, pungent odor as I returned to my pharmacy one evening for some needed supplies. "Mr. Skunk" couldn't sneak up on anybody.

This posed some logistical challenges for me. How does one remove a skunk? Shoot him? Trap him? There was simply no real good solution. It's like the dubious efforts of dogs chasing cars: What do you do when you actually catch one? Sometimes it is better to do nothing than something wrong, so I decided to leave this thing alone for a while. After all, he wasn't in the kitchen, just the garage!

Everybody seemed to be getting along fairly well. The several cats and the skunk were all gaining weight, and the skunk had not sprayed anyone in the house, though he had been encountered in the garage/pharmacy on a regular basis. A sharp "Git!" was usually enough to encourage a hasty exit by Mr. Skunk (by now he had a *name*), and he was usually full by the time I got home, anyway. A skunk—certainly not *my* Mr. Skunk!—had chemically embarrassed the dog on a few occasions, but this had occurred outside the house and no harm had come to the dog, other than his mental anguish at having to spend a few nights in the stock trailer instead of on the floor of the bedroom he so graciously shares with me.

Anyway, I came home one evening, and as was my habit, went back to the pharmacy to supply my truck for the following day. I walked through the door and immediately thought I was seeing double. I rubbed my eyes and looked again only to find that, no I didn't need new glasses, but yes there were *two* skunks in my pharmacy! Later, my fertile imagination envisioned a conversation between Mr. Skunk and his date: "Hey, Baby, I know this nice little place to eat. It ain't much for atmosphere, but the food is great and there's plenty of it!"

Something had to be done. I'm not much of a carpenter, but, quickly, I constructed a hinged door so the "cat door" really was a door, not just a hole in the wall. The plan was to shut the door before dark (prime skunk time) every evening and open it again in the morning. This met with tacit approval of most of the cats; Mr. Skunk was not available for comment.

A couple of nights after I had finished my little construction project, I was enjoying supper in the dining room. A sliding glass door separated the dining room from a deck outside. I had just sat down when Mr. Skunk appeared on the deck at the sliding glass door and reared up on his hind legs, sniffing the air almost as if to say, "Hey! Somebody locked me out, and it's suppertime!" After that, apparently Mr. Skunk got the hint, and I didn't see too much of him for a while.

A couple of weeks later, though it seemed unrelated at the time, one of the cats was absent for a few days. This would happen with other cats from time to time, and I always figured that the hunt just got too good to quit and go home. Butch, on the other hand, was a homebody. He didn't like to roam too far away from his favorite napping spot on top of the refrigerator—a safe, warm place that was also close to the cat food and away from the cold nose of an over-friendly dog. Butch's disappearance was the source of some concern, because cats will commonly go off and hide for a while after they have been sick or become injured. This aggravating characteristic may have evolved as a protective mechanism for cats in the wild, but it worries cat lovers.

Of course, the new cat door situation had also caused Mr. Skunk to be absent during this time, but I wasn't too worried about him. He had survived just fine before the bottomless bag of cat food arrived and I was sure that he would get by just fine without it now.

Then one night I saw Mr. Skunk in the garage again, but he was acting strangely, even for a skunk. He was under the riding mower with his head shaking and obviously a little disoriented, like he couldn't find his way out. This had never been a problem for Mr. Skunk—we had an agreement that he could stay until I got home, and he always found the door quickly.

For four or five months, Mr. Skunk had no problem navigating a course through the garage directly to the cat food and back out again. Now, sure enough, my Mr. Skunk was exhibiting neurologic symptoms. This was a little unsettling, to say the least. Of course, even normal neurologic signs can be hard to evaluate in a skunk, and neither one of us was in the mood for a physical exam.

The next day, Butch showed up after his extended absence. He was sick. He was depressed, and he had a temperature of one hundred and five (normal is one hundred and two). He had a bite wound over the base of his tail very close to the spinal cord. Although it was impossible to determine the source of the bite, the current circumstances were disturbing. *If* the bite had been from a rabid animal, the close proximity of the wound to the spinal cord would mean that the progression of the disease would be rapid. A rabid animal is not capable of transmitting the virus until he demonstrates illness, which of course, with a fever of 105.5, Butch *was* clearly. The frustrating part of neurological diseases is they can present like just about *anything*, so you can't just look at a sick animal and say with absolute certainty that it ain't rabies.

As I mentioned before, non-bite transmission of rabies is rare. However, I had put my hands in Butch's mouth and other orifices to take his temperature and perform a thorough exam. That wouldn't be much of a problem if I didn't always have small cuts on my hands from the nature of my profession. If Butch was shedding rabies virus in his saliva, I had plenty of opportunity to be exposed.

That, by itself, wouldn't have worried me if I hadn't learned of the fact *that a man had died of rabies in our county about three months earlier*! Literature I had recently received from the state indicated that rabies was on the rise, especially in our area. Several house cats had been diagnosed with the disease in our county, and at least two families had undergone post-exposure rabies vaccinations in the past two months because of exposure to their rabid cats. And still, none of this would be any problem at all if I wasn't cursed with such a fertile imagination.

It was time to seek professional help.

"County Animal Control." A voice that could have been a recording gave me a perfunctory greeting the next morning.

"I have a little problem with a skunk," I began.

"Call the Humane Society," the voice said automatically, and gave me the number.

"Thank you," I said to the dial tone.

"Humane Society." Was this the same voice I heard thirty seconds ago?

"I have a little problem with a skunk," I began again. "Can you help me?"

"What seems to be the problem?"

I explained the whole situation, from the history of Mr. Skunk and his cat food habit, to the development of neurologic symptoms and the injury to Butch, the cat.

"That sounds like a normal skunk to me," the voice said.

"I am a veterinarian," I said. "I am concerned about our recent outbreak of rabies, and I have reason to believe that there may be a rabid skunk in my garage."

"Skunks always act like that," the voice asserted.

"Skunks *always* have neurologic symptoms?" I asserted right back. "Are you licensed to practice veterinary medicine in this state, and do you feel comfortable making this diagnosis over the phone? Are you not aware that a man died of rabies in *our* county less than three months ago?" This was followed by a long pause—I expected the dial tone as a reward for my lack of people skills. Then I asked, "What did you say your name was?"

"You'll need to talk to Dr. Jones," the voice answered. "She's the county public health officer. Her number is. . ."

"Thank you," I said to the dial tone, once again.

"County Public Health Office...all of our lines are busy right now. If you'll please leave a message, we'll get right back to you." The recording assured me that my health needs were of great concern to them—all of the efficiency of the US Postal Service with all the compassion of the IRS!

Two hours later, I received a call from Dr. Jones' office.

"What seems to be the problem?" Was this the same voice I had been hearing all morning long? I explained the whole thing...again.

"That sounds like a normal skunk to me. I don't think you have a problem."

It was then that I pulled the rest of my hair out.

"Have you called Animal Control?"

It was then that I knew that this was just a very elaborate, cruel joke that the folks from *Candid Camera* were pulling on me.

"They were the ones that told me to call you!" I didn't scream.

"Okay, just bring the skunk down here," the voice said," and we'll have it tested for rabies for you."

"How do you propose that I catch this thing?" I asked, trying to regain control of my voice.

"Call Animal Control."

"County Animal Control," the same voice answered. At least it wasn't a recording.

"Hello, I called you earlier today about a skunk in my garage. Can you help me?" I said, trying to sound helpless, which was getting easier.

"Like I told you before, it sounds like a normal skunk to me. Have you called the Humane Society?" Miss Bored asked.

"Yes, I have," Doctor Furious replied through clenched teeth.

"Well, I suggest that you call Alice at the Humane Society. If she says that it sounds like a rabid skunk, then we'll send someone out to pick it up for you."

"Humane Society, this is Alice," another voice answered.

Once again, I identified myself and explained to whole situation. I was beginning to wish that I had a recording of my own.

"Well, I'd like to help you, Doc, but you know our funding has been cut, what with the new county budget and all, so I really don't even have a vehicle that I could send someone out with," she said, trying to sound compassionate. "Have you called Animal Control?"

I gave Alice the list of all the state and county agencies that I had called who were diligently working to help me. Thankfully, I *did* get Alice to agree that the skunk sounded suspicious. I called Animal Control again, hoping they would not renege on their earlier promise to help me if *Alice* said it was okay.

"Do you have the animal in a cage?" Miss Bored asked.

"I'm sure you can understand that, if I had the animal in a cage, I would not be troubling you with this problem," I replied, using a thinly veiled attempt to finesse this lady into helping me.

"Well, we can't send someone out unless the animal is in a cage," she said. "It's county policy."

In a state of despair, I walked out to the garage to see if Mr. Skunk was still alive. After all, if he had expired during the night, part of my problem was solved. As much as I didn't want a potentially rabid skunk in my garage, I thought: *Look on the bright side, at least he is sorta' caught and all I gotta do is somehow restrain him, inject euthanasia solution into his amazingly small cephalic vein without getting bit or sprayed and send his head in for testing. Piece of cake! If he doesn't have rabies, I'm in the clear. If he does, at least I know and can get the vaccine.* Pollyanna would have been proud.

I opened the small door that led from the pharmacy into the garage and slowly entered. After a careful search of the garage, apparently one of my problems was solved *and* my worst fear materialized: Mr. Skunk was gone! Not dead, GONE! Now what? How would I ever know whether or not he was rabid? Should I take the shots, or take my chances?

This discussion went on in my head for a couple of hours until a sense of responsibility took control. There was not a reason in the world to take a chance in view of the current situation. The quarantine guidelines for animals who have bitten a person are clear. The offending animal will be quarantined for a week (the duration varies with each state). If he shows illness during that period, regardless of his vaccination status, he is euthanized and his brain tested for the presence of the rabies virus. Since as I've said already, a rabid animal will not shed the virus in his saliva unless he is showing some signs of illness, this gives us time. The virus must travel up the nervous system to the brain before it can replicate, shed in the saliva, and be transmitted by bite or aerosolized in saliva or urine. With this knowledge, we can give a vaccine *after* exposure with a real good chance of preventing the disease. Rabies is the only disease that will respond to "post-exposure" vaccine...and we're glad it does.

What I had was a sick cat with a bite wound of questionable origin and a skunk with equally questionable behavior, which could not be reached for further questioning. If Butch had rabies, he was going to die, and if *I* had rabies...ditto. Sending *his* brain in for testing was a valid consideration, but what if he just had a bite-wound abscess? Sending *my* brain in for testing, well that presented a whole 'nuther set of problems.

I called some of the pharmaceutical firms that supply me with vaccines. Most of these outfits sell human drugs, as well as veterinary products. I found a source of the Human Diploid Cell vaccine, which is the only one cleared for post-exposure use, and ordered enough for the recommended five shot series.

"And you are Doctor...who?" the order-taker at the pharmaceutical company asked. I told her my name, my DEA number (Drug Enforcement Agency permit number—it is required of all vets, dentists, and physicians who purchase prescription drugs). Then, "Can I have your AMA number?"

"I don't have an AMA number. I am a veterinarian. I just gave you my California license number and my DEA number," I replied.

"I'm sorry, we can't deliver any vaccine to you unless you are licensed to practice medicine in California," she said.

"I *am* licensed in California!"

"You are a veterinarian?"

"Yes."

"Uh...I'm afraid that doesn't count," she said. I couldn't help but admire her style. It takes real talent to look down your nose on the phone.

"Thank you very much for your help," I said, thinking, *If your dog gives you fleas, don't come crying to me!*

So, I had to get a human doctor, licensed in California, to order the vaccine for me. This sounded easy, but since I generally "quacked" on myself, I did not have a doctor. I called a phone book doctor—you know, one listed in the Yellow Pages back when they were still around. She wasn't a lot of help and thought that I was foolish for even thinking that post-exposure vaccines were in order, and, "Besides," she said with true compassion, "you are not even my patient!"

Finally, at considerable expense, I got an emergency physician at the local human hospital to sell me the initial vaccine and help me order the rest of the five-shot series that I could give myself at home. Butch survived; so did I...would this be the case without the shots? We'll never know.

_ Elvis

Some of the most common questions posed to me involve genetics and the tendency for horses to pass certain characteristics to their offspring. My response usually begins with an explanation of how genetic data is compiled and formulated into useful information. For example, the genetics of milk production in dairy cows is well understood because of the millions of animals that are included in the Dairy Herd Improvement Association (DHIA) records. These records are now all computerized and genetics experts can accurately predict how much milk a certain cow will produce over her entire career. This is because thousands of dairymen have kept organized, meticulous records of their herds for many years, and their product is something that can be *objectively* measured: pounds of milk. (And yes, it is correct to say "pounds" as milk is measured in pounds by farmers because of tradition and convenience.) *Subjective* information, like how pretty the cow is, or how she holds her tail and picks up her feet at a trot, is not evaluated.

With this in mind, it is easy to see why the genetics of horses is so poorly understood: there are few *objective* selection criteria—the exception being in racehorses, where the stopwatch doesn't lie. It is also easy to see why my standard response to genetic questions ends with "not a clue"!

One such question arose involving the potential transmission of a bad habit from a mare to her colt. Shady was an elegant, classy mare owned by an equally elegant and classy lady named Paula. Shady's one behavioral fault involved her enjoyment of rearing up and falling over backward. This was no graceful accident, like a "levade"—one of the "airs above the ground" practiced in the highest level of classical dressage. This was practiced, quick, and lethal—like a mousetrap—WHAM! I have been on horses like this, and "disoriented" is the best description of what the rider experiences. It feels like the ground moves up and slaps you in the back.

Well, Shady quickly learned that after she pulled this little stunt, people became increasingly reluctant to ride her. Paula decided that Shady might make a good broodmare and proceeded to make the appropriate arrangements.

The following year, Shady presented us with a handsome colt named Elvis. He was perfect in every way, in Paula's eyes, and seemed to lack the unpleasant acrobatic tendencies that his mother had perfected. That is, until the day came to introduce little Elvis to my surgical skills. Paula had wisely decided, even before Elvis was born, that there would be no stallions on the place. So, about the time he was six months old, I was contacted to turn Elvis into even more of a gentleman than he already was.

I had already seen Elvis for routine exams, deworming, and vaccinations, and he had not been unduly stressed by these events. On the day of the surgery, however, things were different. It appeared that Elvis' was aware of his proposed move to the soprano section, and he was not happy about my intentions. As soon as I placed the needle in the jugular vein to inject the sedative, Elvis reared up and only the barn wall kept him from falling over backward. He eventually came back to earth, though somewhat more bug-eyed than he had been during pre-launch preparations and without the needle in his jugular vein. During the impressive display, the needle had found its way deeper into Elvis' neck and had lodged in the carotid artery. This vessel lies just beneath the jugular vein and is the major supply of blood to the head.

Unlike the veins, the blood in the arteries is under significant pressure. For this reason, when an artery is punctured, the blood spurts out, while the same sized hole in a vein would produce only a few drops. Well, with all the jumping around Elvis was doing in his efforts to avoid an incipient voice change, the hole in his carotid artery caused an area about half the size of a football to fill up with blood. In much less time than it takes to tell it, poor little flying Elvis looked like he had almost swallowed a small watermelon. Thankfully, the leak in the artery stopped fairly soon. Elvis never was in any real danger, but the large hematoma (blood clot) in his relatively short neck was going to make it real hard to inject anything into either one of his jugular veins for several days.

Despite the apparent difficulties I was having in trying to anesthetize this colt, I was determined to try at least one more time. He was already mad at me, and I figured that he would not be any less mad if I came back another day. Well, luck or the god of venipuncture was shining down upon me that day because, with the next stick, I had Elvis safely on his way to dreamland and geldinghood. The surgery and recovery were uneventful. The colt soon stood up, albeit somewhat cautiously, and started looking for breakfast. I left aftercare instructions with Paula to exercise Elvis and run cold water over the incision twice daily for twenty minutes during the next week or so, packed up my equipment, and left.

I worked the rest of the day without too much thought about Elvis. Complications following castration are uncommon, and usually do not occur until a few days after the surgery—with one disastrous exception. The anatomy of the male horse is arranged so that the space surrounding the testicles actually communicates with the abdominal cavity. Because the castration incision is not closed with a suture, it is *possible* for a loop of the bowel to find a way into the incision and, subsequently, wind up spilling guts all over the ground. This complication usually occurs within a few hours after surgery and is frequently fatal.

So it is easy to understand why my heart faltered later that day when my pager flashed the emergency signal followed by Paula's name and phone number. My cardiac problems did not improve when I learned that the emergency was not related to the surgery, but that Elvis had only reared over backward and was lying unconscious and bleeding from his nose!

I immediately turned the truck around and headed back to Paula's place at warp speed. When I arrived, the colt was trying, without much success, to stand, and his struggling was making matters worse. A quick examination revealed a youngster in shock. He was bleeding from both nostrils, he was cold and clammy, his gums were white, his pupils were fixed, dilated, and unresponsive to light.

Normally, the eyes respond to bright light by constricting the pupils. Conversely, the pupils dilate or expand when there is less light. The optic nerve in the back of the eye is wired up to a specific region of the brain that controls motor function of the muscles that open or close the pupils. This handy little response is called the "pupillary light reflex" (PLR). The doctor is checking this when he shines that aggravating little light in your eyes. Anyway, abnormal PLR indicates central nervous system (CNS) damage that may be serious. Elvis needed immediate treatment.

I began preparations to place a catheter in his neck through which I would administer the drugs that were essential to save his life. It was the same type of indwelling venous catheter that I've talked about before: a plastic tube fitted tightly over a large bore needle that was inserted into a suitable vein and provided an open line through which large volumes of fluids or drugs could be given directly into the bloodstream.

I looked at the mess in the lower part of his neck—now it was my turn to be in shock. The large blood clot that was formed during the attempted induction of anesthesia earlier in the day had grown even larger and uglier. I was faced with the very real possibility that intravenous medication may not be possible. Of course, there are other veins in the body that could be catheterized, such as the cephalic veins on the inside of the forelegs, but this colt was in shock and thrashing his legs around so much that the cephalic veins were out of the question.

I earnestly prayed that, somehow, I would be able to get a catheter in this colt so that I could start treating him. I shaved and scrubbed a site over the area I suspected contained what was left of the jugular vein, though I sure couldn't see or feel it. Every time I stuck the colt, he would jump, and this just made the situation worse. Miraculously, after the third or fourth attempt, the beautiful sight of blood flowing through the plastic catheter held a glimmer of hope. For the first time in what seemed like several minutes, I allowed myself to breathe.

I immediately started IV fluids, to which I had added the potent anti-inflammatory drugs that were needed to combat the swelling in the brain. The fact that Elvis was in shock presented conflicting treatment goals. We needed to add fluid volume to the bloodstream to treat the shock, but we also needed to remove excessive fluid from the CNS that was producing damaging pressure. It was like trying to squeeze a sponge dry in a sink full of water.

After two hours of intensive care, Elvis was apparently comatose and had occasionally stopped breathing. At this time, I was almost to the point of hoping for a merciful death, because I didn't know to what extent the brain had been damaged or if the colt would ever regain consciousness.

Paula finally asked me, "Is he gonna' live?"

"I really don't feel too hopeful about his chances," was about as tactful as I could be.

After another few minutes, I began to seriously entertain discussing euthanasia. Unbelievably, Elvis rolled up on his sternum, stood up and casually started nibbling on some bits of alfalfa left over from his breakfast. I wouldn't have been more surprised if that other Elvis had just driven up in a pink Caddy. For a long minute, I was speechless.

"I can't believe it," I said. "A few minutes ago, I wouldn't have guessed he'd ever do that again!"

"Do you think this means he's going to be okay?" Paula was hopeful.

"It's sure encouraging," I conceded, "but I can't get my hopes too high. Elvis has sustained a serious injury."

After another hour, Elvis' coordination continued to improve, and he was eating a little. I decided to go home for some supper and planned on returning about midnight to check on his progress. Paula was going to stay with him and would call me if his condition changed.

I returned shortly before midnight and Elvis was with Shady in her stall. He had been nursing, and I was encouraged that he had enough coordination to turn his head into his mama's flank to accomplish this. I spoke to him, and he cocked his nearest ear back to acknowledge my presence. I opened the stall door and gently stroked his back. He stood quietly until I snapped a lead shank to the halter he was still wearing. Suddenly, he spun around to face me and immediately reared up, falling over backward. As he fell back, he hit his head on a steel hay rack that was bolted to the wall, bounced off it and struck his head on the metal automatic waterer that was bolted to the adjacent wall a little lower. It seemed like it took a long time for him to hit the floor, but he finally fell in a heap in front of me.

He was perfectly still, and just like he was five hours earlier, in shock. His pupils were fixed and dilated, but this time there was the extra, added feature of "spontaneous nystagmus," a quick, sideways motion of both eyes that looked like he was watching a ping-pong match. The presence of spontaneous nystagmus usually means that there is damage in the middle ear or further damage in the part of the brain that controls motor function, the "cerebellum"—as if Elvis didn't have enough problems.

Paula showed up about the time that Elvis was demonstrating a textbook example of spontaneous nystagmus. I explained to her that the prognosis just got worse. I went back to the truck and got the same drugs I had used to treat him earlier in the day and was thankful beyond belief that the catheter was still in place and functioning properly. I treated this colt again with even less optimism that I had earlier. I went back to the truck and placed a call to a veterinary neurologist I knew in Southern California. Like most people in my profession, he was used to being disturbed in the middle of the night. Although he did not know me well, he was glad to listen to our problem and was sorry that he could offer no treatment advice other than what had already been done. I thanked him for his help and wished *I* was going back to sleep and telling *him* good luck.

We sat there with Elvis for another agonizing two hours. Like before, he stopped breathing for a long several seconds, and I was, once again, considering euthanasia. Almost on cue, the colt rolled up on his sternum, struggled to his feet, walked over to Shady and started nursing again!

"The first time may have been blind luck," I said, "but this time was a miracle."

As long as there is life, there is hope. I treated Elvis with anti-inflammatory drugs and antibiotics for the next week. With each passing day, he grew stronger and had no lasting effects from the exciting weekend.

_ Equine Herpes—No Shame Here

Early one spring morning, I drove up to a public boarding facility to check on a horse I had seen a few days before. To my astonishment, there was about a mile of yellow plastic police tape wrapped around the entire barn and outside pad-docks, as if some horrendous crime had been committed. It was straight out of one of those detective shows so popular on TV at the time. I was half-expecting to see a chalk line in the dirt, outlining a body. In addition, an armed guard sat in a lawn chair in front of the gate. I knew the management of the place, and to say the least, they were wound up a little tight, with interesting ideas about… everything. But this was just a shade over the top, even for them.

I cautiously drove up to the guard. The scene would have been sorta' com-ical, if he hadn't been armed. He was…portly…but had the requisite sheriff's uniform, gun, badge, night stick, handcuffs, and donut-shop powdered sugar on his tie. His bulk taxed the buttons on his uniform and strained the aluminum/ nylon webbing lawn chair as he dozed in front of the equine facility with its new yellow tape decor.

I got out of my truck, hoping that I had closed the door gently enough that he wouldn't feel the need to come up shooting.

"Mornin,'" I began. "What's goin' on?"

"You can't come in." His professional response was short and to the point, but I was still a little confused.

"I have a patient in here I need to see."

"Nobody goes in. Any horse leaving the premises can't come back."

"How can somebody take a horse off the place without going in," I asked, "and how are the horses being cared for?" These were obvious questions that I should have kept to myself…but didn't.

"Not my problem." If there is a short answer course in cop school, he was at the head of the class.

It took a while, but I eventually found out from one of the boarders that the management had quarantined the place because of an equine herpes out-break at a horse show in Utah. Utah! That was about six hundred miles away. Let's be cautious. Viral diseases are contagious, and some are pretty nasty, but *dang*—get a grip!

I had seen a few cases of this virus, and as is the case with many viral infections involving the nervous system of the horse, if the patient can remain standing, just about all of 'em survive. It's fairly contagious, and though it is not always fatal, it is severe enough to get folks pretty worried.

Diseases of the equine nervous system can cause similar symptoms, regardless of the specific cause. It is generally impossible to make an accurate diagnosis without blood work or nasal swabs, but some of the symptoms presented can give us valuable clues about exactly which virus is the culprit. For example, EHM (Equine Herpes Myelitis) will often cause the horse to sit like a dog. Yep, like your favorite Lab or Heeler. He doesn't wag his tail or pant with his tongue hanging out, but he sure looks like a dog sitting there. Once you've seen this, it has a way of sticking in your mind. This is apparently due to inflammation around the motor nerves that stimulate the skeletal muscles necessary for standing. Why it involves those structures in the hind legs first is a mystery, but typical of the disease. As it progresses, more nerves are involved, and the horse can't stand at all. Eventually, he quits breathing.

I was called one spring afternoon to see a possible colic. Bella wasn't eating with her normal vigor and interest, so I figured the client diagnosis was probably right. When I got there, though, it was obvious that Bella wasn't eating because it was real hard for her to walk to the feed trough and even harder for her to maintain her balance when she put her head down. In addition, when she did walk a little, she was real unsteady on her feet, especially her hind end. By pulling on her tail, I could just about tip her over. This was not normal.

"I think we got something a little more than a colic," I began. "I think this involves the nervous system, and cases like this can get real complicated."

"We're taking her to the State Fair in a couple of weeks, Doc. Darlene is showing her in the reining competition, and she has a real good shot to win it all. Do what you need to do to get her right before the show." Darlene's dad, Dennis, said with concern.

"It may not be that simple," I said, "depending on exactly what is going on here..."

I paused to compose my thoughts. I wasn't optimistic this mare would survive the day, much less compete in the Fair.

"We'll treat her for inflammation and see if we can get her comfortable enough to move around a little better so she can eat," I said, "but this can get pretty serious."

"What do you think she has?" Darlene and Dennis asked, almost in two-part harmony.

"Well, there are a few viruses that can cause this. She's not old enough for arthritic spurs in her spine, and she hasn't had any injuries lately, so I'm thinking virus. Maybe equine herpes. It's a virus."

"What?" Near two-part harmony again.

So I gave 'em my short course in equine virology, easily keeping it brief 'cuz it didn't take long to tell 'em just about all I knew.

We've known about viruses for a little over a century. They were first discovered by trying to filter out a disease-causing organism that was infecting tobacco plants and causing a loss in production. (I guess it had to be a pretty nasty disease, in view of just how toxic nicotine is, though smokers can live a long time in a fairly contaminated environment—but I digress.) They were trying to isolate bacteria with a filter, but as we know now, viruses are many times smaller than bacteria. These infectious agents went right through the filter, so they were called "non-filterable." German biologist Adolf Mayer coined the term "virus," which must be German for "real dang small," I guess.

Earlier, Louis Pasteur had perfected a vaccine against the virus that causes rabies, using techniques he used on the bacterial diseases that were making him famous. But viruses are a whole 'nuther class of bugs. Bacteria are single-celled organisms. But within this single, very complicated cell, they have all the equipment to eat, move around, defend themselves, and make cute little baby bacteria. Viruses, conversely, consist of *only* genetic material so they make cute little baby viruses much differently than other organisms. There is no wasted energy, space, or structure. In fact, there have been some discussions among virologists about whether or not these things are actually alive. (Anyone who has suffered the ravages of the flu can answer this question, even without a PhD!)

While other parasites require some complicated life cycles to maintain themselves as species, viruses have the ability to invade "host" cells and commandeer them to conduct all the functions required to reproduce themselves. They are the perfect parasite. Their presence inside host cells helps them avoid detection by the immune system, thus really challenging our ability to make vaccines for prevention of their invasion, or kill 'em once they're here. And they are very, very small. In fact, most can only be seen with an electron microscope.

The bad news is they are discovering new viruses every day...and changing the names of them just to keep us guessing. Thankfully, most of them either do not cause disease, or the immune system appears to take care of them without any symptoms. We have been studying disease-causing agents ("pathogens") in horses for centuries. The diseases caused by equine herpesviruses have been studied for a long time, and many attempts have been made to produce vaccines to protect horses from them. Initially, there were four classified herpesviruses, cleverly named "EHV 1," "2," "3," and "4." Now there are nine of them. Nine! And it doesn't get less confusing. All of them produce specific symptoms, ranging from respiratory, flu-like cough and runny nose, to abortion, to a potentially fatal neurologic disorder that will render the horse unable to stand.

The one that causes the neuro signs is called equine herpes myeloencephalopathy (EHM, for those who love acronyms—but don't worry, by the time you read this, they will probably have changed the name anyway). This has been the source of much hand-wringing in the horse community over the recent few years, and the reason the rotund deputy mentioned earlier needed so much yellow police tape.

Some viruses can be effectively controlled with vaccines. The vaccines against rabies and West Nile virus, for example, are very safe and effective. EHM, however, has some characteristics of all herpesviruses that makes them a little tricky. One of these is called "latency." Herpesviruses like to hide in the spinal cord. They can hide there for decades, and the so-called "blood brain barrier"—the boundary between the bloodstream and the central nervous system—keeps them isolated from any effects of vaccines. This is the reason that people who had chicken pox as a child are likely to have shingles as an older adult, and why the vaccine for chicken pox may not be quite as effective as advertised.

The herpesvirus particles can easily cross into the CNS because they are very small. The antibodies stimulated by the vaccines are very large molecules, so they stay in the bloodstream. The antibodies may be of some benefit when the virus comes out to do its mischief but can't do much once it returns to its hiding place in the CNS. So the efficacy of the vaccine in this case is questionable at best. Okay, maybe worthless. Though there are several vaccines available, none have been proven effective in the prevention of EHM.

Diagnosis of EHM includes blood tests for antibodies and nasal swabs for the presence of virus particles ("polymerase chain reaction," or PCR, tests—sorry, more acronyms...). These tests are subject to interpretation, as the presence of antibodies may only indicate the animal has been exposed rather than actively carrying the disease or shedding the virus—or demonstrating some protection from it. For example, we can test my blood for influenza, and it would come back positive because I had it this winter. I'm not sick now. (My wife would argue that point. She says I am one sick puppy!) The PCR test will detect the virus in the nasal swab, but if we wait too long, the test may come back negative, as the particles have been cleared, even though the horse is about to get real sick. (This is called a "false negative.")

So...precise diagnosis of herpesvirus is based on clinical presentation, experience, and maybe a little educated guessing.

Treatment involves nursing care, IV fluids, and anti-inflammatory drugs, among other things. Some use of antiviral medications (large, large doses of "valacyclovir") has been tried, but no definitive proof of efficacy has been reported. It appears that patients that can remain standing until they clear themselves of the infection will survive. Those who lay down and stay down, usually do not.

Prevention of the spread of equine herpesvirus is related to the level of "biosecurity" employed. It appears that fairly close contact (between fifty and one hundred feet) with an infected individual—a horse showing symptoms—is required for the disease to spread by virus particles in the air. But, due to the latency—that ability of the virus to hide in the spinal cord that I told you about—it is possible that symptomatic patients contracted the disease a long time before it reared its ugly head.

A three-week quarantine for new horses entering a boarding facility is always suggested but not practical in most settings. This would have to be repeated every time a horse left for some event—even just a trip to the vet—and returned. Foot baths, changing clothes, and working with new horses last during the day may afford some level of security. Disinfection of trailers, tack, and equipment with dilute bleach may reduce exposure potential. But, in reality, we just need to use some common sense. We shouldn't ship sick horses. We should take the temperature of suspected cases twice daily. Anything over one hundred and two needs veterinary attention ASAP.

With this, I finished my lecture.

"That's great, Doc," my clients stated, "but she hasn't been anywhere other than to the trainer's and to a couple of local shows. And nowhere at all since last week."

"This is just one of many aggravating things about viruses," I said and repeated some of my previous lecture on latency and contagion.

I treated Bella with some powerful anti-inflammatory drugs: Banamine*, dexamethasone, and DMSO—that stinky, rotten egg-smelling stuff that is common around many training barns. I took some blood and a nasal swab to send overnight to the UC Davis lab with hopes I was wrong about my diagnosis. The mare was starting to eat a little before I left, and since she could still stand, I left fairly confident we might just get lucky.

My optimism suffered a near-fatal blow the next morning.

"Hey, Doc," Dennis' voice on the phone accompanied my second cup of coffee. "I think you better come look at Bella again. She don't look so good...she's.... sitting like a dog!"

I got to Dennis' place shortly after the call and, sure enough, Bella was sitting like a dog and couldn't get up at all. Dennis could tell by the look on my face that it was not good (that's why I don't play poker).

"I think we should treat her again this morning, but you know I am less than optimistic about her chances." This was code for: *She probably ain't gonna make it.*

I treated Bella just like I had the previous evening, and we prayed over her. I wished I'd prayed over her first, as I needed all the help I could get, and I was rapidly running out of options.

Dennis thanked me for the prayer and all my efforts, but I drove away thinking poor little Darlene was gonna lose her mare and not make it to the Fair, either. We agreed we'd give Bella the day to see how she responded but also that there was the very real possibility of having to make a tough decision soon.

Early the next morning I got an email from the UC Davis lab: positive for EHM. I tried to call Dennis with the bad news, but it went to voicemail immediately. I didn't have another number, so I drove back to see Bella, thinking maybe the family was outside and not near the phone. What I saw when I got to the barn was nothing short of amazing. The mare was standing, had finished most of a flake of hay, and when I opened the gate, she trotted away from me! She didn't walk, she didn't stumble, *she trotted* away from me!

Dennis and Darlene came out a few minutes later, and they were no less astonished than I was. It was a good example of the power of prayer, steroids, and DMSO. As I've said before: where there is life, there's hope, and giving a patient a little more time is seldom a bad idea...even with a scary disease like EHM.

I returned the following day and Bella was just about back to normal. I told Dennis it was a good idea to keep all the horses home for a couple of weeks but that it should be okay to resume normal activity after that, as long as none of the horses appeared sick.

Remember my earlier lecture? Prevention of infectious diseases involves common sense. Use tested, approved vaccines administered by a licensed veterinarian and...quit worrying! More horses die every year of lightning strike than EHM. Horses have been staying healthy a lot longer than there have been vaccine companies and off-duty sheriffs to worry about 'em.

_ **Equine Pain Management**

I have been asked whether or not an animal even feels pain. Certainly, this is a measure of degree, as calves will generally holler more when they are being roped than they do when they are being branded...or worse! Higher brain centers are likely involved. For example, in an old college fraternity "hazing" technique, pledges were subjected to a blindfold, the smell of smoke, and the suggestion they were about to be branded. Instead of a hot brand, a sliver of ice was placed on the skin of the unsuspecting new frat brother. Surprisingly, most would "feel" heat—and protest loudly. But you don't have to vaccinate many horses to know that they do indeed feel pain—and are sometimes willing to inflict some pain on the guy on the other end of the needle.

We know from "histology," the study of microscopic anatomy, that horses have the same pain receptors as other animals. Although these receptors are thought to be fairly specific, as they identify either pressure, sharp, or hot/cold sensations, it is probably a lot more complicated. (Higher brain centers are surely involved, thus the frat brother's confusion between hot and cold.) How do we know when horses are in pain and where they hurt? When should we use pain medications...or not? Which ones should we use?

Inflammation is the major source of pain. First described by the Roman journalist Celsus, inflammation is marked by swelling, heat, redness, *pain,* and loss of function. Horses will exhibit pain in a variety of ways. The loss of normal appetite is a common symptom of abdominal pain. Severe, non-weight-bearing lameness will usually warrant a call to the local vet, and pain management will be on the list of things to do. Other symptoms are a bit more subtle. The reluctance to take a lead, stand for the farrier, or becoming "cinchy" during saddling can be indications of pain. An eye kept partially closed can be the first indication of serious ophthalmic pain. These are common presentations, but sometimes the most subtle symptoms can be a prelude to some serious problems.

There a times when the wait-and-see technique is a good idea. Pain can be our friend, albeit an aggravating one, as it tells us when something is wrong. But this is only one reason that inflammation is a useful process. The extra blood flow to the affected area contains components of the immune system to fight infection and growth factors to repair damaged tissue. Swelling and redness are due to compounds called "vaso-active amines" that change blood flow. This happens quickly after an injury. It doesn't take long for your thumb to demonstrate the activity of these miraculous little molecules after you hit it with a hammer: throbbing, red, with a definite loss of function, while you exhibit a tendency to use words you didn't learn in Sunday School. Of course, the five cardinal signs of inflammation I listed already and the local activity of vaso-active amines are probably not your first thoughts, but these reactions are there to start the healing process automatically. Because of the beneficial effects of inflammation, inhibiting it is not always a good idea.

A trip to the feed store or a cruise through the interweb can provide some help in treating a horse for pain. However, Dr. Google doesn't have a license to practice medicine, and most of the over-the-counter preparations are of questionable benefit. The "all natural" supplements can be a bit suspect, as they have not been subjected to controlled, clinical trials to demonstrate safety and effectiveness. Arsenic is "all natural"; in sufficient doses, it is also "all fatal." I have actually seen a *toxic plant* listed on the label of one of these supplements, so beware.

Once it is determined that pain meds are indicated, we have some choices. For the sake of this discussion, I'll oversimplify it in to three categories: 1) steroids, 2) non-steroidal anti-inflammatory drugs (NSAIDs), and 3) another very broad group let's just call "everything else" (EE). (We can put narcotics and synthetic narcotics in this group). Steroids and NSAIDs suppress pain by reducing inflammation. A certain class called "corticosteroids" are very good at this, but they also have a tendency to suppress the immune system, which may cause some infections to get worse. NSAIDs don't suppress the immune system, they just kill the cells in the liver, kidneys, and lining of the gut. Some EE's are very good pain relievers that tie up specific receptors in nerve cells, but they do little for inflammation, can become highly addictive, and don't last very long.

So, yeah, we have some choices. Things ain't always as simple as they seem.

The "risk versus benefit" is a factor that must be considered in just about any treatment. The short duration of narcotics or their synthetic analogues may be a good choice for some cases of colic but of little benefit to long-term lameness. Steroids are excellent in some neurologic cases but may be harmful in certain infections as they suppress the immune system. Long-term NSAIDs have been reported to cause problems with kidneys and gastric ulcers, but I have several old rope horses in my practice that won't eat grain if it's not flavored with a little "bute."

In the horse, NSAIDs are the most commonly used drugs. Aspirin, ibuprofen, phenylbutazone ("bute"), Banamine˚, and Previcox˚ are in this class. Tylenol˚ has recently been removed from the NSAIDs club. Apparently, it does not reduce inflammation in the musculoskeletal system, but, rather, in the *nervous* system. (This sounds like splitting hairs to me. It is still *not* a steroid and it still *is* anti-inflammatory, but what do I know.) In a recent study, Tylenol has been reported as beneficial in cases of laminitis. However, the potential toxic side-effects have not been evaluated. (There is a wide range of tolerance in many drugs, which varies with species. For example, one Tylenol tablet, while well tolerated by a person, will kill a cat.)

It appears that pain and the ability to manage it is a broad, confusing subject. New modalities including therapeutic ultrasound, electromagnetic pulses, lasers, and new chemical variations on old drugs hold great promise. But we should not lose sight of the amazing power of healing the Creator has put into all animals. As the saying goes, "Time heals all wounds." In some cases, I think that is right.

_ Buddy and the Picnic Table

Head trauma can be a frightening experience for all parties involved. I'm not talking about the type of head trauma sustained when you discover that you are being audited by the friendly folks at the IRS, but rather, blunt force trauma. This can be due to contact with anything harder than the skull: a tree limb, baseball bat, or locomotive.

The head of a horse is well-constructed with a thick skull bone (this anatomical feature is not limited to the horse), and an inner brain case that suspends the brain within the structure called the "cranium." Air pockets, the "sinuses," are dispersed within the skull to make the cranium stronger and lighter than it would be if it were made of solid bone. Like rafters in the roof of a house, the air spaces may have no specific function, but the design of the cross-braces makes a stronger, lighter package. The "brain case" is somewhat spherical and perforated with several holes called "foraminae" that allow the passage of blood vessels, nerves, and the spinal cord. Through these pathways, the brain receives sensory information from the body and sends out the appropriate responses.

When the head is traumatized, even to the extent of a fractured skull, the sinuses provide a buffer between the brain and the offending hard object. Most of the time, the cranial structure serves its protective function quite well.

Occasionally, the brain gets rattled around a little bit within the protective shell and is bruised. With severe head trauma, the symptoms may be obvious. Among these are lack of coordination, blindness, coma, dilated pupils (equally or unequally), or the presence of a head tilt. In other cases, symptoms may be more subtle. If overlooked, covert damage can lead to serious problems, so all head injuries should be treated as serious emergencies.

When small vessels are broken and bleeding occurs between the brain and the lining of the skull, it is called a "subdural hematoma." Because the skull is so well-designed for strength, there may not be a way for the blood to escape. As the bleeding continues, the pressure rises in the skull and nerve function is altered. Prolonged pressure on vital nerve centers can produce coma, and eventually, death.

In humans, most physicians will recommend a standard skull series—an X-ray or "computer assisted tomography" (CAT) scan—to look for fractures or a subdural hematoma. These problems are relatively easy to diagnose, and if treated in time, the victim can be saved.

Swelling of the brain, or "cerebral edema," is another serious sequel to head trauma that is easy to detect with CAT-scan equipment. (Unfortunately, although these machines are available for horses, they are not portable for use in the field.) The rigid structure of the skull will not allow for the expansion of swollen nervous tissue and the pressure of cerebral edema can cause permanent damage and death.

In the horse, radiology is not always performed on head trauma cases due to the inability of most portable X-ray machines to penetrate the skull of an adult beast. Immediate transport to a referral facility equipped with a high-powered X-ray machine may not be practical due to the hazards associated with hauling unstable animals. A horse that has trouble standing in a relatively motionless barn may find it impossible to remain upright in a trailer being driven by a frantic owner racing to the nearest referral horse hospital.

Since even a modest amount of brain swelling can be serious, I treat most cases of head trauma with anti-inflammatory drugs. Although some patients do not show any serious symptoms, it is wise to treat them as a preventive measure. As mentioned, I start with DMSO, an industrial solvent with remarkable anti-inflammatory properties, and dexamethasone, a short-acting steroid—the drugs of choice for cerebral edema. In some cases, "mannitol" can be used with good results. This is a sugar that, when injected intravenously, helps pull water out of brain tissue the same way that Epsom salts can pull swelling out of a sprained ankle.

When I am not out terrorizing the local horse population, I am at home providing high quality aggravation to my own horses. One of these beasts was an almost-green-broke, too big, too smart Thoroughbred gelding I call Buddy. Over the six years I was blessed to have him, we gave each other many hours of what can be euphemistically called "quality time" together. For the last forty-five years or so, I have spent a fair amount of time trying to figure out how a horse thinks. There are some fairly consistent concepts: They do not like change, windy days, or the smell of pigs. But the only thing about horse behavior that remains a surety is that all the "fairly consistent concepts" are subject to change. At any time. On very short notice. Buddy often reminded me of this, and one time gave me a good reason to think about head trauma in the horse.

We had just finished a ride on one of our favorite trails on Mt. Madonna in Santa Clara County, California. As we loaded up to go home, Buddy balked a little at the trailer. In my younger days there were times, just occasionally, where I lacked patience. This was one of those times. He hesitated a little before loading, and I gave him a little encouragement on the rump with my hand. His response was a little love pat of his own: a hind foot to my right thigh. After I quit hollering, cussing, and limping around the parking lot, much to the amusement of others at the park that day, I vigorously massaged his southern end with the ragged end of a short cotton lead rope. This made a lot of noise, but I knew it did not inflict much pain. Still…I've made smarter choices in life.

Buddy, never being one to pass up a chance at an Academy Award, started backing away from me all bug-eyed like he expected that the world was about to end. He was so worried about Armageddon that he neglected to see a big section of redwood log that was right behind him. The park service had placed these logs around the parking lot to prevent pickups and trailers from wandering around unsupervised among the picnic tables.

Well old acrobatic Buddy hit one of these logs and completed a perfect reverse somersault with a half-twist. With amazing athleticism, he landed upside-down and wedged precisely between the log and one of the aforementioned picnic tables. If there had been Olympic judges present, I expect they would have held up little cards with 8s and 9s on them based on his artistic expression and flawless landing.

Buddy just lay there quietly...too quietly. He had a normal "palpebral reflex." This is noted by a blink when a hand is waved in front of the eye, and it indicates that some of the cranial nerves are intact. His breathing was about as normal as it would be in any upside-down horse, and his gums were pink. This meant that his heart and lungs were still working and adequately supplying his tissues with blood. I was concerned that he may have been seriously injured because he wasn't struggling to get up. I thought: *Maybe he's just smart enough.... Well, you never know...this is Buddy!*

I figured that I would just move the picnic table and roll him over so he could get up. I was planning on either treating him medically or finishing the spanking, whichever seemed appropriate. I hadn't counted on the untrusting nature of the park service folks, however. They had bolted this particular table to a big piece of cement that was buried somewhere in southern China. The log was also a problem. This thing was about ten feet long and half of its three-foot diameter was buried in the loose gravel of the parking lot.

I'm nothing, if not resourceful. I unhitched my trailer and drove the pickup around so that I could back it up next to the log. I looped my famous, double stout nylon lariat around the log and tied the end to the trailer hitch of the pickup. I jumped in the cab, eased the truck forward and promptly buried that rascal hub deep to a Ferris wheel in the loose gravel of the parking lot. Neither log nor horse budged.

Trying not to panic, I backed the truck up to make another run at moving the log. I hit the throttle hard. This spattered gravel all over Buddy, and I could see in the mirror that he was still capable of closing his eyes. *Not the textbook way of testing cranial nerve reflexes,* I thought, but it was comforting to know that Buddy was still alive enough to squint and cuss.

With two more tries, the truck finally pulled the log out far enough to give us some working room. Murphy's Law still lives. Instead of rolling *away* from the picnic table into the clear parking lot, Buddy rolled the other way, getting his legs mixed up with those of the table. I was glad that I took all those anatomy courses back in my college days, because it didn't take very long to sort out the Buddy legs from the non-Buddy legs. I looped the lariat over his legs, this time without the use of the pickup, and rolled him over so he could get up. A quick exam assured me that he was miraculously uninjured and about as normal as he ever was.

Buddy just stood there with a stupid grin on his face, shook himself off, and jumped in the trailer while he mumbled something under his breath about a bunch of gravel and a letter to the Humane Society.

He never kicked me again.

How to Breed a Mare…with a Paralyzed Stallion

The yellow carpet of poplar leaves in the yard, combined with a bit of a bite in the morning air, told me the summer heat was just about over and we had some cool fall days ahead. The other signal of the fall season were the flies that instinctively filled the cab of my truck—a warmer environment—as if they knew their days were numbered (or maybe they liked my singing better now than back in midsummer). I loved the century-old trees in the yard between my house and my clinic, but it was the signal that, along with the cool weather, some joyous hours of leaf-raking were in my near future.

For now, my focus turned away from leaves and flies, as I was on my way to see a horse for a new client with concerns that his aging stallion could not stand up. Cases like this can be a real challenge, cuz you never know what happened till you get there. It could be a case of colic, broken bones, or primary neurological disease—which opened up a whole new can of possibilities.

I arrived at the farmhouse on a quiet country road a few miles out of town. The horse was easy to spot, because my client had one of those pop-up awnings with the screen on three corners placed over a very large bay stallion, lying in the front yard. The poor old horse was covered with flies, even more than the season and location would warrant—not a good sign, as flies often sense impending doom. The awning just barely covered the horse, so with me, the stallion, and about a jillion flies, it could get a little crowded in there if he started to thrash around while trying to stand up.

I introduced myself to the owner, Scott, and suggested we move the awning. This seemed to annoy Scott a little.

"We put it there to keep the flies off him!" He said this with just enough emphasis to suggest his disapproval. The futility of having a *three-sided* enclosure for this function was apparently wasted on him, as about half the flies in southern Idaho had taken up residence on this poor, debilitated horse. In a rare instance of self-control, I decided not to argue the obvious.

"Well, it might be a little safer for us if we just used some fly spray and moved the awning. I'd hate to see him get tangled up in it," I said tactfully. I had visions of me and the stallion, fighting our way out of the contraption as it folded around us, like two panicked fish in a net. As the smaller of the two "fish," I was not likely to fare well.

I've noted before that any time you have a potential equine wreck on your hands, the audience swells to an amazing population. Though we started with a few barefooted kids, the number of "supervisors" soon expanded to an alarming level.

"Let's put a halter and lead shank on him." This was my typical starting point for down horses.

"He CAN"T GET UP!" came the emphatic reply from one of the short bystanders.

Sometimes, older down horses have been lying on one side so long, the muscles sort of "go to sleep," like how your leg feels all tingly when you been sitting wrong watching *Oprah* reruns. I have found that if you roll these horses over to the *other* side, some can stand rather easily.

"We don't have a halter," Scott replied.

"Ooooooookay," I started. Now things were about to get interesting. "How long have you had him?" I ventured, thinking this "horse thing" was a new experience for Scott and his family, as there really wasn't a lot of stuff around one would expect to see at a horse outfit (bent pipe panels, fence boards chewed away to toothpicks, well-used crutches...).

"Twenty-seven years. He was born right over there." Scott pointed to a corner in the same yard that would likely be the site of his demise.

"He's always been a good boy. In fact, we just got his feet trimmed for the first time a few months ago. He just stood right there and let the guy do it," he said with pride. "You're the first vet who has ever seen him."

"Well, he's sure a good-natured stallion," was about all I could say. *Twenty-seven years* and had just stood well for his *first* trim? Not too many ways to reply to that!

So I put a halter I had in my truck on him and tugged on it a little, trying to encourage this fine old horse to stand. This elicited another chorus of, "He CAN'T GET UP!" from the audience.

He rolled up on his front legs and tried to stand, but his hind legs couldn't bear the weight...you guessed it: HE COULDN'T STAND UP.

We were faced with the challenges of an older horse that was either paralyzed or just too weak to stand. In cases like this, I have two problems...at least. First, I need to advocate for the horse. I could tell this poor guy had been down for a while—probably days—evidenced by "bed sores," called "pressure necrosis," from the weight of the horse mashing one side of his body. And, at twenty-seven years, even if we could figure out what was wrong and could successfully treat it, how much time could we hope to buy him? Second, how much suffering are we willing to subject a horse to while we wait to see if a treatment is gonna help him?

I brought up the idea of intravenous fluids, steroids, and antibiotics, but that got shot down right away.

"We really don't have a lot of money to spend on this horse," Scott began, "but we wanted you to collect some sperm from him so we could breed some mares later."

While this may have seemed like a reasonable request, it posed a few challenges. The first limitation was "we don't have a lot of money to spend." Any horse outfit that doesn't have a halter and lead shank appears to have some real basic economic limitations. And that may make the collection, freezing, and storage of semen a very unlikely dream.

It gets better.

In order to collect a stallion, we need a mare in heat, an artificial vagina, and some more technical equipment to store the semen until it can be packaged for freezing— and, oh yeah, one more thing: a stallion that can stand up to breed a mare! You can see where I'm going with this.

There are some techniques available to extract small numbers of sperm cells from the epididymis, the storage tube at the base of the testicle. *But,* and that's a pretty big qualifier, this adds a whole 'nother level of technology not for the faint-of-heart-financially-challenged paralyzed stallion owner. At the level of the epididymis, it is not technically semen. Although the sperm cells are stored there in high concentrations, they are also undergoing a maturation process that is required before they perform their intended function. Most of the volume of seminal fluid comes from accessory glands. Their secretions are added during ejaculation, in addition to some important factors required for the nutrition and maturation of the sperm cells as they travel to their target inside the mare.

Harvesting epidydimal sperm is a little tricky. The process requires sedation, a needle, and a steady hand to spear the precise place where the sperm cells are stored. Once the cells are collected, they can be prepared for freezing by various methods. The key here is to get the cells suspended in a protective medium. All tissues are subject to "freezer burn," like we can see in meat that has been in your freezer too long in the plastic wrap. Sperm cells don't like freezer burn. The average home freezer can chill things to about ten degrees Fahrenheit, but sperm cells can only survive if they are frozen at about three hundred degrees below zero. Three hundred below! Even winter in Idaho seldom gets that cold! You can't just put this stuff in a mayo jar and chuck it in the back of the old Frigidaire. It requires liquid nitrogen and a special container to hold it—neither of which are available at your local Walmart. This type of freezer is not cheap to buy *and* maintain, as it must be re-charged with the liquid nitrogen several times a year to keep the temperature low enough to ensure the survival of the samples. If it goes dry, all the samples are dead.

Although this technology has been around for a long time—there have been semen samples stored from bulls for over fifty years that are still viable—there are other aspects that should be considered before we freeze stallion semen. It is interesting that, once the frozen stallion semen has been thawed just prior to inseminating a mare, the sample looks great. The "motility," or number of sperm cells we can see actively swimming under the microscope, is impressive. However, the "fertility"—the ability to establish pregnancy—is considerably lower than that of fresh cooled semen or that derived the old-fashioned way (just let him breed her!). This may be due to microscopic damage or freezer burn the sperm cells experience during the process. The mechanism of the damage is not exactly clear, it just is.

A normal stallion can be collected with an artificial vagina using a "jump mare"—a willing female accomplice of the same species, in an almost natural setting. For epididymal cells, it gets more complicated. Because the volume and numbers are so low, we can't just inseminate mares "the old-fashioned way." It requires fertilization in a test tube where a single sperm cell can be inserted into an egg harvested from a mare. In some cases, a very small volume can be surgically injected directly into the uterine tube, or oviduct, of the mare.

These are highly advanced, technical procedures that are only available in university settings or at some specialty hospitals. AND, if you don't want to do all that, cloning techniques are also available. All of this is available; none of this is cheap.

Simply harvesting the cells and storing them is not the end of the process. The best way to manage frozen semen is to thaw a few samples and breed test mares with 'em. This, in itself, requires another level of technology not available to most backyard breeders. Once we know we can establish pregnancy with thawed semen, it's a pretty good bet we can do it again if we store the samples properly. Of course, regardless of how many scientific tests we can run on stallions and mares, the ultimate evidence of fertility is when we see the little nose and front feet of a foal emerging from the mare.

I explained this to Scott, his family, and the ever-expanding audience present on an apparently slow news day in real rural southern Idaho. It was not well-received. It appeared as though they still believed in the mayo-jar-Frigidaire version of how this could happen. There was an awkward silence.

"What are we gonna do?"

This is where I had to tread lightly. While I seldom, if ever, suggest euthanasia, there comes a time when the "quality-of-life" discussion becomes necessary in so many cases. End-of-life issues are among the most challenging and painful parts of our journeys with horses, but we will all face it eventually.

Finally, after what seemed like a really long time and with a more-than-average volume of tears, the decision was made to do the kind thing for the poor guy. Thankfully, the audience vanished, the tears dried, and the final, humane procedure went mercifully well. As I drove away from this most unusual case, all I could feel was empathy for these folks and the horse. There was no way of knowing what they were thinking during those final hours, but I was glad that they did the right thing for the old stallion. The right thing is not often the easy thing, but kindness is never wrong.

_ Lonesome

It was a rainy day, typical for California in the fall. The hills were tinged with the pale green promise of early grass and there was the kind of nip in the air that makes even the old horses hump up their back and snort a little when you pull the cinch tight. The weather set the mood for the day, as I had just given a lethal injection to a good young horse that had tolerated many injections from me in the past. Well, maybe he did not exactly *tolerate* the injections, but he certainly experienced them. It was never easy for me to lose a patient. It was especially difficult when a young one failed to respond to treatment or had problems that simply couldn't be treated. This was the case with Lonesome.

I first met the colt when he was still on his mama, a massive Quarter Horse mare that, from the long hair around her fetlocks, you might suspect had ancestors with experience in farming. I had been asked to evaluate the little fellow as a prospective riding horse for my good friend and client, Teresa. I almost never work on Sundays, but due to our busy schedules, that was the only day that was mutually available. She arranged lunch at a favorite restaurant as a bribe to get me to work on my one day off. My own horses were glad for the rest, and I was not really looking forward to another one of my Sunday morning adventures in cooking.

I examined the colt and couldn't find anything wrong enough to prevent the sale. Some folks would not think of having a purchase exam done on a foal, but there are several serious problems to be avoided when buying young and old horses alike. Even a cheap horse can get real expensive when problems don't become obvious until after the check has cleared the bank and you get him home. Oftentimes these are problems that would have been obvious to the trained eye.

We finished up our business with a delightful breakfast, and I didn't see Lonesome again for a while.

About a year later, I got a call from Teresa. She had vaccinated Lonesome earlier in the day and now it appeared that he was having a mild bout of colic, and she wanted me to come look at him. I treated him with analgesics and a little mineral oil. He really didn't act like a typical colic, and I thought it was too soon for a vaccine reaction to occur, but the treatment I gave wouldn't hurt him. I left thinking that he would be better in the morning, and I really wasn't too worried about him. I called a few hours later and Lonesome wasn't any better. I returned and examined him again. His gut sounds were still a little depressed and his pulse was elevated. He was not interested in feed, and the analgesics I gave him earlier seemed to have had no effect.

We discussed further treatment options, and Teresa said she would feel more comfortable if we sent him to a referral hospital for observation overnight. This was fine with me, and there was a good facility about two hours away. In less time than it takes to tell it, we had Lonesome loaded in a trailer, and he and Teresa were on their way.

By the time they got to the hospital, Lonesome was fine. They stayed a few hours just to be on the safe side but came back home the same day.

"Next time, I'll just get you to vaccinate him," an exhausted Teresa said. "I don't know if I did something wrong, but I don't want to take the chance."

So the next time, *I* vaccinated the colt. I used fresh vaccine from a reliable source. I used a clean, sharp, small gauge needle, and with the perfect professional skill of an almost painless technique, injected the vaccine. I refer to this as an *almost* painless procedure, but for Lonesome, *almost* was still way too much. He demonstrated his low opinion of my technique by stomping on my foot. By this time, Lonesome was a big, stout soon-to-be two-year-old of about twelve hundred pounds. The colt had long legs and a short fuse; it didn't take very much to elicit an unpleasant reaction, and a needle would do it every time.

But an injection wasn't the only trigger. Lonesome's bouts of ill temper could come on suddenly, with explosive results. On more than one occasion, for no apparent reason, I had seen the colt go from a state of absolute calmness to a rearing, striking, one-horse wrecking crew. The behavior was more than a little unsettling—it was downright dangerous.

About six hours after the professional, almost painless, don't-try-this-at-home-folks-these-are-the-hands-of-a-trained-expert vaccination, Lonesome presented with the same symptoms that he had when Teresa vaccinated him. This time, we gave him *oral* analgesics and observed him closely through the night. The next morning, he was fine. I have seen many vaccine reactions, but most of them take a couple of days and they appear in the form of pain and swelling at the injection site and an occasional loss of appetite. They usually last for a day or two and are almost never serious. However, I had never seen a vaccine reaction like the one Lonesome had. I knew he wasn't "faking it" to see me, because I was not his favorite human and instead the source of at least some of his problems.

The vaccine reaction and the random acts of violence were not the only ways that Lonesome was unusual. I would soon learn he had others.

As a three-year-old the colt presented a poorly defined but significant lameness in a hind limb. Though I spent several hours trying to determine the source of the pain, I was unsuccessful. The way that I usually work up a lameness is by a series of diagnostic nerve blocks. Most horses will not tell us where it hurts. Although there are some folks that think they can diagnose a lameness "in the front shoulder" by the signs of the moon or by the way a horse holds his ears or chews a carrot, I cannot. So, like most veterinarians, I use use a local anesthetic, like the dentist uses to numb your jaw before he fills a tooth. If, after a block to a certain part of the foot or leg, the horse's gait improves, I know that at least part of the problem involves the specific area that was blocked.

Well, as you can imagine, this can be a challenge when dealing with a horse with such an aversion to needles. After several hours and *many* injections, it became obvious that I was not close to diagnosing Lonesome's problem, but I was real close to getting killed by a generally good-natured though somewhat unpredictable horse.

I hate to admit defeat, but over the years, I have learned to ask for help when I cannot find answers on my own. My friend and colleague, Dr. Doug, had a great clinic a few hours south with all the diagnostic toys imaginable and experience to match. He had been kind enough to help me through some difficult cases in the past, and a visit with him was always a learning experience for me. I made arrangements for Dr. Doug to look at Lonesome the following week and took time away from my own practice to go with him.

When we arrived at Dr. Doug's clinic, Lonesome got off the trailer with his predictably unpredictable personality intact. As he stepped away from the back of the trailer, he immediately spun around and kicked at Teresa with both back feet *hard*. It was not just a playful little buck, but a purposeful, double-barreled attempt at decapitation. Dr. Doug and I helplessly witnessed the narrow escape and exchanged a silent sigh of relief with a nervous chuckle.

Lonesome underwent an extensive battery of diagnostic tests, including "radiography" and what was then a relatively new medical technique called "scintigraphy."

Radiography (X-ray) is an imaging technique that involves penetrating radiation and photographic film, or an electronically sensitive computer chip enclosed in a light-proof cassette. The X-ray itself is generated electrically, passes through the part of the body to be imaged, and is captured on the film or computer chip. Dense structures, like bone, do not allow much of the X-ray beam to penetrate, so not much radiation exposes the film. Boney structures are, therefore, projected on the film as white, or "negative" images. Soft-tissue structures and air allow most of the radiation to pass through, so the film is exposed to produce a dark image. Radiography has been around for about a century and most veterinarians have radiographic equipment.

Scintigraphy, or "bone scan," on the other hand, is relatively new technology and not widely available. The technique uses radioactive isotopes injected into the bloodstream of the patient as the source of energy to expose the photographic film. Blood flow is often increased (or altered) to an inflamed or diseased area, so the radiation is abnormally concentrated, producing more intense images that are picked up by the gamma camera. The images are interpreted by a computer and printed on film similar to that of conventional radiographs, but in a positive mode. In other words, whereas bone is mostly white, or "negative," on a conventional radiograph, it is dark, or "positive," on a scintigraph.

In addition to the thorough physical exam, Lonesome was tested for "equine protozoal myelitis" (EPM) because Dr. Doug was concerned that there might be a neurological component to the lameness. (I'll talk about this disease in detail later.)

Despite the thoroughness of the tests, nothing remarkable was found. There was a small chip fracture of the extensor process of the right rear coffin bone and a suspicious area in his stifle, but we were not convinced that either one of these was enough to make Lonesome lame. We sent him home on a regimen of anti-inflammatory drugs and stall rest. This sure wouldn't hurt, and it would give us enough time for the problem to either resolve itself or get bad enough to be real easy to diagnose.

The next year passed uneventfully for Lonesome. His lameness apparently went away, and he was started under saddle by a local trainer.

"He broke out okay," the trainer told me after the first month, "but he's lazy as a stump. Sittin' on him is like trying to ride a butane tank. He's about that big and about as hard to move."

Lonesome went to another trainer. Her assessment was similar, but less eloquently stated. She said that he didn't "seem right behind," which echoed Dr. Doug's suspicions that there was some nervous system involvement with his earlier lameness.

I was still puzzled by the colt's case and wondered if I would ever figure it out. I didn't have to wait long. About a month after Lonesome went to the new trainer, I got an emergency call from Teresa late one evening.

"I just got a call from Lonesome's new trainer," Teresa said. "It seems that Lonesome has a serious neurological problem. They had their vet out earlier this evening and the horse doesn't seem to know where his back legs are. He said we ought to take him to the veterinary college at UC Davis, but he didn't know if the colt could stand the trailer ride up there."

Now I was certain that the problem could only be in his spinal cord. "Not knowing where his rear end is" is a classic, textbook symptom of spinal cord disease. The first phase is proprioceptive deficits. You don't have to look at your feet to know where they are—that's "proprioception." Because the nerves that carry this function are located on the outside of the spinal cord, this is usually the first symptom noted.

"We need to get him somewhere where we can radiograph his neck," I told Teresa. "I'm convinced now that is what his problem has been all along, but we need to confirm it before we do anything else."

We made arrangements to move the colt to a clinic nearby that had an X-ray generator powerful enough to radiograph the neck of an elephant. I drove up there and met with Teresa, Lonesome, and the referral vet, Dr. Gabriel. The radiographs showed remodeling and compression between the fifth and sixth vertebrae in the neck. We stood facing the brightly lit plastic box that illuminated the X-ray films and cast strange shadows on our faces. I was uncharacteristically silent as the past several months scrolled rapidly through my mind like credits at the end of a movie on "fast forward." I knew what had happened.

It was obvious from the radiographs that this had been a long-term process, as the changes in the bone could not have occurred overnight. It was equally obvious that the lesions in the bones of his neck were the source of all the problems Lonesome had been experiencing for the recent year and a half. Lonesome was a "wobbler."

Some rapidly growing, vigorous weanlings and yearlings are prone to the so-called "developmental orthopedic disease" (DOD). This is the newer term for a group of diseases we used to call "metabolic bone diseases." These include "epiphysitis," "osteochondrosis" (OCD), "wobbler syndrome," and maybe "navicular disease." It is a very complicated, poorly understood process that occurs due to abnormalities in the quality of bone growth. Unfortunately, it is most often found in the biggest, most rapidly growing colts and fillies. When the process involves the bones of the spinal column, the vertebrae and the ligaments connecting them can become unstable or have abnormal junctions. This, in turn, causes pressure on the spinal cord, which in Lonesome produced the mild, poorly defined lameness and intermittent loss of proprioception that made him "not right behind" and is commonly associated with "wobblers."

Occasionally, the nerves of the spinal cord would become pinched and produce severe pain. This accounted for Lonesome's sometimes explosive temper. The colt would experience a severe and literal "pain in the neck." Not knowing the source of the pain, he could only assume that it was from the individual standing closest at the time and responded accordingly.

Although an experimental surgery has been successful in some mildly affected cases with breeding potential, there is no treatment that will allow horses with this disease to continue an athletic career. Severely affected individuals are sometimes left to live out their lives as a pet or companion for another horse. However, I am convinced that many of these patients are occasionally in severe pain. In addition, they oftentimes have difficulty walking or standing and can fall without warning, posing a danger to themselves and to the people around them. For this reason, euthanasia is justified in some cases.

The humane destruction of an animal is sometimes necessary, but it is never easy. With a tear in my eye, I said goodbye and walked back to my truck in the rain. As I drove away from Lonesome for the last time, I was discouraged by the outcome of the case, but convinced that, for the duration of his illness, we had done all that was possible. I could only hope that someday we would figure out a way of preventing developmental vertebral problems in horses.

_ Sleeping Sickness?

"I think my horse is lame. Can you come look at him?" The caller's request was typical, the case was not.

I arrived at the palatial home of Mrs. Elizabeth Kraus, an elegant wife of a big business lawyer. The personality of this delightful lady belied her high society background, as she was really down-to-earth and not at all aloof. Her horse, Slick, was a racing Quarter Horse type whose ancestry was mostly Thoroughbred. He was a big, red, honest horse, and he sure was lame.

I picked up his right forefoot after feeling the blood vessels on either side of his ankle. The vessels revealed a pounding digital pulse. Although all arteries possess a pulse, the arteries that provide blood to the pastern and foot of the horse usually don't have much of one. When it is present, it often means inflammation in the foot. It is not diagnostic for anything specific, but it is usually good evidence that the problem is in the foot, not higher up the leg.

I cleaned the foot out with the blunt end of my hoof knife and removed about a quarter cup of black, tarry, smelly goop that was evidence of "thrush." This is a common disease of horses that I call "industrial strength athlete's foot." It is caused by the same class of organism that is a fungus or higher bacteria that produces athlete's foot in people. In severe cases in horses, it can cause lameness and even abscesses in deeper tissues of the hoof. I see most cases during the rainy season or in horses housed in wet or unsanitary conditions. When the ground dries up, or somebody keeps the stall clean and dry and the horse's feet picked out for a couple of weeks, many cases of thrush will disappear.

I put a poultice of Epsom salts and oil of wintergreen on the foot to draw out the inflammation and gave Slick an injection of phenybutazone to make him feel better. This would make him more comfortable, and he would want to bear more weight on the sore foot. This would increase circulation in the area and the healing process would be enhanced. I gave Beth instructions to remove the poultice in two days and start soaking the foot in a dilute bleach solution (about one part bleach to fifteen parts water) for a few days. There were other ways to address thrush, but this was the best treatment I knew of.

"There's something else I've noticed, too," she said. "He acts funny when you tighten the saddle on him. I know it sounds strange, but I'm afraid to hurt him, and I don't know if maybe the saddle is pinching him somewhere."

"Let's get your saddle on him and see how it fits," I said. Lots of horses are a little "cinchy," meaning they hump up their back a little when you tighten the cinch. That is why it always a good idea to walk the horse around a few steps after saddling but before you step on. (The Vaqueros have a name for this in Spanish that is loosely translated to "the step of death.")

We put the saddle on this good horse, tightened the cinch and led him off. He walked out nice and gentle as you please. The saddle fit well. I determined this by putting it up on his back without a pad, first, and sliding my hand flat under the tree. Ideally, you want as much of the saddle as possible to contact his back. Lots of saddles fit well toward the front and toward the back, but there's a gap in the middle. This puts uneven pressure on the horse and usually makes for a sore back. Adding more pads just tends to accentuate the poor fit and makes the sore back worse. The best solution to this problem is to get a pad with blocks of felt that are adjustable to fill the gaps. When the pad and the saddle fit the horse, you won't be able to feel a space between the tree of the saddle and the back.

"Oh, well, I guess it was just that one time," Beth said, when I told her the saddle fit Slick perfectly. "Maybe there was a burr under the saddle or something."

About a month later, Beth called me again.

"Do you remember what I told you about Slick acting strange when I saddled him?" she asked.

"Yeah," I said. "Is he up to his old tricks again?"

"It almost looks like he is going to sleep," she replied. "His eyes close and he starts to buckle his knees. When I loosen the saddle, he straightens up and seems okay. I can ride him bareback, and he doesn't have a problem."

It was about time to vaccinate Slick and give him his annual dental exam, so we made arrangements for me to come by.

This time, sure enough, when I cinched up ol' Slick, his eyes closed and his knees buckled in front like he was giving a nap some serious consideration. Once I loosened the cinch, his eyes opened, he stood back up and he looked at me out of the corner of his eye almost like he wanted to say, "How did you do that?"

I repeated the process a couple of times with similar results. During these episodes, his heart rate and respiration never changed, he just acted like some cowboys I have known: As soon as it was time to go to work, he would fall asleep.

"It is possible that he has 'narcolepsy,'" I stated.

"I've heard of that, but I didn't think animals could get it," Beth said.

"Well, if that's what this is, it is extremely rare," I continued. "There's two schools of thought about equine narcolepsy. One suggests that the symptoms Slick was showing us were not truly those of narcolepsy but a response to pain. Or, it was due to a lack of sleep because he was housed in a place where normal sleep was not possible. On the other hand, he could have had a deficiency in the neurotransmitter. This is one in a class of hormone-like compounds that helps fine-tune the nervous system. Epinephrine, or adrenaline, is the most commonly known neurotransmitter that can be found in many of the 'synapses,' or junctions, between nerve fibers throughout the body. 'Hypocretin,' the neurotransmitter that helps control appetite and sleep, is located only in the brain. Like so many of the complex aspects of physiology, it is only noticed when it is missing.

"In people, there are several medications for this rare disease," I went on. "These drugs are basically antidepressants, some of which have effects similar to 'speed,' or amphetamines. This treatment does not replace the missing hormone, it just makes the naturally occurring effects of adrenaline last longer, and the patient stays awake."

I had tried these treatments in patients I suspected of having narcolepsy with little or no effect. Since it appeared that the trigger for Slick's inappropriate snooze was the cinch, Beth was okay with just riding on a bareback pad with the stirrups cut off. (The first thing to do with *any* bareback pad is to cut off the stirrups—they are very dangerous and easy to get hung up in and dragged.) Apparently, Slick was okay with this arrangement, too.

_ Teaching a Lesson

One of the most aggravating and dangerous habits for a horse to develop is the art of rearing up and falling over backward (remember my story of Shady and her colt Elvis?). I can only guess about the psychology of this particular habit—it may be a stretch to put the words "thinking" and "horse" in the same sentence—but it seems like a fairly painful thing to want to do. Any horse that rears up does so out of a reluctance to move forward, and most horses can be cured of this vice simply by encouraging them to do so. A few horses, in my experience, have honed this maneuver into one that is clearly designed to cripple, maim, or kill the rider by flipping over backward.

This is obviously dangerous to the horse, rider, and your brand new, custom-stamped, basket-weave saddle. As far as the horse is concerned, however, it is the one almost fool-proof method of unseating a rider. He may not be able to buck you off or run away with you or rub you off under a tree limb, but pinning you like an Olympic wrestler is a trick that works every time. The effect of this method is compounded by "positive reinforcement" when you don't get right back on him because your saddle is busted or you are dead. A horse doesn't have to do this many times to become convinced of its effectiveness, and armed with this knowledge, become a repeat offender.

My suggestion to an owner of one of these "wrestling horses" is to sell the horse at an auction or to someone you don't like. However, there are still some folks that are hard-headed enough to think that they can break a horse of this nerve-wracking tendency just for the challenge of it. One such individual was a salty old horse trainer I knew named Will Walters. Will was about seventy years old and had become more of an institution than just a horse trainer. Although he dealt mostly with Western horses, more than a few very expensive jumpers and dressage horses spent a summer vacation at Will's ranch for an attitude adjustment. I never knew him to abuse a horse, but he was definitely a no-nonsense kind of guy.

Will's method of dealing with the rearing-up-and-falling-over-backward horses was not original, but it seemed to be effective. He had to be agile, fearless, and prepared for the event, as it was not for the faint of heart. Once a horse had pulled his little trick but before he could get back up, Will tied his feet together so that he *couldn't* get back up. Then he covered him up with a tarp or a piece of plastic and left him "tied to the ground" for a little "time out" to make it unpleasant for the horse when he had thrown himself on the ground. Will didn't have to take it any further—just being given this time under a nice, warm tarp to think about the error of his ways was insulting enough to the offender. Will would regularly look under the tarp to check the horse's eye for palpebral reflex (wave a hand and watch for a blink in response, as I did with Buddy, earlier in the book) and mucous membrane color to assess consciousness and and watch for signs of shock (depressed palpebral reflex or pale or white instead of pink mucous membranes can indicate shock).

Although this psychological method might not be approved by Dr. Phil, it must be remembered that this type of horse is a dangerous animal. Any horse that will hurt you should be respected. However, any horse that will hurt himself in order to hurt you should be *sold.*

One warm, spring day Will had just such an individual on his ranch to begin charm school. I don't know why anyone would go to the time and expense of having a horse like this trained, but Will liked the challenge. This particular day, one of Will's young apprentices had been involved in a lengthy discussion about wrestling maneuvers with a great big, expensive, opinionated filly when she reared up, fell over backward, and died.

Will's colleague, a young cowboy called Buster, escaped with only an elevated heart rate and some minor incontinence. Of course, now he was faced with a couple of new problems. The first was, what to do with the body? It was not like he could just get the tractor and drag the filly to the back forty—there were several riding students and potential horse buyers on the place at the time. Second, how to discretely tell the boss that one of his client's horses had just died while he was busy with other customers? Well, the first problem could be solved by covering the body with a tarp in standard operating procedure. The boy figured that the second problem would just have to wait.

Will's guests were curious about the covered, recumbent horse, lying quietly in one of the corrals. Will explained that the horse was there for alteration of dangerous behavior and that one of his boys was involved in "the lesson." By then, Buster had ambled over to where Will was talking.

Will asked, "How's her eye?"

"Oh, her *eye* is just fine, boss," Buster replied truthfully.

"She sure is lying still," one of the visitors observed. "Are you sure she's okay?"

Will assured the visitor that the horse was fine, and that after a while under the tarp, they would allow the horse to stand. He went on to explain the filly's habit and elaborated on the dangers of head trauma.

"We'd like to teach her about avoiding the dangers of head trauma," Will drawled. "I don't want her banging either her head *or* my head on the ground."

"How long will she have to be on the ground like that?" someone asked.

"Oh, it may be more than just a few minutes," Buster suggested. "This one will be a particularly tough case." He grinned sheepishly, almost to himself. By this time, a few more of Will's hands had gathered nearby, and there were a few audible snickers and comments about just how long the horse would be under the tarp.

In medical terms, the horse's condition was stable—she wasn't getting any better or any worse.

Thankfully, it wasn't too long until most of the visitors had left Will's ranch, and his boys gently broke the news to him.

"That flippin' bronc filly is deader than a hammer, boss," Buster related tactfully.

"What?" Will was used to the rough jokes common with most cowboys, so he wasn't really alarmed. "Good, then we can roast her back strap for supper if the fall didn't bruise it too bad." Will *thought* he was joking back.

"No, *really*, boss," Buster insisted. "That filly flipped over backward an' busted her head like a ripe melon. She was dead before her feet hit the dirt."

"Really?"

"Yeah, really. What are you gonna tell the owner?"

Will paused for a long moment and replied, "I'm gonna tell her that you would like to have a word with her about her filly!"

_ The "Waltzing" Horse

"Howdy, Doc," a cheerful voice greeted me over the phone one crisp, fall afternoon. "Angus McCheatem here."

(Of course, that's not his real name, but it fits him better than the one his parents gave him.)

"Do you have any time today to come out and look at a horse for us?"

Any time a new client invokes the name of Angus McCheatem, I tend to get a little cautious. When it's *him* calling, I'm on high alert. Angus is a pretty good ole' boy, as they say, but I know him as a very shrewd horse trader with an occasional tinge of larceny in his blood. When he's not making a lot of money as an engineer, he has been known to extract a few dollars from some unsuspecting horseman. I don't think he needs the money. I think he does it for the sheer sport of it—but that's a whole 'nuther story.

We scheduled an appointment for later in the week, and I arrived with my usual cheerful punctuality. He showed me his new purchase, a nice little mare that was strictly fancy, and at first glance, a proud addition to any man's remuda.

"A trader sold me this little mare a couple of weeks ago," he said. "He told me the mare was such a fancy mover that she fairly dances around the arena. I've heard of a Walkin' horse," he went on, "but I never heard of a *waltzin'* horse!"

The chuckle at the end of this statement was one of guarded curiosity more than humor, and I was wondering if maybe ole Angus had just got a dose of his own medicine.

"Well, anyway, she just waltzed right out from under herself a few times and fell on me once! Like broke my leg and scratched up my brand new saddle!" At this point, it was hard to tell which injury bothered him more.

I examined the mare, and she did have a funny way of moving. Although it wasn't real obvious at first, she swayed around a little, almost like her rear end wanted to go east while her front end was going north. There was no apparent lameness, and her front feet were not sensitive to hoof testers, though she was reluctant to let me pick up her back feet as she kept them spread wide under her.

"I had a colt about twenty years ago that we ended up taking to Davis—you know, up to the vet school—and they said he was a 'wobbler.' This mare is too old to be a wobbler, ain't she, Doc? I mean, that's just in young colts, ain't it?"

"I'm beginning to think that she may have some problem with her spinal cord, Angus," I said cautiously. "The term 'wobbler' can include any one of a number of problems involving the central nervous system, the brain, or the spinal cord."

Horses with neurological problems can be a diagnostic challenge. We can't just sit them up on a table and tap on their knee with that little red rubber hammer or get them to look at ink blots on folded pieces of paper. And they sure can't *tell* us what's wrong; that would be too easy. This mare definitely had neurological problems, but the cause in such cases is often evasive. The nervous system is really an electrical structure, so it's not unlike electrical problems in your pickup truck: the source may be very hard to find. In the horse, these symptoms can also be caused by the viruses that cause sleeping sickness (Eastern, Western, and Venezuelan equine encephalomyelitis, EEE, WEE, VEE), West Nile virus, equine herpesvirus (EHV), and even rabies!

I continued the examination by feeling the mare's spine all the way from her ears to her tail. I figured that if she was real sore right behind her ears, I might be close to a diagnosis. Well, this mare didn't appear to be terribly sore anywhere. So much for wishful thinking. Next, I put my hand under her chin and raised her head about as high as I could while I asked her to back up. She took a couple of tentative steps straight back and then stumbled back two or three more at a 45-degree angle, trying hard not to fall down.

"Angus," I said, "I don't think this mare knows where her rear end is."

"Well, I can see she has a little problem backin' up with her head in the air, Doc, but I don't want her to back up with her head in the air!"

"That was a diagnostic procedure, not a training exercise," I quipped. "The fact that she lost the last few steps backing indicates that her proprioception is a little off."

I went on to explain that it was possible that the horse had suffered nerve damage for some as-yet-unknown reason. You may remember that in Sarah's story, I explained how spinal cord damage occurs in three stages. The first is loss of proprioception—the ability to know where your feet are without looking at them. When you are first learning how to dance, you may not think you can do that, but as it turns out, your brain and spinal cord *can* do that, and it comes in right handy for dancing...or walking in the dark. I knew this mare had lost some of that ability by the way she "waltzed" around at the walk—her rear legs didn't exactly follow her front ones. In addition, as I'd noticed at the beginning of the exam, she stood with her rear legs more apart than normal and had difficulty backing up with her head elevated. To the untrained eye, these symptoms might have seemed fairly subtle, but combined with her history of falling for no apparent reason, they were the hallmarks of a significant neurological problem.

The nervous system of a horse or just about any other animal is a set of living "wires" that conduct electrical impulses. These impulses send messages both ways: that is, some go toward the brain and some away from it. As a general rule, sensory information travels from the body toward the brain and motor impulses are sent out to the various organs. For some horses, when a person with a halter stimulates sensory input from the horse's eye, motor impulses to the muscles of the legs are activated so the horse will walk or run *away*. Miraculously, an image of the same person with a couple of flakes of alfalfa in hand will stimulate the leg muscles of the same horse to walk *toward* the person or even *follow* for a considerable distance!

Neurology is amazing, ain't it?

Although the concept of nervous impulses is fairly simple, their interaction with each other and the way that sensory information is processed is highly complex. In fact, much of what is known about brain function has been determined by studies of human accident victims. Medical records of people with damage to specific areas of the brain or spinal cord have provided us with a sort of "map" of various functions in the brain. For example, the function of the olfactory center of the brain was unknown until somebody had this area damaged in a gun fight and lost his sense of smell. This map is by no means complete, but a rather large body of knowledge has been assembled, and much of what is known about human neuro-anatomy translates closely to other animals.

The spinal cord is a large cable of millions of nerve fibers, like the main cable of a telephone system. As I explained earlier in the book, the nervous pathways for proprioception travel in the outer layers, so minor pressure or irritation in this area will cause problems with knowing where your feet are. More severe pressure, lacerations, or inflammation will involve deeper layers of the cord and result in loss of motor function. So the second stage of nerve damage is indicated when the animal cannot bear weight. The final, most severe form of nerve damage is evidenced when there is the loss of deep-pain sensation. A dog with this type of injury after a car hits him will drag his hind end and not yelp when a back toe is pinched with a forceps.

The diagnosis of horses that are in the latter stages of nerve damage is often of "academic interest." This term translates literally to mean only those people in academic institutions with unlimited time, resources, and lots of students to do most of the work could attempt to diagnose the problem. At this stage of the disease, the diagnosis doesn't really matter because treatment is rarely beneficial.

The first stage of neurological disease, however, presents challenges in both diagnosis and treatment because *some* of these patients can be helped.

"What're we gonna do to fix my mare, Doc?"

"Well, before we can fix her, we have to figure out what is wrong with her," I said.

"How do you propose to do that?"

"It's fairly clear that the mare has a disease of the central nervous system. What is not so clear," I continued, "is what is causing it. We should start by trying to rule out the most common problems first. The old saying is: If you hear hoof beats, don't look for a herd of zebras. The bad news is, this process may take some time and a little money."

"How much time and how little money? I got lots of one, and not much of tha' other," Angus replied.

"It may not be as bad as you think," I said. "I've already made my truck payment this month! Seriously, we could start by shooting some X-rays of her neck. Neurological symptoms in a young horse like her could be caused by trauma, like when a horse pulls back hard on the halter."

"I'd of thought she'd be dead if she broke her neck," Angus said. "Wouldn't you?"

"Surprisingly enough, it's possible for her to have a fracture in one of her vertebrae that's just bad enough to cause inflammation in the outer parts of the spinal cord. That would cause symptoms like hers but wouldn't necessarily be fatal right away. The other thing that we will look for with the radiographic study is a malformation of the boney canal that the spinal cord travels through. We can do this with something called a 'myelogram.' We inject some dye into her spinal canal to see if it is a little 'pinched'" on one or more areas. A constriction of the canal could cause similar symptoms."

"Like a 'wobbler,'" he mused, apparently remembering the colt he had mentioned earlier.

"The other thing to consider is a disease called equine protozoal myelitis, or EPM for short. It is an infectious disease of horses in which a nasty little parasite gets into the spinal cord and causes real problems."

"It can't be that," he said. "I worm her regularly and she gets her shots every year!"

"Well", I replied, "this type of parasite can't be killed with a paste dewormer. It takes something with a little more kick." I also explained that there was no effective vaccine for EPM yet. The disease has a very complex life cycle involving two hosts. One is a carnivore, like a cat or opossum, and the other an herbivore—in this case, the horse. Breaking this cycle or helping the immune system fight off the infection is not nearly as easy as it is with other diseases.

Although there are blood tests for EPM, they only indicate the horse has been exposed to the parasites; they are not considered "diagnostic" for active disease. The only way to definitively find out if Angus's mare was actively infected was by analyzing her spinal fluid. In this procedure, a special needle is placed into her spine just behind her ears, and very carefully, a sample of fluid is withdrawn. The sample is sent to a lab and analyzed for the presence of DNA specific to the parasite. This is called the polymerase chain reaction (PCR) test (I've mentioned it before), and it is very specific.

One of the challenges with this or any diagnostic plan is the fact that sometimes the results are negative. In the case of a negative test for EPM, we can *probably* say a horse does not have the disease, but there are some "what ifs" in the test. There are reports of "false negatives" with the PCR. It is not clear why, but a negative test does not mean it's not a case of EPM. And there is always the possibility that the problems are caused by one of the viruses I've mentioned before in this book—all neurological problems can present with very similar symptoms.

I've told you that one of the frustrating things about veterinary medicine is that money often plays a part in what we can do for the horse. In this mare's scenario, there was no guarantee that all the diagnostic tests available were going to tell us what the problem was. To make things more complicated, even if we made a definitive diagnosis, there was no promise that a treatment would work. In reality, my experience had been that horses with the degree of neurological damage that appeared to be present in Angus's mare may never return to use as a riding horse at any level. My concern is always for the horse, obviously, but in these cases, there is a distinct possibility that a rider could be seriously injured, as well.

So Angus thanked me for my time and information, and told me he would think about it. I never did hear back from him, and I never saw the mare again. I guess somebody in another county probably bought "the waltzing mare"—lucky him.

Boys and Girls Will Get Together

Mammalian reproduction is a miracle that nobody
really understands. Inject semen in the shoulder
of a mare and you get a nasty abscess. Put the same sample
in her uterus and you get a foal…with a little luck
and three hundred and forty-five days, or so.
The pages ahead address the reason we call
castration "brain surgery," what happens when
it goes wrong, and why it's always a good idea
to wait a while before you make rash decisions.

CHAPTER

6

_ Cut Willie

Mrs. Wiggins had been a good friend and client for many years. She often called me for advice or even just to let me know how one of her horses did at a recent show. Although she was a good horseman, she often sought advice from other horse people, trainers, veterinarians, and Dr. Google before she made a decision regarding one of her horses. Then, armed with a gold mine of conflicting information, she would call me, hoping for a simple answer to a complicated question.

The main problem with all the free advice is that it is often overpriced.

"Mrs. W" was a kind lady. She had a good sense of humor and took a joke well. Her skepticism about *everything*, however, had occasionally taken me to the edge of my already questionable sanity. She called me one day before I had left on my morning rounds.

"I'm calling you about Willie," she began. "You know, my yearling colt. He's getting bad about biting and striking at me with his front feet. I punish him for that, but he just can't seem to help himself. He's started to get interested in mares, and we've had to cut him out of the fences a couple of times."

I replied with unusual succinctness, "There's a surgery for that."

"Really?" She said with more interest than I had expected. I guess she was thinking some new miracle cure that had just been discovered up at the state college.

"How much does it cost?"

"'Bout a hundred dollars."

"Will it really work? I mean, is it successful and is it dangerous?"

"Mrs. Wiggins," I said smoothly, "you can't buy a *dangerous* operation for only a hundred dollars!"

"Do you mean *castrate* him?" she exclaimed with surprise that surprised me.

"Yep." I do my best Gary Cooper first thing in the morning.

"Well...I don't know. Don't you think we should wait another year? I mean, I wouldn't want to stunt his growth. I don't even think that he's 'dropped' yet," she said.

These were good questions commonly asked by soon-to-be-gelding owners. There are many myths about the descent of the testes into the scrotum of colts and of their long-term effects on stature, musculature, and behavior. I get most of these calls when colts are about two, because, like teenage boys, they will often show symptoms of testosterone toxicity at this age.

The "gonads"—ovaries or testes—in fillies and colts are formed very early in pregnancy and are located just behind the fetal kidney in the abdomen of the developing foal. In fillies, the gonads stay behind the kidneys and become the ovaries. The testes of the colt, however, will descend into the scrotal sac *before* birth. Although there are exceptions to the rule, a colt born without testicles in the scrotum will not "drop" at any magical age. There are several terms used to describe colts with one or both testicles undescended. "Ridgelings," "high-flank-ers," "cryps," and "one-lungers" have all been used to describe what veterinarians call "cryptorchids." Surgery for the removal of retained testicles is a little more complicated than a routine castration, but it should be done because the re-tained testicle will continue to make testosterone, the hormone responsible for stallion behavior, even though it cannot make sperm cells. A horse with one or two retained testicles will be just as obnoxious as a normal stallion, but sterile, unless one testicle is on the outside.

"My colts were never cut before they were two or three and they have always been big and muscular," Mrs. Wiggins commented. "But Willie is so full of himself, I may have to sacrifice some size so that I don't have to shoot him first! Is there anything you can give him so that he will develop normally, but not be so silly?"

I explained to her that the muscle-building effects of testosterone, the male hormone, is lost as soon as the colt is gelded. Geldings always look like geldings, so there is no lasting effect from keeping them intact for a certain length of time. For example, some bodybuilders take anabolic steroids to improve their strength and muscle definition. These drugs are all synthetic forms of testosterone, and if used repeatedly, they are very dangerous. Unfortunately, they *must* be used repeatedly in order to be effective because, like the naturally occurring hormone, these compounds are constantly being removed from the body. Once the hormone is removed, there is no lasting effect on muscle development.

There is, however, a lasting effect of testosterone on adult size. The presence of sex hormones in both males and females will stop long bone growth at puberty. This fact was well illustrated by my friend Butch Bordeen, who was a kid in my sixth-grade class. Butch was big, strong, and not destined for the Dean's List, but he was the envy of every boy in the class because he had to *shave*. By the time we were all in the ninth grade, everybody called him "Shorty" (only behind his back).

Colts that are castrated before the onset of puberty (usually about twelve months) will grow taller than their unaltered herdmates. The reason that some stallions may *look* bigger than many geldings is that they are way overweight. After all, fat is the prettiest color of a show horse.

Although testosterone disappears from the bloodstream within twenty-four hours after surgery, it can take up to a month for the psychological effects to sink into little colt brains. Rarely, a colt will continue to act like a stallion indefinitely. These horses are called "proud cut," but there is no known reason why these colts continue stallion-like behavior. One old myth contends that "if you don't cut 'em right, they'll still squeal like a stud." In reality, if both testicles are removed and the horse survives the surgery, he was "cut right." No other tissue in the equine body makes testosterone.

Mrs. Wiggins was surprisingly silent during my explanation of pubertal physiology and offered little argument. I attributed this to my brilliantly thorough treatise on the subject.

"I'm really not worried about him not getting very big because you cut him too early," she remarked. "I'm afraid of the anesthesia. My friend lost a horse that way. Do you have to knock him out?"

"We can do him standing with a mild sedative and local anesthesia," I explained, "but he'll feel more of it than if a general anesthetic is used. It's up to you, but there is usually nothing to worry about." I realized too late that the quickest way to make somebody worry was to tell them not to. When somebody says, "Don't think of a pink elephant," what happens?

"This is one of the oldest known surgical procedures," I tried again. "It was practiced in Egypt over four thousand years before the invention of anesthesia and is usually quite safe." I didn't know for sure if Egyptians anesthetized their surgical candidates, but my guess was that they didn't.

"I don't know." She was still apprehensive. "You keep using the word 'usually.' Are you sure you know how to do this? How many colts have you *successfully* castrated?"

"Everyone I ever cut stayed castrated," I said, unable to resist a smart retort. "I never get a repeat patient for this type of surgery." I hoped my humor would reassure her that this was well within the range of my capability.

After a long, thoughtful pause, Mrs. W asked me if we could set up a time to make a gentleman out of Willie sometime in the next few days.

I arrived at the appointed time and began preparations for the anesthesia and surgery. Willie was upset because he had missed his breakfast, per my instructions, and he seemed to know that something was up.

Mrs. Wiggins was apprehensive. "Maybe we should wait for another day," she said. "I think it looks like rain," though most everybody thought that we were in the midst of a three-year drought.

During the next two months, Mrs. W made and canceled two more appointments for the proposed brain surgery on her prized colt, Willie. Late one Sunday night, I received a call from her. I usually only answer emergency calls on Sunday, so I figured that she must have a real problem.

"Doc," she almost screamed, "I want you to come cut this @#$%^& colt right now!"

"Well, I'd like to help you," I began, "but I rarely perform emergency castrations on Sunday night. Do you think he could wait till tomorrow morning? I'd like for him to be off feed for about twelve hours before the anesthesia," I explained. "That way there's less chance that he will colic after he recovers."

Finally, she made and kept an appointment. This time, I was ready.

I arrived on time, as usual, and arranged my surgical instruments and shining stainless steel buckets with precision. I answered Mrs. W's onslaught of questions with the skill and finesse of a true professional, and then, I exacted my revenge.

I took out a surgery book and turned to the section marked "Equine Castration" and pretended to read it with interest. After about five minutes I slammed the book shut and said, "This ain't gonna be too hard. Where is he?"

After she resumed breathing, we both had a good laugh. The surgery was uneventful. Mrs. Wiggins followed the postoperative care of cold-water therapy over the surgical wound and forced exercise for twenty minutes twice daily with her usual dedication. Willie is alive and well and doesn't aggravate the mares anymore.

_ Mares and Pregnancy: Timing, Hormones, and a Little Luck

There is one thing more complicated than reproduction: discussing it. I always try to use the proper names for the anatomy involved, as professional-sounding terms are much clearer than "that thing." But these discussions tend to be delicate and require no small measure of finesse and adjustments to fit the audience.

A few years ago, a friend of mine was faced with just such a discussion with his six-year-old son. He was ready for the questions, as this was not his first child. One morning, the expected query became the topic of discussion over the oatmeal.

"Dad, where did I come from?"

My friend answered with a short course in obstetrics and gynecology, including a brief glossary of anatomical terms suitable for an inquisitive first-grader. When he finished, *he* was fairly pleased with his answer. He had almost regained his normal breathing pattern when his son replied: "Oh…Billy says he came from Chicago!"

So when clients ask about reproduction, I always want to be *certain* of the question so I can know if the answer should include detailed physiology or "Chicago." In reality, the processes that start with a willing mare and stallion and result in the foal standing to nurse, are masterpieces of creation and miracles of timing.

It is the classic "chicken or egg" conundrum, but let's start with fertilization. The mare has the egg, or ovum, and the stallion has the sperm. How they get together…go ask your mother. The fact that it works at all is a major miracle. A normal horse has sixty-four chromosomes in almost every cell in the body. *Almost* every cell. The sex cells, the egg and sperm, have exactly half that number. During the process of "syngamy," or fertilization, these two halves become a whole and a new horse begins to form. *Completely new.* Of course, there will be some similarities due to breed characteristics and other factors—a Shire horse won't often deliver a Shetland pony—but a new, genetically unique individual is formed.

The act of breeding is somewhat physically demanding. If you have ever seen this performance…wow! But at a very basic, immunological level, several obstacles must be surmounted before fertilization can occur. Semen placed in the uterus, with the right timing, will produce a foal. But a new foal growing in the mare's body presents a set of immune challenges. In organ transplant patients, the donor must be "matched" genetically very close to the recipient. This is why family members, while seldom a first choice for a loan, are the best bet for a kidney. Even with a close match, the recipients will usually need anti-rejection drugs for the rest of their lives. Though the foal is genetically distinct from the moment of conception, he thrives in the uterus of the mare without any man-made drugs at all. How the immune response, which would normally expel the "little parasite," is temporarily suppressed is not understood, but it obviously works.

The entire symphony of procreation involves a vast array of hormonal inter-actions that we are not even close to understanding. By definition, "hormones" are chemicals created in the body that have actions away from their site of manu-facture. They are responsible for the manufacture of other products, as well, and modify behavior directed at survival. For example, "epinephrine," or "adrenaline," is responsible for "fight or flight." It is manufactured by the adrenal gland (hence the name "adrenaline"), which is a little lump of tissue that lives next to a kidney. Although this gland seems pretty insignificant when compared to the heart or liv-er, it secretes the hormone that can cause the horse to react in a most unpredict-able manner. (The sudden appearance of a carnivorous balloon or tarp is capable of eliciting a memorable, explosive expression of the effects of epinephrine.)

In a similar theme, the sex hormones, "estrogen," "progesterone," and "andro-gens," have profound effects on behavior, as well as other, though less obvious, changes in physiology. The hormone-producing cells found in the ovaries and testicles comprise a relatively small portion of the population of cells. The bulk of testicular tissue is made up of microscopic tubules that constantly produce sperm cells by the billions, but the effects of the hormonal products from these tissues can be profound. They are primarily involved in reproduction and are found in *both* sexes. Estrogen prepares the reproductive system for the release of the ovum. It also modifies behavior, making the mare receptive to the amo-rous advances of the stallion for a few days a month. This receptivity occurs only during the "breeding season." The rest of the time she would just as soon kick his fool head in if he gets too close to her.

We think of estrogen as a "girl thing," but the stallion produces more estrogen than any other animal! What they do with all this female hormone poses a great physiologic question. Biological systems are amazingly efficient with very little waste, so stallion estrogen production has *some* function, we just don't know what it is yet. Progesterone is considered the hormone of pregnancy, but it also has a tranquilizing effect. Pregnant mares are "settled" due to this, and there is some recently discovered evidence that it sedates foals during pregnancy as well.

In some brilliant research conducted by the same Dr. John Madigan I mentioned in an earlier story, the function of progesterone in newborn horses and autistic human babies may have something in common. "Dummy syndrome," from which Lisa's colt suffered, has baffled veterinarians for a long time. As you learned, these foals are not capable of nursing, but if they can be kept alive for a few weeks, most of them will develop typical behavior and mature into normal horses. As I mentioned, Dr. Madigan found that these "dummy foals" lacked the normal mechanisms to clear these *progestogens,* the progesterone class of hormones, retaining the high levels that kept them sedated. What is even more astounding is the association between high levels of progestogens and autism in children. Dr. Madigan is currently conducting a study with the Stanford Medical Center in this area with hopes for a prevention of this growing problem.

Although the physiology of reproduction and the miracle of timing are truly astounding phenomena, they get forgotten as the 345-day marvel ends with that excited question: "Is it a colt or a filly?"

_ Ol' Buck's "Thing"

"Doc, this is Henry," the familiar voice greeted me over the phone early one morning. "It's ol' Buck. He has a couple a' problems and I think you better come look at 'im soon. We got a team pennin' this weekend an' I don't wanna miss it."

Henry and his wife Edna were the long-time friends you met in the story of Clyde earlier in these pages. They were a couple of "old school" ranch folks and always a delight. For over twenty years I enjoyed Edna's home-cooked meals and Henry's sage advice and tales about the old days. Though their kids were grown and the town had moved out to surround them, they still had a menagerie of hound dogs, horses, and an occasional orphaned calf in the yard.

As I drove into the yard, I was greeted by barking dogs and scampering chickens. Edna hollered at me to come into the kitchen for some coffee. I enjoyed the hospitality while she and Henry filled me in on the recent antics of the grandkids and local gossip.

"Ol' Buck's legs are swelled up big as fence posts." Henry decided to get to the point of my visit. "I think he got bit by a snake."

We went out to where the old gelding was standing in a lot behind the house, and sure enough, Buck looked like he had a pair of tight-fitting, black-and-tan jeans on his back legs that were neatly tucked into his hooves. In addition, he had a band of swollen tissue under his belly that was about eight inches wide and three inches thick and extended from his flanks to his elbows.

"There's something else that Edna is kinda' worried about," Henry said with predictable embarrassment. This is the way he always brought up something *he* didn't want to talk about. "Ol' Buck's got some awful scaly stuff on his...'thing'... and Edna is worried that he may have some kind of infection."

Lots of folks are shy when it comes to talking about certain parts of anatomy. This can create some confusion if we fail to use proper terms when we are trying to explain a medical problem. A few years ago, I was examining a well-endowed stallion because the owner thought that there was something wrong with "Zippy's pee-pee." About the third time I heard her use the term "pee-pee" I said, "Look at the size of this thing! Do you really think it qualifies as a 'pee-pee'?"

That was not my best exercise in people skills, but the client used the correct term every time after!

Back to Buck: He had "pitting edema" from the coronary bands of both hind feet, extending up his legs and along his belly all the way to his elbows. This refers to a swelling that is due to a collection of water between the cells. Because this tissue is swollen like a sponge, there is no "pocket" that can be lanced to relieve the pressure like you could if there was an abscess present. It is called "pitting" edema because when you press into the area with your finger, it leaves a little depression that will persist for several seconds. He was not lame and there were no other signs of illness.

"How long has he been like this?"

"Just noticed it yesterday. What do you think it is? And what about his 'thing'?"

Now was my chance to really shine in the eyes of this client. I knew I could fix Ol' Buck's problem and eloquently explain the situation in the process.

"I think I can fix him by cleaning his sheath," I said confidently. "The problem is in his lymphatic vessels," I added.

"Okay...what are they?"

I went on to explain that there are four basic types of vessels in the body: "arteries," "capillaries," "veins," and "lymphatic channels." Arteries carry oxygenated blood to the muscles and other organs of the body. The capillaries are very small vessels that allow the passage of oxygen and nutrients to the tissues. (These vessels are small enough that about fifty of them could fit inside a human hair!) Once the blood has delivered oxygen and nutrients to the tissues, the veins carry it back to the heart. During the transfer in the capillaries, some of the fluid in the blood leaks out into the minute spaces between the cells. Most of it winds up back in small veins, but some of it is collected in lymphatic channels.

These lymph vessels are a vital part of the immune system and are connected to "lymph nodes," which act as filters to catch foreign particles invading the body. In addition to their function as filters, the lymph nodes are involved in processing of information needed by the immune system. The production of antibodies, which will be essential in the body's fight against infection, is initiated here. This is the reason that those little "glands" swell up behind your jaw when you get the flu or a bad cold. (You can *claim* that this phenomenon has occurred if you don't want to go to school.) The lymph vessels draining your eyes, nose, and throat pass through these nodes, which become inflamed due to the infection that is making your nose, throat, and chest hate you. When the nodes under your jaw swell up, it is obvious that the source of the infection is somewhere in your head. Consequently, understanding the lymphatic drainage of the body can help us to locate the source of infection or inflammation in some cases.

There are three major "lymphocenters" in the body of the horse: "submandibular," just under and behind the jaw; "prescapular," in front of the shoulder; and "inguinal," tucked up under the flank. Ol' Buck had a dirty sheath: the tissues around his "thing"—aka his penis. The inflammation from this region caused the lymphatic drainage to "back up," and the rear legs and underside of his belly retained water because of it.

Henry's response to this eloquent discourse was silence and a blank stare. He broke a long quiet: "But why the heck are his back legs swole up because his sheath needs cleanin' and what about his 'thing'?"

Knowing my shine was beginning to fade, I tried another approach.

"Did you ever notice that the shower starts draining slow a couple of days before the toilet backs up?"

"I thought you was a medical genius, not a plumber."

"That's what I'm trying to tell you!" I said, waving my arms as if it would improve my communication skills. "His plumbing is backing up. Something has plugged up the lymphatic vessels around his sheath. As long as that blockage is there, his legs and belly will stay swollen. I may be wrong, but I think if we clean his sheath, we can fix his problem."

In about half a minute, I saw a flicker in Henry's eye like a reading light in a trailer suddenly switched on so a balky horse will load. Henry was a really sharp fellow and educated in his own way…or all that arm waving of mine paid off. I'm pretty sure it was the former.

I figured Ol' Buck was going to be embarrassed about me examining his private parts, so I gave him a sedative that would prolapse his penis and relax him enough to let me clean his sheath thoroughly without getting kicked over the fence. I gently reflected the tissues surrounding the "urethra" (the passageway for urine) so that I could explore the little crevices around it. Then I removed a waxy "smegma bean"—an accumulation of dead skin and sebaceous secretions about the size of a large lima bean.

"There's the problem," I said, holding the trophy-sized bean in my gloved hand. "This thing was plugging up the works. If Buck didn't have to put up with you, he might have a chance at the penning Friday night."

I explained that some folks wanted the sheath of their horse cleaned periodically for cosmetic reasons, but unless the horse was stocked up like Buck was, there was no medical reason for the procedure.

"Thanks, Doc. Now what about his 'thing'?"

_ Stallion Hygiene

It was an unseasonably cold, early spring evening. There was an icy warning in the strong southern wind that a cold rain would soon deliver *more* water to the already swollen creeks and soggy pastures. But I was getting used to the changes between *both* seasons in California: the muddy one and the dusty one. Although the water in the stainless steel bucket was warm, my hands chilled and stiffened quickly in the night air as I attempted to wash the stallion's "private parts" just before he was to breed the mare.

The stallion was less than enthusiastic about my intervention in his personal life, and he squealed a little as I completed the process of prenuptial hygiene. This had almost become a ritual in which neither of us was a willing participant. The stallion, for obvious reasons, and me, for a less apparent medical dilemma. Linda, the stallion owner, and I had been 'round and 'round about stallion hygiene. She was meticulous, to say the least, and we had been embroiled in a friendly battle about cleanliness in the breeding shed for some time. The use of strong disinfectants may seem like an obvious part of good breeding management, especially in these modern times as folks are becoming more aware of the spread of infectious diseases. However, things in nature are not always as they appear.

Nature is amazingly adept at protecting the health of all forms of life. Even in the delicate balance between host and parasite, predator and prey, there is a precarious parity that provides the environment for an astounding array of plants, animals, and *protista* (bacteria and other microscopic life) to flourish. Although we are literally covered by bacteria, viruses, and other microbes in unimaginable numbers, our immune systems and other factors protect us from disease.

Of course, the immune system plays a big role in protecting all animals from disease, but the balance of the ever-present microbial population is involved, as well. This is clearly illustrated in cases where well-meaning stallion owners have actually caused infections by overzealous hygiene. There is a normal, constant population of bacteria that lives on the skin of all animals, including horses. These microbes are usually harmless and have apparently established an agreement with the stallion to live and let live. Of course, there are good and bad among us all, and the good bugs in the microbial population tend to keep the bad ones in check.

This harmony becomes discord when, with good intentions, we come along with a bottle of Betadine˚ and a roll of cotton to be sure that Mr. Ed's equipment is good and clean before his date. What happens is that *all* the bacteria are wiped out. This does not cause an immediate problem. However, if the stallion is washed a few times with the strong disinfectant, all of the good bugs are killed repeatedly and only the pathogenic bad bugs return. This is like putting a broad-spectrum herbicide on your lawn. *All* the plants would be killed, but only the weeds would grow back. The grass that was keeping the weeds in check was wiped out when the botanical equivalent to Betadine˚ was applied. Virtually every case of venereal infection in stallions has been due to the use of strong disinfectants (Betadine˚ or Nolvasan˚) for genital hygiene.

After lengthy discussion, Linda and I reached a compromise. I would wash the stallion with warm water *only*. This would not disrupt much of the normal flora, and that would keep me and the microbial population happy, but it would remove some surface debris, and that would keep Linda's aesthetic sensibilities happy. It still didn't make her stallion real happy. He didn't care about microbiology; all he cared about was...well, you know what he cared about.

About the time of the great depression, horses were still used for work and transportation, as well as pleasure, so breeding mares was more of a necessity than a hobby. My friend Hugh Bishop told me a story about his dad breeding a buggy horse back in the nineteen twenties.

Young Neil Bishop grew up in the vast, sparsely populated Kansas farmlands. There were considerable distances between farms and towns in those days, and a fast buggy horse was a real asset to farmers who couldn't afford an automobile. Hugh's grandfather owned a *great* buggy horse: a mare named Dolly. Grandpa Bishop appreciated Dolly's style and stamina as she swept the countryside with the smooth, effortless power of a champion. While she may not have won the Hambletonian Stakes, she could pull a buggy through Kansas with style and speed that made him proud.

As Dolly got a little older, Grandpa Bishop realized that he would eventually need a replacement for her. So arrangements were made to breed her to a neighbor's stallion. As all the men in the family were involved in the spring planting, the duty of transporting Dolly to the stallion was given to Neil. Lacking a horse trailer and a one-ton Ford diesel to pull it, the younger Bishop, who was about eight years old at the time, swung on the mare bareback early one morning and rode her to the neighbor's farm.

He arrived in the mid-afternoon. Just like at home, all the grown men were working in the fields—only the farmer's wife and infant child were present. The younger Bishop, not wanting to repeat the day-long journey, convinced the farmer's wife that he could hold the mare if she could lead the stallion. Being a tough, resourceful Kansas farm woman, not bothering even to remove her apron, she stepped into the stallion's corral and slipped a halter on him.

Neil stood with Dolly in quiet awe as the proudly prancing stallion neighed his amorous intentions loud enough to be heard in St. Louis. He lunged toward the mare with youthful exuberance. The surprised mare stepped nervously to the side just enough to momentarily interrupt the event. The stallion, more eager than accurate, became increasingly frustrated at his apparently poor aim. The farmer's wife was in a position where she could correct the stallion's aiming deficiency, but she was just a bit squeamish about actually *touching* the passionate appendage. In a moment of quick thinking she would live to regret, she placed her hand under the hem of her apron and using the cloth like a pot holder for a hot skillet handle, directed the stallion to the target.

That was all the encouragement the stud needed. As soon as he realized he was in the right place, he was *in the right place*! Unfortunately, the clean, dry calico of the apron stuck fast to the slightly damp skin of the organ and the cloth, which had so recently been an apron, was quickly transformed into a calico condom! As young Bishop watched in dumbfounded silence, the hardy Kansas woman, still tied to the apron by some stout, cotton strings, was picked up by the ardent thrusting of the young stallion and became an involuntary member of an unlikely threesome. Thankfully, the stallion completed his mission quickly and oblivious to the presence of an accidental participant. No one was injured, and miraculously, the mare conceived.

Less than a year later, Dolly presented the Bishops with a beautiful, long-legged filly who would be a worthy legacy to her elegant dam. At a church social a short time after the birth of the filly, the Bishops were visiting with the owner of the stallion and his wife. Grandpa Bishop commented on what a beautiful foal their stallion had produced with his mare, Dolly.

The farmer's wife stood silently, apparently reflecting on the truly unforgettable event of the previous year. Then she said, "Well it ought to be—it was strained through my prettiest calico apron!"

_ The Traveling Pregnant Mare

The mare stood patiently as I invaded her depths with the probe of my ultrasound machine. Both Barbara and I looked anxiously at the small black screen but did not see the image we had hoped for. It could have been worse—there could have been twins, or extra fluid—but the black, quarter-sized circle indicative of a single, fourteen-day pregnancy was conspicuously absent.

But the mare *felt* pregnant. I had learned to palpate mares ten years before portable ultrasound had been invented, so I learned the "feel" long before I learned what they looked like on the very expensive six-inch black-and-white TV screen. (My first one cost more than a new truck.) Without ultrasound, I would have *called* her pregnant and that would be the end of the story. But, as you have probably guessed by now, this is not the end of the story.

Mrs. Barbara Goodrich had contacted me in the early spring, asking about the possibility of breeding her mare artificially. She had her eye on a real fancy, blue-blooded stallion in Colorado but didn't want to take the mare on a long, expensive trip. I told her we could help her avoid the trailer ride by using shipped, fresh-cooled semen and artificial insemination, but it wasn't cheap, and timing was critical. They weren't going to send a sample in a pickle jar that we could just use when we had time. The mare had to be in heat, the semen had to be placed in the uterus, and she had to ovulate within forty-eight hours. Fertility is not a function of how *many* times the mare is bred. One time is sufficient if it is the *right* time. Of course, if we *didn't* want the mare to conceive, she could get pregnant *any* time—especially by the dink, fence-jumping two-year-old down the road that should have been gelded at birth—but that's a whole 'nother story.

I went on to explain that the entire process could take several visits, and the synchronization of several factors was critical. We made an appointment for the following week.

After examining the mare, I told Mrs. Goodrich that we were very lucky. Normally, the first exam (the one with the long plastic sleeve) indicates where the mare is in her cycle, but more visits are usually needed to improve the chances of predicting ovulation. I told her that if we could have a sample in forty-eight hours, I thought the mare would be ready. I stressed how lucky we were, as it seldom happened so quickly. I thought to myself that it might be a sign that this case would be easy.

I was wrong.

The practice of veterinary medicine has taught me a lot of things over the years. It has taught me some things about horses...and lots of stuff about people. After all, this is not an "animal business," it's a "people business"...and the people own horses. As much as I like a horse, I have yet to have one call me on the phone. So my interaction with Mrs. Goodrich took a surprising turn in the next thirty seconds.

"The next step is for you to call the stallion owner and have the semen shipped to you. If you can call me when it arrives, I can make arrangements to be here within a couple of hours so we can get the sample in your mare."

"Well, I have to work on Thursday," she replied, "so I won't be here until after six. I have a neighbor who can keep an eye out for the UPS truck, and she can call me when the shipment gets here...I can't even go outside without her knowing about it, so this will be one time where a nosey neighbor comes in handy!"

"That should work," I said. "Just give me your gate code so I can get back to the barn so you won't even need to be here." The mare was real gentle, but the barn was about one hundred yards in back of the house. Mrs. Goodrich was quite cautious, maybe even a little paranoid, as she kept the gate closed, sometimes even locked, when I was still back there.

"Oh, I couldn't do that," she said. "You can just crawl through the fence."

I had to stop and digest what had just been fed to me. I was thinking, but for once in my life did not say: *You trust me with your very expensive mare, a fairly* *expensive semen sample, and my ability to perform a rather complicated proce-dure, but **not** with your gate code?*

The thought of "crawling through the fence," making several trips to the barn with my equipment, the semen container, and my pride, would have been hu-morous, if it hadn't been true. In those days, my practice was fairly new in the area, and I found myself doing things I wouldn't even consider later in my career. So we made arrangements for the semen shipment and a phone call from Ms. Nosey sometime Thursday.

I received the call in the middle of the day Thursday and drove to the Goodrich place. She still did not offer the gate code, and I didn't ask, figuring, *What's the point?*

When I got to her place I was in for a pleasant surprise. Her zealous security system had one small hole in it: The front gate was on strap hinges secured to the fence post by heavy bolts with a 90-degree bend to accommodate a loop in the hinge. Normally, the top hinge is pointed down, and the bottom hinge is pointed up. This keeps somebody from simply lifting the gate off its hinges, thus seriously limiting the function of the lock and chain.

To my amazement, both of the hinges were pointed *up*, so I easily lifted the aluminum gate off its hinges, swung it open, as it was still chained to the closing end, and drove back to the barn. (I *may* have failed to later mention the security flaw to the ever-so-cautious Mrs. G....)

It is always a good idea to recheck the mare in forty-eight hours to ensure ovulation, and this mare did so, exactly as predicted. Though the whole process started out dang near textbook perfect, it didn't stay that way.

I recommend the first ultrasound on day fourteen after ovulation. This will *usually*—and the key word here is *usually*—tell us if she is pregnant or coming back into heat. An exam at this early date also helps us manage twin pregnancies more easily. Although twins sound like a cheap way to expand your herd, they almost always end in disaster.

Before I place the ultrasound probe in the right location (this also requires a long plastic sleeve, a lot of nerve, and a very cooperative patient), I feel the cervix and uterus. In a mare during early pregnancy, the cervix feels like a pencil and the uterus feels like a banana or large sausage. That is the way this mare *felt*, but the image on the screen suggested my fingers were either lying to me or they were thinking about something else. The embryo is about the size of a quarter by fourteen days, and the uterus is about the size of a large banana, so there ain't a lot of room to hide. However, these sneaky rascals have occasionally played hide and seek with me, and I just can't find 'em. In mares that really *feel* pregnant, I like to scan again in a couple of days. This often results in the good news that the mare is, indeed, pregnant. On this occasion, however, this was not going to happen.

Mrs. Goodrich was *livid*.

"I can't believe I spent *all this money...*" (I think her bill totaled about two hundred and fifty dollars at that point, unbelievably cheap for the amount of service provided, even twenty-five years ago) "...and you can't see anything on this stupid machine!"

I told her again how fortunate we were that things had gone this smoothly and that I was fairly confident that we would see the embryo in two days.

Nope.

"I can't believe I thought we could actually do this artificially in the first place," she fumed. "I am going to take her to Colorado and let things happen naturally. It's what I should have done in the first place!"

She did.

Three months later I got a call from the farm manager at the blue-blood stallion station in Danglongwaysfromhere, Colorado.

"Mrs. Goodrich brought us a mare a few months back and listed you as the vet of record," he started, "but she said she had already spent a *FORTUNE* with you and didn't want to spend another dime on unnecessary vet bills. We have been teasing this mare every other day for about three months, but she hasn't showed the slightest interest in our stallion. I thought I'd find out if you did something to bring her in heat. Mrs. Goodrich was fairly adamant about 'no vets.'"

I told him the condensed version of the story and that maybe another exam would be helpful. He called me back in a few hours with the news that his vet had examined her and said she was in foal...about ninety days!

Sometimes just one more try will give us a victory. It's not like we had been breeding this mare for six cycles with no luck; we had been very fortunate with the timing of the whole process. But let's think about Mrs. G's decision. One more ultrasound exam would have cost her about fifty dollars. Instead, she took a week off work, drove twelve hundred miles to Colorado—twice—to deliver and retrieve her mare, paid for ninety days board, *and* eventually, another vet exam anyway to determine the mare was pregnant all along.

With that exercise in economics, I'm sure she has a promising future in politics.

_ Train Wreck (Even If You Can't Define It, You'll Know One When You See It)

I've been working with horses professionally for a long time—just short of fifty years. This is nothing short of a blessing from God, as it is the best job there is. Although it is almost always very rewarding, it does have its occasional downside, and that's the topic here. Even though this case started out normally, the course of events was anything but normal.

I was called out to see a nice two-year-old colt that the client wanted gelded. Debbie was clearly proud of this nice colt, and he followed her toward my truck without the typical young wannabe-stud-horse-ruler-of-the-world antics that compels so many of us to consider castration a life-saving surgery. Ben exemplified good manners in a young stallion.

Although some veterinarians perform castration on the heavily sedated, standing horse, with an injection of local anesthetic directly into the testicle (!), most of us prefer general anesthesia. This is less painful for the victim and much safer for the surgeon.

Ben's response to anesthesia was textbook. I performed the surgery as planned and he recovered uneventfully. To remove the testicles, we cut the "spermatic cord," the structure that contains the testicular artery, vein, and nerve, and the "vas deferens," as well as a thin segment of abdominal muscle. The Modified White's Emasculator is the instrument of choice for many of us. It is a century-old design that cuts the cord close to the belly wall and crimps the vessels above the cut to stop the bleeding. On mature stallions, I tie off the whole bundle with a large suture, just to be sure there's no hemorrhage. The instrument works very well, but the extra ligature has *usually* given me a little extra security on the more "well endowed" colts. (Emphasis on the "usually" part.)

No matter how we secure the testicular vessels, the skin is left un-sutured, as the surgical site needs to be left open to drain. It is common for some of the skin bleeders to drip for a few minutes after recovery, but they *almost* always stop by the time I clean up my toys and get ready to go. (Emphasis on the "almost" part.)

As textbook as Ben was on the anesthesia, he was woefully lacking on "hemostasis." (That's the ten-dollar word for the body's ability to stop bleeding.) The incision was still dripping when I left, but the rule of thumb is: if you can count the drips, it's not a steady stream, so the bleeding will stop on its own. So I gave post-surgical care instructions to Debbie, confident that Ben would *probably* be okay. (Emphasis on the "probably" part.)

Later in the day, Debbie called to report that she couldn't count the drips. This was not a math problem; it was a clotting problem. I returned to the scene and was discouraged to see Ben had lost a couple of pints of blood. A little blood looks like a lot of blood when it's your horse. However, a mature horse has about ten gallons, so losing a couple of pints is less than a donation to the blood bank, though a bit worrying nonetheless.

I explained the options to Debbie, and we decided to anesthetize Ben again and try to find the bleeder. Castration is the most common surgery in equine practice. Over the recent three decades, I have performed hundreds of them, and the rate of any complication is less than two percent, and hemorrhage, less common than that. However, in re-anesthesia to look for the source of the hemorrhage, I am batting a thousand, as I have *never* found one. The anesthetic drugs lower the blood pressure and the simple act of lying down must crimp or displace whatever is bleeding so we just don't see the source. It's just basic plumbing: an unseen leak can't be repaired. So I packed the cavity that once held the family jewels with gauze sponges, put a couple of big sutures in the skin to hold the absorbent material in place and waited for Ben to recover. He did. I expected the packing to stop the bleeding. It didn't. It wasn't streaming out like before, but it was still dripping.

At the risk of succumbing to the insanity of doing the same thing looking for a different result, we reinstituted the "count the drips" (CTD) plan, and I left, again hoping our efforts would finally stop the bleeding and we could get some rest. Twelve hours later, the hemorrhage had escalated beyond the CTD monitor. Anesthesia, round three. This time I re-ligated the left stump, as the initial one had fallen off. The right stump, however, demonstrated a reflex due to the slip of muscle present in the spermatic cord. This is part of the system designed to regulate temperature by pulling the testis toward the body when it is cold. During a normal castration, stimulating the cord with a blade or other instrument will commonly cause the muscle to contract and pull the testicle toward the abdomen. It's almost like the colt is saying: "NOOO! I WANT THAT!" When I tried to retract the cord to tie it off, the same reflex occurred, so it was impossible to tie it off. Since I couldn't see bleeding from either cord, it seemed like a fruitless effort, anyway, so I shoved more gauze sponges in the hole and waited for Ben to get up and stop bleeding. He did and it didn't...had we been here before?

I decided to employ another method—one that I *hate*, but it works, sometimes: WAS (wait and see). I knew Ben would not die with this amount of blood loss. I did not really want to remove the packing until the dripping stopped, but this constituted another challenge: The packing could become the source of infection, potentially into the abdominal cavity causing peritonitis—commonly *fatal* in horses.

Ben dripped for three more days, tried to breed a mare through the fence (a whole 'nuther story about "proud cut geldings"), and the dripping increased. Early on day four, the risk of peritonitis creeping up on my pillow with me drove me to pull the packing. He dropped a blood clot the size of a cat and dripped for another day, but I am glad to report Ben survived and grew up fine and healthy, and I could once again sleep with no bleeding colts in bed with me.

Neoplasia: There's No Nice Word for Cancer

The "C word" is terrible in general, but thankfully,
serious cancer is not common in horses.
Most of this type of disease involves skin,
and some of 'em, while not fatal, can be a real challenge
to manage. Here I discuss the cause and treatment
of some common neoplasia, and one real uncommon one.

CHAPTER

7

"Secrets"

_ Sarcoids

Nothing makes people more nervous than the thought of cancer, in themselves or their pets. There are many forms of "neoplasia," or cancer, that affect animals and, fortunately, not many are common in horses. A fellow named Al called me out one morning a few years ago to look at a mare that he had recently added to his menagerie of horses, cattle, goats, and chickens.

Dolly was a middle-aged Morgan mare that was as pretty as one of those "artist's conception" paintings of what a particular breed of horse is supposed to look like, but few have ever seen. Dolly was just about perfect in every way—with one exception: a large, ugly spot over her withers just where the saddle would sit. The skin in this area looked like something you would find on a sick elephant. It was hairless, thick, and wrinkled, with ulcerated, raw areas that looked like terminal saddle sores.

"We bought her off of ole' GW, across town," Al began. "He said that this spot was just a touch of ringworm that we could kill with this medicine." He handed me a bottle of patent medicine that had been purchased at a local feed store. The label on the bottle claimed that the stuff would do everything but teach horses conversational Mandarin. I was a little skeptical.

"He said she would be all right," Al said, "and the price was hard to beat, so I thought I'd take a chance. Then I got to thinkin': I've bought horses that came with a halter, or even a saddle and bridle, but buyin' a horse that comes with a bottle of medicine...I don't know." He paused, leaving the sentence unfinished. Apparently, I wasn't the only one who was skeptical. "Anyway, I've been doctoring her every day, but the spot just keeps getting bigger. I figure I've quacked on her long enough." Al grinned. "Now it's your turn."

I examined the good mare after feeding her a customary carrot and giving her a few pets and scratches on the jaw just to get acquainted. I looked at the suspect area over her withers. It was about five inches across, hairless, and oozing some bloody serum.

"Where the heck did she get ringworm, anyway?" Al was never one to mince words. "And why didn't this medicine work?"

"Ringworm is not really a worm," I replied. "It is a fungus, like athlete's foot. They call it 'ringworm' because the lesion it causes is sometimes round, but that's beside the point. This ain't ringworm." I suspected that the mare had a fairly harmless skin tumor, but the discussion of neoplasia requires some tact...not my long suit.

"I figured as much. What *is* it?"

"A sarcoid."

"What the heck is that?"

"It is the most common skin tumor in horses," I said with all the finesse of a freight train. Before I could explain that it was no big deal, Al exploded.

"Tumor! You mean she's got cancer? Is she gonna die? She's *awful* young for that, Doc, are you sure?" After another long pause, Al chuckled. "Dirn that GW. He's got a memory like a elephant. I bet he's gettin' even with me for sellin' him that half-bronc rope horse two years ago."

Al had been known to buy and sell a few horses and cows occasionally. He would freely admit to being somewhat creative when describing the many attributes of his animals. His sense of humor was always intact, however, even when he was the victim of similar transgressions by one of his trading buddies. He was a firm believer in the "don't get mad, get even" school of horse trading.

The only way to be sure of the diagnosis was to submit a biopsy sample to the lab. I injected some local anesthetic into the area and cut a piece of the affected skin, including some of the normal tissue surrounding the suspicious lesion. Since the area was anesthetized, the mare never felt the minor surgery. I placed the sample in a plastic jar of formal buffered saline ("formaldehyde") for submission to the lab. A few sutures through the skin closed the wound so that it looked about like it did before the biopsy.

Within a few days, the pathology report confirmed my initial suspicion that the lesion was a sarcoid. This is a common skin tumor that comes in three flavors: 1) Flat, 2) wart-like, and 3) ulcerated. A flat sarcoid can look like a fungal infection in the skin of the horse, but it will not respond to topical anti-fungal medications because it is not an infection.

"How serious is this really?" Al asked when I phoned him with the news of the biopsy report.

"These things are usually not very serious at all, Al," I said, trying to reassure him. We were past the joking stage, as any form of cancer, no matter how minor, is not a joking matter. "In fact, sometimes I don't even remove them unless they are growing rapidly or are in a place where they would get irritated by the saddle or bridle," I went on. "They are almost never fatal. Sarcoids, like the one Dolly has, are almost always benign. In the language of the pathologist, 'benign' is not what you do after you be "eight"...okay, it's not a good joke, but it is good news because it means that the tumor will probably not spread to other organs of the body."

"But it *is* cancer, right? And how did she get it?" He was still worried.

"Yes, it is technically 'cancer' but not the dangerous kind," I explained. "The most likely cause is from the same virus that causes warts in cattle—even if she has never been near a cow. I can't explain how she got it, but sarcoids are almost never serious, they are just something we will need to manage occasionally."

It is curious that the warts on the noses of two-year-old horses, from the horse "papilloma virus," will fall off by themselves and never come back. So why do sarcoids, from the cow virus, never go away without treatment and *always* come back? At least they are benign.

A malignant tumor will have little bits of it break off and spread to the organs that are rich in blood vessels, like the liver, lungs, and kidneys. Cancer cells, once they take up residence in another organ in a process called "metastasis," will not function like the normal cells of that organ. Metastatic cells just go crazy. They divide rapidly and generally cause havoc in the body. That is why malignant cancer is so dangerous. Benign tumors can also be dangerous if they are rapidly growing and become locally invasive in the wrong place. This means that, even though they won't spread to other organs, their growth crowds local tissue, and the resulting pressure can be deadly—a benign, but rapidly-growing brain tumor, for example, is bad.

"Well, that's good to know." He sounded somewhat relieved. "But how we gonna' treat it? I can't ride her like she is. The saddle rubs that thing pretty bad."

"There's several ways to attack these things," I said. "Freeze, fry, cut, or chemo."

"Okay. What's the best way to fix it and how many new pickup trucks am I gonna' get to buy you for the pleasure of your professional company?" he asked sarcastically.

"You already bought me two new pickups because of all the bad horse trades you've made over the years that I have known you," I retaliated. "This time, you get to send me to Tahiti for a couple of months!"

"Good, I could use a break from you!"

After further discussion of the pros and cons of each treatment, we decided on injecting the tumor with an immune stimulant called "Bacille Calumet-Guérin," or BCG, for short. I think it was actually invented as a vaccine against tuberculosis in man. Apparently, it didn't work, and I have always wondered who decided to inject it in equine sarcoids. What were they doing? I visualize a bunch of guys sitting around in white lab coats trying to figure out what to do with a few thousand gallons of stuff that failed in its intended purpose. I guess it just falls in with other scientific accidents, like Teflon™ and "sticky notes."

In theory, after it is injected into a tumor, BCG attracts a specific type of white blood cell called "T lymphocytes" that remove the foreign BCG proteins along with the tumor cells. (I had some real good luck with this drug, but unfortunately it is no longer available. I guess it just took thirty years to run out, and they didn't want to chance making another batch, or maybe the "White Coat" with the recipe died...something to think about.)

I treated the Morgan's tumor three times at two-week intervals until all of the cancerous tissue had sloughed and normal skin and hair appeared. Within three months, the mare had returned to work under saddle, and everybody was happy.

Over the years, I have learned to never say never and always avoid always. However, regardless of the type of treatment, sarcoids *always* come back. Two years after the initial treatment, Dolly's tumor returned in the same spot. The same treatment protocol was followed with the same result. For obvious reasons, early medical intervention is advised in cases like this.

There are newer treatments available now, but the "cure" rates depend on the duration of the "follow-up." Most treatments are successful for six months, but every treatment I know of will fail within a few years. To be continued...

_ Ed, "Mom," and Intestinal Cancer

I was headed home late one Saturday night when the familiar buzzing sensation erupted along the right side of my belt announcing a page. (This was a long time ago when cell phones were still unreliable, but a "pager" was considered fairly high tech.) A page at this time of the night usually meant an emergency. Bonnie, one of my indispensable answering service ladies, told me that the lady was frantic and I needed to call right away. Sure enough, the woman was just short of hysterical when she answered the phone.

"My horse is colicking again and my vet can't get out here. If *you* can't, tell me now and I'll call somebody else!" she fairly screamed into my ear. I knew where the horse was, as I had other clients in the same barn. So I turned the truck around and headed for the place, once again amazed that virtually every emergency is in the opposite direction of my travel.

The new client, a young lady named Bobbi, had calmed down a little once I reached her, and I began examining her big, almost black Warmblood horse she called Ed. He was experiencing a lot of pain and was trying to go down and roll. Bobbi kept him walking, and I administered an intravenous injection of Banamine®. Intravenous injection on a moving horse is not taught in vet school, as most of the school horses are gentle and stationary, but when the pain is real bad some horses just naturally walk out to try to alleviate the agony. Hitting the vein in some of these moving targets can be a real trick.

Within minutes, the pain medication had taken effect and Ed was standing more comfortably but still in distress, as his pulse was over eighty beats per minute (normal is about forty) and he had almost no gut sounds. I passed a stomach tube and gave him a gallon of mineral oil. After thirty minutes, he was still in pain and wanting to lie down and roll. I was getting worried.

"He colicked about a week ago," Bobbi said after a momentary lull in the activity. "We took him up to the vet college. They kept him there for a day and told us to take him home—that he was okay."

"Did they X-ray his abdomen or endoscope his stomach?" I asked, hopeful for some useful information. An X-ray may have shown an enterolith, or stone, formed in the intestine. An endoscopic exam is usually required to diagnose a gastric ulcer. Either one of these can produce recurrent signs of colic and could have been the source of Ed's problems.

"No. They just gave him some fluids through a stomach tube and watched him overnight. Then we brought him home."

I suspected they hadn't given Ed any IV fluids because there wasn't a shaved area on his neck where a catheter would have been placed. I was curious why they hadn't done *some* diagnostic tests, though, because *I* sure would have if I had the fancy equipment they did. It's never a good idea to second-guess another veterinarian, so I said nothing. Silence has always been hard for me, but the horse may have presented a very different clinical picture a few weeks ago. No use dragging your abdominal surgeon out of bed when a shot of Banamine˙ will fix the problem.

Ed wasn't getting any better. I placed an IV catheter in his jugular vein and started giving him fluids and a narcotic, a more serious painkiller. He lowered his head to half-mast when the synthetic morphine hit his central nervous system, and for a while, he didn't care about much of anything. He started breathing easier and you could see that the drug really relaxed him. I continued to administer IV fluids and hoped that rehydration would fix him. I guessed he was about five or six percent dehydrated. Since he was about an eleven-hundred-pound horse, that meant twenty-five or thirty liters of IV fluids would be required to correct the dehydration. At a rate of about six minutes per liter, we would spend the remainder of the evening watching fluids flow into the bloodstream of the fairly ill horse.

After a couple of hours, Ed started to have pain again. I repeated the doses of synthetic morphine at fifteen-minute intervals, but they weren't much help. The presence of unrelenting pain in colic cases is never a good sign.

"Are ya'll up for another trailer ride tonight?" I asked.

"What do you mean?" Bobbi, and her mother who had joined us, asked simultaneously.

"I'm pretty worried about Ed. Even though we have given him high doses of some very strong medicine, we can't seem to control the pain. That usually means that it is time to consider surgical intervention."

"You mean take him back up to the vet college?"

"Well, that's an option." I hesitated a second.

"Where would you suggest?"

I had been sending surgical cases to a private clinic about two hours away, so that was my suggestion.

While Mom and Bobbi were hooking up the trailer, Ed and I were strolling around the barn trying to keep his mind off the pain in his abdomen. I was concerned that his attempts to lie down and roll wouldn't stop just because he was in the trailer. We took the center divider out of the small, two-horse trailer, but this would still pose some potential dangers to a horse as big as Ed if he tried to get down during the trip.

Ed was needing more and more pain medication to keep him comfortable, so it was obvious that someone would have to ride in the trailer with him to do this. In the most literal sense of "don't try this at home, folks," I volunteered. We shoe-horned me and Ed into Bobbi's "size-seven" trailer, which was a trick, since

Ed was a "size-eight" horse. It was crowded even without me. I was really hoping he wouldn't go down. Mom followed us in my truck, just in case we needed emergency supplies and so I could get back home once we delivered Ed to the referral hospital.

The trip to the referral clinic normally took me about two hours and fifteen minutes. I looked at my watch, and Mickey Mouse grinned at me over distorted arms that indicated one in the morning. Bobbi piloted the rig quite expertly. It was my first ride in a horse trailer. It was interesting. Really. I think that anybody who plans on moving a horse in one of these aluminum-and-steel nightmares ought to actually ride in one, at least once. If the cab of a pickup truck was as uncomfortable as a horse trailer, everybody would just ride the horse! Even the nicer ones rattle, squeak, and leak. The bright lights and loud road noises of trucks and other vehicles flash by in unpredictable patterns that tended to spook *me* a little. I can only imagine what must be going through the mind of a horse traveling in one of those things.

I kept giving Ed pain medication through the intravenous catheter, which made injecting a horse in a moving vehicle possible, but not easy. Otherwise, it would have been like trying to thread a needle during a two-hour earthquake. Ed and I kept each other company. (He promised not to lie down if I promised to quit singing.)

Finally, I recognized the sound of tires on gravel that signaled the end of our journey. As we pulled into the drive at the clinic, I looked at my watch, and it was not yet two-thirty. We had made the trip in under ninety minutes. I was amazed.

Bobbi unloaded Ed and unfolded me like some cowboy origami. It's a funny feeling, knowing you can't get out of the trailer until somebody *lets* you out. I guess it could have been worse—at least she didn't have my head tied in a corner. We walked in the big door of the clinic exam room, and I made all the appropriate introductions. Ed had arrived in fairly good shape, but he was still showing signs of pain. As the referral vet's exam and clinical impressions were similar to mine, he began making preparations to take Ed to surgery. He had adequate staff to handle the case, so I wished everybody good luck and headed back home. I had a full day planned and was thinking about a short nap before I began morning rounds in my own practice.

Later in the day I called to get a progress report on Ed. The surgeon was busy with other patients and his secretary told me he would call me back later. I called him back later in the evening and finally got through to him.

"This was an unusual one," he began. "He had a mass in the 'lumen' of his 'jejunum' that I was able to completely remove. There were other, small masses in the 'mesentery' that I was able to sample, but I couldn't get all of 'em. It was the strangest thing I've seen in a while."

"Do you have any idea of what it is?" I asked. "It almost sounds like a primary tumor in the bowel with metastatic lesions in the mesentery." "Metastatic lesions," more tumors that have spread, are the most dangerous aspects of any cancer. They are like little seeds of disease, and almost always indicate the end is near.

"That's what I'm worried about, too. We won't know until we get the results back from histopath. In the meantime, we plan on keeping him here for a few days before we send him back home. I'll let you know the results of the lab tests as soon as they come in."

Intestinal cancer in horses is quite rare. In fact, I later searched the literature, and in the recent sixteen years, there had only been thirty-six cases of intestinal cancer reported in the horse worldwide. Every reported case had been fatal. In Ed's case, it looked like there was one mass (tumor) in the small bowel (the "jejunum" is the longest part of the small intestine) and that smaller, "metastatic," or "spreading," tumors had moved into the filmy, skirt-like "mesentery" that suspends the small bowel from the base of the lumbar spine. It did not look good, but to be sure, we had to wait for the results from the lab.

"Histopathology" is the study of diseased tissue under the microscope. Small samples of each of the tumors would be analyzed microscopically in very thin sections put on glass slides and stained so that the cells could be more easily seen. The reports usually come back in a couple of days. In Ed's case, however, things took a little longer.

After about a week, Ed had apparently recovered from surgery and Bobbi took him home to her mother's, rather than the boarding barn, where they could easily monitor him. About ten minutes after they arrived at home, I got another panic-stricken call from Bobbi's Mom. Ed was in pain again. I knew things were getting worse, I just wouldn't know the extent of "worse" until a few minutes later. I gave a quick explanation/apology to the client I was with at the time of the call and left in a cloud of dust.

Bobbi's Mom and Ed were in an exclusive gated community on the outskirts of town. In her haste to alert me of Ed's declining condition, "Mom" gave me the directions to her barn but forgot to give me the gate code. I called her from my truck and got her answering machine. This was no surprise, as she was obviously out with Ed, walking him or doing something to try to help (in those days, cell phones were pretty rare).

I waited patiently for somebody else—another resident, the UPS guy, Santa Claus, *anybody*—to drive up with the gate code. Finally, somebody did. I explained my *emergency* situation, complete with the name and address of my client. The response I got amazes me to this day. The resident of the exclusive gated community politely listened to my request for entrance, looked at my truck—unmistakably a vet's truck and told me, "No. I don't know you, I don't know her, and if you are who you say you are, you *have* the gate code!"

So I waited for his car to disappear around the hill, hopped over the gate, and walked a mile to Mom's house. She was a little upset at my lack of punctuality, and the fact that I *walked* to her house with no equipment. I explained my predicament and she calmed down a little, gave me a ride to the exclusive gate, and I returned to her barn—this time with my truck.

I examined and treated Ed much the same as I had on our initial visit, without the IV fluids. He responded to the pain medication, but his gut motility was still poor. I phoned the surgeon from my truck for some advice. He suggested that I use a new, human drug that had shown some promise in stimulating gut motility in horses after surgery for colic. I didn't have any of this on the truck, so I called a local pharmacy, and they had a prescription ready for me when I got there. So back I drove to Ed's house (this time with the gate code memorized!).

I pulled up the drive to a fearful sight: Ed was lying down and Bobbi was crouched over him. In the half hour it had taken me to retrieve the new medicine, it appeared as though Ed had died. Just about the time I was thinking about how hard it is to lose a patient, he swished his tail, rolled up on his sternum, and put his head in Bobbi's lap! I heaved a sigh of relief and wiped some dirt or something out of the corner of my eye.

We got Ed up on his feet, and he started nibbling around the yard a little. I gave him some of the medicine that was supposed to help his gut motility. I stood there watching him for another hour. After I was sure that he was comfortable, I left instructions to feed him lightly several times daily and call me if he looked like he was in pain or wouldn't eat. I drove away, still not knowing exactly what to think about this case, but thankful that Ed had survived so far.

The following months are a story all by itself—not a good one, but painfully true, all the same. It began with repeated phone calls to the surgeon's office, hoping for the lab results that would tell us exactly what the mass in Ed's small bowel was and if it was malignant.

"We still haven't heard from the lab," he told me. "I sent it to Colorado. They have an oncologist there at CSU that has treated more of these than anyone, so I thought that would be the place to send the sample. I've called them several times, but they haven't got back to me. There's really nothing to worry about, we wouldn't want to start any chemotherapy for four months post-surgically, anyway. I'll call them again and let you know."

In the meantime, I had been in touch with Bobbi several times. Ed was doing well, though he had lost some—okay *a lot*—of weight after the stress of surgery and probably the cancer. Of course, we were anxious to know the results of the histopath. I told her we had to wait, and that the surgeon was recommending against any other treatment for a few months, anyway.

Finally, almost six months after Ed underwent surgery, I received a preliminary report from the diagnostic lab. The preliminary report gave a tentative diagnosis of "lymphosarcoma" but did not elaborate on the relative malignancy of the tumor, or whether the smaller, mesenteric lesions were products of the larger mass. So now we had an apparently well patient with an unknown prognosis, a somewhat impatient client, and a vague diagnosis. This was something they didn't prepare me for in veterinary college!

As unsettling as it was to not know exactly what the mass in Ed's jejunum was, having even a vague diagnosis was better than an outright guess. A literature search revealed that intestinal lymphosarcoma in the horse is exceedingly rare, and treatment has been futile. I called three well-known veterinary oncologists and asked their opinions about how to treat the case. The management plan ranged from treatment with three potent chemotherapeutic agents immediately after surgery to the more conservative approach of waiting until abnormal cells appeared in the bloodstream or abdominal fluid and *then* starting chemotherapy.

The fact that there were only thirty-six cases of the disease in horses reported in the entire world over the recent sixteen years, *all* of which were dead, was not a resounding endorsement of our vast advances in veterinary medicine. With this kind of a record, I decided to seek help elsewhere.

I am fortunate to have a friend who is on the staff at the Stanford Medical Center. Let's just call him Dr. Joe. Over the years, he has been not only a friend and fellow horse fanatic, but a valuable resource for my practice. He is in a very specialized area of oncology, and he may be the smartest man I know. (When he was about to take his board exams for his specialty, someone asked, "Who in the world is smart enough to test *him*!")

I explained the case to Dr. Joe and asked him if he had ever seen any human cases like it before. He said that he couldn't count the number of cases of lymphosarcoma that he saw in a year. Well, then I knew I had come to the right place. We formulated a plan of treatment for Ed that would minimize untoward side effects and probably prolong his life.

I called Bobbi and outlined our treatment protocol. Initially, we would monitor Ed's blood and abdominal fluid every month. If any abnormal cells appeared or he became ill, we would start him on a moderated dose of "prednisone," a very safe drug in most cases, and one I had used extensively to treat other problems in horses. Even at twice the dose we would use on Ed, I had seen no side-effects other than weight gain and increased water consumption. Bobbi agreed that this plan sounded reasonable.

We made an appointment for the following week to do some blood counts and abdominal fluid analysis. This involves a couple of needle sticks but is not unduly stressful for most horses. Ed passed the first round of tests like he'd been studying for them.

Two weeks later, Bobbi called me and said that she was worried about Ed. She thought he was having problems with his rear legs, almost like he was losing control of them. Fearing the worst, I rushed to the barn.

By the time I got there, Ed was doing okay as far as I could tell. He was a little stiff about his rear legs, but I really couldn't find anything wrong with him. There was a possibility that he had a dirty sheath and that it could account for his stiff gait (remember Ol' Buck?). I sedated him so he would prolapse his penis and allow me to examine him and clean his sheath, but I didn't find anything abnormal.

Since Bobbi had described symptoms that were potentially neurologic in origin, I was concerned that maybe the tumor had spread to one of the large vessels supplying his rear legs or possibly be pressing on a nerve. I examined him *per rectum* but found nothing abnormal in the part of his abdominal cavity that I could reach. We decided to give him a combination of anti-inflammatory drugs, just to be safe. I drew up the drugs in three large syringes and administered them intravenously. I have used these drugs in thousands of horses and had never seen any adverse reactions.

Until then.

Within two minutes of receiving the injections, Ed nickered plaintively and fell over. I thought I had killed him...again. He was still breathing, and he was still conscious, but we were both scared. I ran back to the truck, grabbed a catheter and in less time than it takes to tell it, I had a fast drip of IV fluids flowing into Ed's jugular vein. During all this Bobbi and Mom were just about as hysterical as humans can be and maintain consciousness. It didn't take long, maybe fifteen or twenty minutes, and Ed rolled up on his sternum, stood up, shook himself a little and looked around like he was wondering what all the fuss was about. Bobbi calmed down; Mom got mad. Real mad.

"Why did you have to give him *so much*!" she screamed. "Why didn't you just give him something by mouth. I studied nursing, you know, I know a little something about medicine!"

"I have used this combination of drugs on literally thousands of horses," I said. I tried to explain that this was a very rare reaction, one I had never seen before, but as far as Mom knew, I had just about killed her horse...again.

"I have never seen a reaction like this before," I continued. "He apparently had his blood pressure crash for some reason. A little time and some IV fluids allowed the pressure to rise, and now, I think, he's going to be okay."

We made an appointment for the following Monday to do some more blood-work and another abdominal tap. According to our plan, once Ed showed signs of illness, we were going to monitor him closely and seriously consider starting chemotherapy. I left the barn glad we were both still alive, but somewhat shaken from the unpleasant events of the recent two hours.

The next round of tests came back abnormal. His liver function had been altered and the blood count was abnormal in a way that is characteristic of cancer patients. I conferred with Dr. Joe by phone, and we agreed that it was time to start Ed on the prednisone.

I made arrangements to meet Bobbi at the barn to give her the medicine and instructions. When I got there, Bobbi hadn't arrived yet, but Mom had. And she was still mad. Real mad. Like fine wine, her anger had aged and ripened over the weekend to a robust, full-bodied maturity.

In over forty-five years as a professional horseman, I confess I have made a few folks a little agitated at me. However, I cannot remember anger of such intensity and duration. Mom proceeded to verbally abuse me for half an hour. I really admired her style. I would never have believed that anyone could be that mad for that long and without repeating herself or cussing even once. It was amazing!

I left the prednisone with Mom and drove away from the barn for the second time in as many days not necessarily glad to be alive, just glad to have survived and thinking that it couldn't get worse.

I was wrong.

A couple of days after I had experienced radiation therapy from Mom, I got another phone call. "I just talked to the surgeon on the phone, and he says that the dose of prednisone you prescribed is ten times the recommended dose. I'm a little concerned about that. Are you sure that you are giving him the right dose?"

"Yes. Ed's body surface area is about four-and-one-half square meters and the dose I prescribed is precisely that which is required for his illness. In fact, I have given many horses twice the dose that I prescribed for Ed, though for other conditions, and I have not seen any untoward side effects because of it," I replied.

I have rarely quit a case, but one definition of wisdom is knowing which bridges to cross and which ones to burn. I spoke frankly to the client. The surgeon and I were in obvious disagreement about several aspects of this case, and it would be wise to seek medical assistance from someone she could trust fully, and forget the rest. She was kind enough to call me a few days later to tell me that she had decided to follow another treatment protocol.

Two months later, I called to check on Ed's progress and learned he was doing well and had regained all of his weight, but I do not know what happened after that. As a veterinarian, I have found that good judgment comes from suffering the consequences of bad decisions. However, second-guessing is rarely educational and tends to drive us nuts. But...I still question the decision to allow Ed to even recover from the surgery. The mass in his small bowel was serious enough to consider euthanasia right then and there, and the presence of other small lesions was compelling evidence that Ed had a terminal problem. In some cases, the best we can hope for is simply buying the horse a little time. In Ed's case, this would likely lead to future bouts of colic and inevitably, eventually, doing the "kind thing" for him. In the end, we will never know, but I am thankful that cases of equine lymphosarcoma are rare, and I will not likely be faced with decisions like the ones that Ed's case presented ever again.

_ Gender Confusion and Ovarian Cancer

Jack Osborne was one of the toughest men I have ever known. He wasn't mean, he was just a no-nonsense type of fellow who instilled respect in his horses, as well as his employees. He was a professional stockman. It was demanding work and required the same durability and self-reliance in both man and beast. That was why I was generally surprised when I heard from him. He did most of his own doctoring so, on the rare occasions that he called me, it was either interesting, a wreck, or both.

"I don't know what to think about this mare, Doc," he said, truly perplexed. "She'll go along just fine as you please, and then, for no reason, just break in two and quit the ground. You know I like tough horses," he continued, "but I like 'em predictable. This mare ain't predictable. When she's good, she's good as anything you ever threw a leg over...that's why I put up with her. But when she ain't, well..." he paused. "And when she's horsin', she's worse, and it seems like she's always horsin'. I swear, this mare has been in heat for two solid months. She's got the studs real confused. The only time she isn't acting like she's in heat, she's acting like she's one of the studs! Maybe you can give her a shot, or somethin'," he said finally.

Psychological problems in horses are difficult to define. As a general rule, horse *people* are a fairly opinionated bunch, especially when it comes to training, nutrition, genetics, breeding, color, lameness, shoeing, tack, trailers...but other than that....

You get my point.

During the course of my day, many of these subjects come up, so I must rely on science. Behavior, however, is a bit more subjective, and I try to ask questions before I venture an opinion. A thorough history and a good physical exam can help rule out physical reasons for behavioral problems. Bad teeth or a sore back or feet can cause a lot of "bad" behavior, and it is best to eliminate these possibilities before you haul the ornery rascal to the neighborhood horse whisperer or auction barn.

I examined the mare. I started my exam with the usual "temperature, pulse, and respiration" (TPR). It is amazing how much information you can get from something as simple as that. When I placed my stethoscope on the mare's chest, she squealed and tried to bite me. I quickly agreed with Jack's assessment—what we call a "working diagnosis": "She's tough." As the stethoscope was going to be the *easiest* part of the exam, I was beginning to wonder about the rest of it, especially the "T" part. The horse's temperature has to be taken rectally, not under the tongue or a swipe across the forehead, though I wondered if I'd be able to do even *that*. Since I had already experienced the biting end of the mare, I was a little apprehensive about the kicking end. I slowly worked my way back, gently petting along the mare's back and croup until I could touch her tail. She kicked me so fast that any self-respecting mule would have been envious. For speed and accuracy, it was a thing of beauty.

I limped a few, ungraceful steps away from the mare and saw that Jack wasn't doing a very good job of stifling a laugh. I was trying not to cuss, so I attempted to defuse the situation with light conversation.

"And quick, too. Ain't she," I said through clenched teeth. "What do you call her?"

"Pet."

"Pet?"

"Yeah. We figured she was so dang mean anyway, if we named her something that would fit better it would just encourage her! We already got one we call Widow-Maker," he added laconically.

I eventually caught my breath and said, "She's a little opinionated, I see. Is she eating okay?"

"She's never missed a meal," Jack replied.

"Well, if she's eating normally, she's probably not running a fever. I suggest we assume that her temperature is normal. What do ya' say?"

"Good thinkin', Doc. I don't think she likes thermometers!"

I carefully continued with the exam. I looked at her feet and legs, her back, eyes, teeth, and anything else I could think of that could cause pain, thus be responsible for the mare's interesting behavior. By the time I finished my exam, the only sore spot I could find was just above *my* knee, but nothing on the mare seemed to be wrong.

I stood there, looking at the mare and mentally going through the list of things that could cause a problem. One of the cowboys rode by just about then and the mare raised her tail for a long moment and expelled a small amount of urine.

"See what I mean, Doc!" Jack exclaimed. "She's doin' that all the time!" Nods from a couple of the boys assured me that this was a consensus.

"Well, this time of the year, she could just be in transition. You know, most mares don't cycle in the wintertime. Along about late February or March, their reproductive systems begin to wake up, and it's not uncommon for a mare to be in heat for a month during late winter and early spring," I said.

"This is July!" Jack's observation was correct, but I had more to add.

"That's why this type of behavior is so unusual. Normally, a mare is only in heat this time of year for four to seven days. Now, some mares can be a little testy when they are in heat so that it seems a lot longer, but normally it's a week or less. If a mare has prolonged heat periods during the summer, when she should be cycling normally, it could indicate a problem," I explained.

"Oh, we already know she has a problem, Doc!" one of the boys joked. "That's what you're here for."

"What kind of problem are you talking about?" Jack asked, more seriously now.

"A tumor on one ovary can sure make a mare act like that," I said. "It can also make a mare act like a stallion."

"That fits our little Pet," Jack replied. "We were startin' to think she was bisexual," he added with a laugh. "How would you diagnose something like that?"

"I was afraid you'd ask that," I said as I walked back to the truck for a plastic sleeve and some obstetrical lubricant…and a dose of sedative—a large one.

This time, I was prepared. The drug would not guarantee my safety—I have been kicked real hard by sedated horses, but I hoped that it would at least spoil her aim. I performed an exam of her reproductive organs *per rectum*, hence the need for the long plastic glove. The heavy sedation relaxed her considerably, and the examination was completed without incident. I peeled the sleeve off my arm, wiped a little manure off my shoulder, and heaved a mental sigh of relief at having survived the tenuous procedure.

"Your Pet mare has a 'theca-granulosa cell tumor' on her right ovary," I said.

"That's easy for you to say, Doc. What the heck does it mean?"

"One ovary is real large, about the size of grapefruit, I'd say. It's working over-time, making a bunch of male hormone that has her brain confused about wheth-er she *is* the head stud around here or would just like to meet him. All this extra hormone suppresses the other ovary, and it is shrunk down to about nothing. In view of her behavior, this is a fairly straightforward diagnosis."

"What do we do now? I guess cancer means we have to put her to sleep," Jack said with a tinge of remorse.

"Not at all. These things are almost never malignant, meaning that they don't spread. The surgery to remove one ovary can be done right here with her standing, under heavy sedation, of course." I gave her a sideways glance. She was still standing with her head at half-mast from the tranquilizer.

We made arrangements for me to return to his place in a few days for the surgery. The procedure is fairly simple. The approach is by "colpotomy," an incision through the deepest part of the vagina. This way, there are no sutures on the outside and the risk of infection is minimal. The mare is sedated heavily, and a small tear is made with a scissors in the anterior vagina, next to the cervix. Then an "ecraseur," a crushing instrument, is passed through the hole in the vagina and a little chain is looped around the ovary. An assistant tightens the instrument from the outside and the artery, vessel, and nerve of the ovary are severed with almost no bleeding. The surgeon catches the ovary once it is severed and removes it by the hole in the vagina that was made earlier.

Although this procedure sounds a tad barbaric, it is usually well-tolerated under standing sedation. The mare may experience slight discomfort when the ovarian vessels are crushed, but for the rest of the procedure, most mares act as if they are absolutely unaffected. For safety reasons, I try to do most surgeries with the horse standing under sedation with local anesthesia. Some surgeries require general anesthesia, but as you read in some of my earlier stories, recovery can be dangerous as horses lack coordination when they initially try to rise after the anesthetic wears off.

Pet recovered from the surgery and resumed work within two weeks. She is still as tough as she was with two ovaries but has normal reproductive cycles. She never did show any signs of cancer in the other ovary, but she really resented the name "Pet," and was still not helpful during any medical procedures—even ones that did not involve a long plastic sleeve.

Truth Is Stranger Than Fiction

*I kinda got a late start in horses—I did not develop
a true love for 'em until I was about seven years old.
But I can't really separate my private life on my horses
from my professional life under (or in) those of my clients.
This is a group of stories that didn't fit anywhere else,
but I find so intriguing that they should be included.
They illustrate how horses have become an integral
part of my life: how I treat them, handle them,
and relate to the folks that love them…
some of them better than others.*

CHAPTER
8

one step "closer"

Michael Simmons '06

_ Buddy

Most folks that have horses for very long develop some attachment to them. For all the expense and aggravation these beasts are capable of imposing on mankind, we must at least like them, though I've known a few horsemen who were touched with apparently uncontrollable masochism. If you are ever fortunate enough to own one really good one, you can consider your life truly blessed. Everyone remembers a first horse with some degree of affection. Unfortunately, most first horses are generally a sorry lot. This is why a horse owner must become a repeat offender to ever have a chance of knowing a really good one.

I consider horses an addictive disease, only slightly less destructive than whiskey, tobacco, or credit cards. There is no cure. All that an addicted individual can do is treat the symptoms by applying manure to his boots, horse sweat to his clothing, and an occasional bruise, sprain, or broken bone to his person. An empty bank account seems to be common among "equiholics," but I think that this is a symptom of the disease, not a form of treatment. I have noticed that marriage to a non-horse person can be helpful in controlling the affected spouse, but conversion of the previously unaffected individual can be disastrous. A skinny couple with two cars that won't start often have two fat horses in the back yard.

As I get older (too soon older, too late smarter), I think about the things I could have done better in my life. As many folks reach maturity, it is natural to consider past disappointments in themselves or others—bad business decisions or poor choices in their personal lives. As my knees, ankles, elbows, and just about everything else that used to move freely quit doing so, I think that maybe I am approaching maturity. As I think of horses I have known, I remember some with fondness, some with bland indifference, and a few with outright terror. Although I cannot tell you most of what I got for my birthday six months ago, the memory of a good horse remains in my mind a certitude like the first roller coaster ride, the taste of watermelon, or the smell of fresh coffee on a cold, winter dawn. Thinking back over the last thirty years, I have known only one really good one that was mine. He died of colic. I will never forget him.

His registered name was Brave Reason. The fact that he had registration papers and a blue-blooded pedigree was largely wasted on him, as he was not at all stuck up about it. He was twelve hundred pounds, over sixteen hands on the outside and a pussy cat on the inside. If you had known him for about three minutes, you'd have known that the fancy name fit him like earrings on a pig. I called him Buddy. (You'll remember his run-in with the picnic table, earlier in these pages.)

Buddy had been donated to the teaching hospital where I was a resident back in the 1980s. We were involved in experiments involving stallion fertility, and Buddy was one of seventeen horses on my project. He was quite fertile. In addition, he was the gentlest stallion I have ever known. Handling a breeding stallion can elevate the blood pressure of an experienced horseman, let alone a young veterinary student, hoping to become an equine practitioner. Other stallions would give me some cause for worry when my students were handling them. Not Buddy. He could be handled with only a nylon halter any time. We never had to use a stud chain on Buddy, and because he was such a gentleman, all of the students fell in love with him. This was especially so when they were able to compare his behavior with that of the other stallions.

Frequently, students would ask me how I could perform experiments on horses that would ultimately be placed on terminal projects—those studies that required the humane destruction of the animals. I would usually respond by saying that none of the animals in my care *ever* suffered any discomfort and that the alternative for most of the donated horses would have been the killer market. My idea at the time, and still is, was that we had to sacrifice a few individuals for the benefit of the species. It is dangerous for a research scientist to fall in love with his experimental subjects.

Well, after two years of knowing Buddy, I couldn't bear the thought of him ending up on a terminal project. I worked through my residency in blissful denial that it would ever happen to him. I even managed to get him changed to some non-lethal studies while I was there. Two weeks before I was scheduled to leave academia and return to private practice, the worst happened. Buddy had been placed on the "pineal experiment."

The "pineal gland" is a little thing about the size of a pea that lives right in the middle of the brain. It may not be essential for life, but you generally can't remove it from a horse that could survive such a surgery, so most studies on this gland require sacrificing the donor. Although I was saddened by the prospect of losing Buddy, I kept reminding myself about the benefit of the species and all that cavalier stuff I had been preaching to my students. I kept thinking these thoughts all the way to Dr. Janson's office, the project leader. I figured I'd formulate my plan for groveling once I got there. With any luck at all, I hoped she wouldn't be there, and I'd have time to steal him. Lady Luck was on sabbatical, Dr. Janson was in.

I spilled my guts to her without shedding a single tear.

"What about not falling in love with research subjects?" She grinned knowingly.

"That rule has temporarily been suspended by the Dean, I think," I replied, using as much charm as I could muster.

"The university has tightened regulations concerning donated horses," she said after a couple of more digs at my expense. Dr. Janson was my superior on the faculty, but she was also my friend. We had spent many hours together working on our stallion project, and I think we shared mutual admiration and respect. "I'll talk to the administration, and we'll see what can be done."

During my tenure in academia, I loved the learning environment and working with some of the brightest faculty and students in our country. The past two years, however, I had been butting heads with some of the ivory tower residents in "The Administration." I had come to the conclusion that a few folks in academia were there because they would starve to death anywhere else. Unfortunately, some of these underachievers were well placed in The Administration. For that reason, I had decided not to extend my contract with the university (as if they would have me!). With this in mind, my hopes for rescuing Buddy from the pineal project plummeted.

Two days later I got one of the most surprising calls in my life from Dr. Janson. She had made arrangements for me to purchase Buddy legally from the university. I couldn't believe my ears. She admitted that she was also partial to the horse, and she was so glad that I was going to buy him, she'd made arrangements to have him delivered to the ranch I was renting.

I had no use for a stallion, and as gentle as Buddy was, I decided that he would be easier to manage and move around as a gelding. Opportunities for castrating horses were wanting in the teaching hospital at that time, and most students were eager to get as much experience as possible. The last year of academics is the only chance for them to gain hands-on, clinical experience before they are thrust upon the unsuspecting horse owners of the world. So I had no trouble finding a volunteer to perform a different (non-lethal) brain surgery on Buddy. I selected a competent student (who later went on to become a very successful practitioner), and we made arrangements to meet at the research center before I was due to accept delivery of Buddy at my ranch.

Because Buddy was a favorite, but mostly because a research project required it, Buddy got to breed one more mare before his career as a stallion would be ended at the hands of an eager young student. This concession to Buddy's masculinity emerged as a mixed blessing as, just after he dismounted the mare, she let loose with a well-placed kick to the front of his knee. He limped outside to the grassy area where the surgery was planned, bleeding profusely from a deep cut that just barely missed the joint. He stood there, those big brown eyes alternately looking at me and the surgical instruments strategically placed on the tailgate of my pickup. He would later use those eyes quite successfully against me, but at that time, he had not yet honed his technique. I felt so sorry for him that I almost canceled the surgery, but as I said, his "look" was as yet unpracticed, so under the knife he went.

We anesthetized him and, despite the presurgical trauma, he went down uneventfully. While the student got started on the castration, I was considerably more worried about the cut on his knee. Repeatedly, the student asked me for help, observation, and encouragement, to no avail. Finally, she said, "You're so worried about his damned knee,'" she nearly screamed. "What if the surgery kills him?"

"Either way his problem is solved," I replied, shamelessly plagiarizing a line from a movie, "and besides, if you don't fail my rotation by killing *my* horse, in two weeks, they'll be calling you 'Doctor' and I won't be within a hundred miles of you! What will you do then?"

"Thanks for the vote of confidence."

"No problem. That's why I didn't win that teaching award."

Buddy and the student both recovered uneventfully.

_ Buddy and the "Beach Camper"

Since I am an incurable horse fanatic, one of the best parts about being a veterinarian is getting to visit with folks that share my affliction. This is not a "support group," since we don't help each other stay away from horses. In fact, it's usually just the opposite. Occasionally, one will ask me a question of a personal nature that really does not have anything to do with medicine.

"Why do you carry a lariat in your truck? Are you plannin' on ropin' something?"

"No. Most of my clients wouldn't tolerate it well if I handled their 'little darling' like that. I use this rope on clients that won't pay. I just sorta casually shake the rope and say something like, What do you mean, *credit*? Did it take *me* thirty days to get here?'" I have been accused of the occasional use of sarcasm.

The real reason is that a good, strong, nylon lariat is real handy sometimes. I rarely resort to roping a patient because I'm not that good a roper, and it is not the textbook way of establishing good client rapport. When I'm not saving lives and stamping out pestilence among the local horse population, I spend a fair amount of time aggravating my own horses with a saddle and bridle. I have been afflicted with the horse disease since I was old enough to hold both ends of a halter off the ground and, by now, have about given up hope for a cure.

I have read that people with addictions are prone to irrational behavior. I demonstrated this tendency when I bought Buddy—the five-year-old, almost-halter-broke stallion with one leg too crooked to withstand the rigors of race training—to save him from death by experiment.

Buddy should make a great riding horse, I thought to myself. Now I was faced with the prospect of having to ride this beast without getting killed before I finished repaying my student loans and while we were both still young enough to stand the strain.

Several ways of approaching this training project had crossed my mind. I thought, *I'll just snub him to a nice, gentle oak tree, sack him out for a couple of hours and get on him. Of course, I don't bounce as well as I used to. I sure won't be able to do much surgery if I am in a body cast! How 'bout that Indian trick where they took horses to a creek where it was harder to buck? No, on second thought, and with my luck, I'd probably hit my head on something and drown.*

It should be noted here that I met Buddy way before the "horse whisperer" craze had hit the world and "natural horsemanship" had not yet been invented. So I decided to saddle the Thoroughbred up and use the lariat to fasten him to a nice, friendly piece of railroad iron, about thirty feet long, via the saddle horn. I let him drag this toy around for a few hours and hoped that this little exercise would render him too tired to buck. This worked well.

For the first eight saddlings, Buddy was willing, intelligent, and gentle. He only occasionally bucked me off, just to make sure I was paying attention and to further demonstrate his sense of humor. For this reason, I always had my trusty lariat secured to his halter and rigged so that the long end would drag the ground if I left the saddle involuntarily. He was easier to catch if he was draggin' a long rope.

By the ninth saddling he was doing so well that I decided to take him to the Salinas River Beach. I thought it would do *him* some good to see the ocean and a bikini or two. We arrived at the beach on a crisp, spring morning, just as the sun was peeking over the eastern hills and a foggy mist was rising over the translucent green surf with nary a bikini in sight.

As soon as Buddy saw the waves thunderously crashing on the beach, he decided that he was more of a dry-land type of a colt and immediately headed back to the trailer. As frightening as he found creeks and ponds, he wanted no part of *any* loud water that comes rushing up to get you! I gave him some iron injections (it isn't professional to "spur" a horse, so I use a more technical, medical term instead) to allay his fears about the ocean and to assure him that I fully intended to ride on the beach. He became rather annoyed by my form of therapy and proceeded to give me his best audition for one-horse beach volleyball. Of course, being a former rodeo star, I stayed right with him for at least two seconds before I was launched.

These days, *that* much time in the air usually involves a flight attendant and the beverage of your choice—have your credit card handy. Preparing for reentry, I saw Buddy, my two-hundred-dollar-horse, encouraged by the success of losing his rider, trying to lose my four-hundred-dollar-saddle. As he bucked off into the distance, I had time to be thankful that, at least this time, I would land in some soft sand. It could only have been the cruel hand of fate at work that day, as my trajectory terminated directly on the only rock within twenty miles. It is a miracle that portions of my liver, spleen, and last two ribs are not still on that rock as a memento of that day.

I stood up gingerly and examined myself to make sure that all my bendable parts still did and all my non-bendable parts still didn't. Then I saw Buddy, motionless, either having tired of one-horse beach volleyball or simply standing on the lariat and thinking he had suddenly become tied to the beach. His attention was directed at some poor, semi-conscious "camper" lying on the beach, clutching a blue plastic tarp in one hand and a bottle of cheap wine in the other. The now wide-awake, petrified "gentleman of leisure" was wide-eyed and face-to-face with a crazed, bucking bronco. It was impossible to tell who was more surprised.

While Buddy was distracted by the spectator under the blue tarp, it was easy to grab the end of the lariat and capture him. I stepped back into the saddle and rode away, certain that both Buddy and the tarp dweller were wishing they had not come to the beach that morning. Although this was not the first or last time that Buddy left me to go somewhere unsupervised, it is a good illustration of one of the many uses of a good, strong lariat.

_ Dancer and Her "Fly Allergy"

It was a balmy, late spring afternoon. The rains of winter had brought the annual green blanket of grass to the California hills, which was turning to the familiar parched, golden brown of summer. The oat hay was ready for harvest and lay mown in neat rows that looked like long bread sticks casting brown shadows late in the day, smelling sweet and fresh. A bumper crop of flies and dust was also apparent, though no worse than any other year. Of course, we always complained that the flies *were* worse than last year and blamed them on the heavy rain, or the lack of it—whichever was appropriate.

I received a call from a lady who had just moved into the area. She needed some medicine for her mare, Dancer, who apparently had some problem with her eyes.

"I just need some BNP with cortisone," the caller, Mrs. Webster, said. "Can I stop by your office and pick some up?"

"I haven't seen your horse before," I questioned, "have I?"

"No," she replied. "I just moved up here from Los Angeles. My vet down there always gave me the eye medicine for Dancer. She always has trouble with flies and dust irritating her eyes this time of year. It's some kind of allergy."

Mrs. Webster had asked for an ophthalmic antibiotic ointment that also contained "hydrocortisone," a steroid used to control inflammation.

"I can't prescribe any medication for a horse I haven't seen," I began.

"Oh, I *know* all that," she said impatiently. "I just need some medicine for her eyes. I know what her problem is."

"I understand this seems like an inconvenience," I explained, "but this is not just a matter of my preference. It would be a violation of the Practice Acts, state law, for me to give *any* medication for an animal I have not seen. If you called a doctor up and asked him for a prescription, do you think he would just give it to you?" I asked. "Even though this medication has helped her in the past, things in that eye may have changed, and we wouldn't want to give her the wrong medicine now, would we? The BNP-hydrocortisone ointment is a very good medication, for some things," I went on, "but, if your horse has a scratch or ulcer on her cornea, for instance, this drug could cause serious side effects and maybe even the loss of the eye."

"Well, I *know* what her problem is," she repeated. "I guess I'll just have to call someone else."

"Okay," I replied, "just let me know if I can be of any help."

A few days later Mrs. Webster was back on the phone. "I guess I'll have to get you to come out here and look at Dancer," she said with resignation. "I've called some other vets and they tell me the same thing you did. Once you have seen her, though, will I be able to get the medicine without another examination?"

"If she has an ongoing problem that requires repeated treatment, I will be glad to dispense you the appropriate medication," I said, "but that is something that is always up to *my* judgment." I paused and added, "I'm sure you understand that I am just thinking about the health of your mare."

I made an appointment to see Dancer the next day. Mrs. Webster was cordial but still a little irritated at the inconvenience of having me out to examine her horse. After the proper introductions, I fed Dancer my customary carrot and began my examination. She was a pretty Paint mare. She appreciated the carrot, but she was not interested in having me examine her left eye, which was almost completely closed. There was a thick, yellow discharge coming from it, though the right eye was apparently normal.

"How long has she been like this, Mrs. Webster?" I asked.

"Oh, she's had problems with her eyes off and on for years. Just like I told you on the phone, it's just a fly-and-dust allergy. I do a little cutting and team penning with her, and the dust in those arenas drives us nuts. Like I said, my vet down in LA always lets me come get the medicine for her."

"I mean, this time. How long has she been holding her eye closed and had the discharge?" I asked.

"Ever since we got here—three or four days."

"Well, I'm afraid that Dancer may have a more serious problem than just a little irritation from dust and flies. I don't like the way she's holding her eye closed," I said. "We really need to stain her cornea to make sure there isn't an ulcer or scratch on it."

"Why would you want to do that? Is it really necessary?"

"Yes, ma'am," I assured her, "I really think it is. A little goop running from an open eye is usually not a big deal. But, when a horse holds the eye closed or partially closed, it usually means that there is some pain in the eye. This is called 'blepharospasm,' an involuntary constriction of the eyelids, or 'photo-phobia,' which literally means 'afraid of light.' A painful eye can be the result of severe inflammation in the 'anterior chamber,' or front part of the eye, that may indicate underlying disease. The first thing to do is to put a little temporary stain on the 'cornea,' the outer, clear membrane of the eye," I explained, "to see if the cornea is intact."

I went to the truck and prepared a couple of ccs of "fluorescein dye," an orange liquid that turns green when you squirt it into the eye. Dancer was not real happy about me putting this cold stain into her already painful eye, but with a little patience and an extra carrot, I successfully stained her left cornea. After a couple of minutes, I gently pried her eyelids open and noticed that the stain had adhered to a circular area about half the size of a dime right in the middle of her eye.

The cornea is made of collagen fibers that are so precisely arranged that it is normally completely clear. Like carbon atoms, they can be arranged in a precise, geometrical pattern that produces the clarity and light refractive properties of a diamond. Or, the same carbon atoms can be arranged differently to form charcoal or pencil lead. Skin is also mostly collagen, but the fibers are lined up differently and contain more elastin fibers and pigments so that most skin is not transparent. When the alignment of the collagen fibers of the cornea have been disrupted by a scratch, or a larger area, like an ulcer, the frayed ends of the fibers take up the stain and are quite visible.

"See how the stain is taken up by that spot in the middle of her eye?" I said, still holding the eyelid open so Mrs. Webster could see.

"Yes, I do," she said, now more concerned. "What does that mean?"

"It means that she has a corneal ulcer. I am glad you let me come out here and see her. This is something that needs to be treated right away," I said.

"How did she get an ulcer there?" she asked. "How are we going to treat it? You said she might lose her eye?"

"There is a slight possibility," I said, "but that probably won't happen."

"No," she argued. "You said on the phone the other day that an ulcer could make her lose her eye!" she said, more sharply.

"What I said was," repeating part of our earlier conversation, "if the wrong medication was put in an eye with a corneal ulcer, BNP with hydrocortisone, to be exact, the mare could lose her eye because of the steroid. This is *exactly* the reason that you can't buy this stuff at the feed store and *exactly* the reason that I will not dispense it without first examining the patient. I know you only want the best for this sweet mare," I added while bribing Dancer with another carrot and petting her silky neck. The mare was starting to think that this visit wasn't going to be so bad, after all.

"What could possibly have caused such a thing to happen?" she asked.

I put on a sterile glove and carefully placed my little finger between Dancer's eyeball and boney orbit, the hole in the skull that houses the eyeball. The orbit is pretty deep in a horse, and I could stick my pinkie in it up to about the second knuckle all the way around the eyeball. Dancer was a real good sport about this seemingly painful process and didn't object too much. I was looking for a foreign body, a splinter or piece of straw that may have caused the scratch on the cornea. I didn't find anything suspicious.

"There isn't anything still around the eye that would have caused an ulcer," I said, "so there's no telling exactly what happened. It's possible that she bumped her eye during the trailer ride, or after she got here. It's hard to say. The important thing now," I emphasized, "is that she gets treated properly. I'm going to leave you with two types of medication. The first is 'atropine sulfate.' This needs to be applied to the eye twice daily. It will dilate the pupil, prevent the 'iris,' or colored part of the eye around the pupil, from sticking to the lens or cornea, and help to reduce some of the pain. In addition, she will need an antibiotic ointment put in there every four hours. Most ophthalmic preparations are readily washed out of the eye, so frequent application is important to maintain adequate levels of the medicine in the place where it is needed."

"Every four hours!" Mrs. Webster exclaimed. "The other vet only had me giving the ointment twice a day!"

"That medication was not for a corneal ulcer. The situation is different now, and more serious. A normal cornea can heal in a couple of days, if things go right, but it's important to treat the eye frequently."

I left the farm after Mrs. Webster assured me that she would be able to treat Dancer as I had indicated. I planned to return and stain the eye again in a couple of days.

Two days later, I went back and examined Dancer's eye again. This time, she was not holding it quite so closed as she had previously, but she was still showing signs of some discomfort.

"See how much better she is, Doc?" Mrs. Webster was encouraged. "She has just been a real trooper, too. I haven't had any trouble treating her. Of course," she smiled, "a little bribery with a handful of grain or a carrot, has helped."

I stained the cornea again and noticed that, although it did not take the stain as intensely as it had two days earlier, there was a small area in the center that was completely clear. This was alarming.

"It looks like the part in the center is completely healed," Mrs. Webster observed. "Isn't that wonderful?" She scratched Dancer on the chin. Dancer pulled her head away and began searching coat pockets on both of us in hopes of finding a treat.

"This is not good," I said, with some disappointment. "The clear area in the center of the ulcer is *not* healing; it's getting dangerously thin."

"What!" she was a bit surprised. "I thought it was getting better."

"It's called a 'descemetocele.' That's a hernia of the very thin, fragile membrane that separates the cornea from the rest of the eye. It's serious. If it ruptures, we could lose the eye."

"What do we do now?"

"Well, we have to provide some support for the cornea, to try to keep it from rupturing. We'll have to give her a general anesthetic and pull the third eyelid over the cornea and sew her top and bottom eyelids together. After that, a 'subpalpebral lavage system,' a little plastic tube that I can place under the eyelid, will be installed so that you can medicate the eye, even with her eyelids sewed shut."

"What?"

"I know that all sounds kind of crazy," I explained, "but it is necessary in order to save the eye."

"What's the *third* eyelid? I thought everybody just had two."

"Lots of animals have a 'third eyelid.' It's a fairly thick, pink membrane that is usually under the 'medial canthus,' the corner of the eye closest to the nose. Occasionally you'll see one prolapse, as it will flash across the eye after a horse yawns. The third eyelid has a fairly large gland in it that helps make tears, but other than that, I'm not sure what the function of it really is. It does comes in handy when a horse has a serious eye problem, like Dancer does now, but I don't know exactly what God had in mind when He invented it. Anyway, we can use it like a kind of natural Band-Aid to support the cornea, keeping it moist and in the dark so the pupil will stay dilated. By sewing a soft plastic tube under the fold of the upper eyelid, you'll be able to treat her with a liquid form of the ointment I gave you the other day. If we do all this, and you are able to provide the nursing care she needs, we just might save the eye," I said with all the optimism I could muster.

"What other options do we have? I'm a little nervous about general anesthesia. What are her chances of recovery, with and without the surgery?" she asked.

"These are good questions," I replied. "I'm sure you understand that there is no guarantee, regardless of what we do."

"I know that, but what are the chances that her eye will be okay without all this treatment?"

"Anything is possible, but I seriously doubt that she will recover fully without some extensive treatment. In fact, she will probably have a scar on that eye for the rest of her life, even *with* treatment. The questions I always have to ask myself are: what are the risks versus the benefits of any treatment, and how would I treat it if she was my mare? The answer in this case is, we don't have any choice. The chances as regards her eye are not all that good, no matter what we do. This is really a minor surgery, and it is definitely the way I would treat Dancer if she was my horse."

I did the surgery. Although this procedure *can* be done on a standing horse, without general anesthesia, Dancer was getting a little narrow-minded about me even being *close* to that eye, and therefore, prone to move around. Since I didn't want her doing this while I had sharp instruments near her eye, I encouraged Mrs. Webster to go for the general anesthesia. She did.

The surgery and subsequent anesthetic recovery were uneventful. It was an amazingly short procedure, and Dancer was back on her feet in no time, although slightly unsteady and slowly adjusting to seeing only half of her world. We had to be careful with her and approach her from her right side until she got used to listening for us. I braided a long plastic tube into her mane so that the medication containing antibiotic, atropine, artificial tears, and another drug, "n-acetyl cystiene," which would stop production of the enzyme "collagenase" that added to the destruction of the cornea. This concoction could be flushed through the tube and over her cornea six times daily. The "subpalpebral" (under the eyelid) lavage system is also real handy for treating the eyes of horses that won't let you jam that little metal tube of ointment in their eye six times a day, even if the eyelids aren't sewn shut.

Dancer's treatment required diligence and patience in all of us involved. Treating eyes like this can be slightly frustrating because you can't see whether or not you're making any progress since the eyelids are sewn shut. All you can do is keep treating the horse and hope that everything is going all right on the inside.

Ten days later, I removed the sutures holding Dancer's eyelids together. Thankfully, instead of a giant hole in the cornea, there was a plug of pink, healthy scar tissue where the dangerously clear descemetocele had been previously. The "third eyelid flap" and Mrs. Webster's diligent nursing care had worked.

"What about the scar," Mrs. Webster asked.

"I'm just glad she'll keep her eye," I retorted, slightly amazed that this lady never did seem to realize how close we had come to *that*. "I think that it will shrink, with time and a little steroid ointment. She probably won't have any obvious visual impairment. It may be a little aggravating, though, like trying to read the latest issue of *The Quarter Horse Journal* with a spot on your glasses, but I think she'll learn to adjust. She'd probably rather read *Cosmo,* anyway." I took a chance on a very small joke.

Two years later, the mare still had a small, bluish dot of corneal "edema," or swelling, about as big as the fat end of a ball point pen in the middle of her cornea. This didn't slow her down any, however, and she was still going down the trail and terrorizing calves as good as she ever did.

_ It's Just a...Scratch?

Horse skin. *Ughhhh.* Just the thought of dermatology sends some veterinarians into early retirement, or at least wondering why they didn't attend motel management school like Cousin Jake did. (He's doing very well now, you know.) Though the skin is the largest organ in man and beast, it is one of the least understood of the body's systems. It keeps all our inside parts contained, and all the necessary fluids in and bugs—bacteria, viruses, and fungi—out. It does not usually cause problems, so we tend to ignore it...until there's a problem.

The most common skin disease in horses involves foreign objects: tempestuous T-posts, barbaric barbed wire, and felonious fence board fragments (say *that* three times fast), just to name a few. These cases rarely present a diagnostic challenge for real obvious reasons: The poor horse is cut! Though some of the simplest wounds can become devastating injuries, others can *look* much worse than they really are. A simple examination will usually provide a successful treatment plan. However, some skin things ain't always what they seem. Throw in the panic factor when a neighbor has diagnosed your horse with fatal, contagious, untreatable cancer "just like the thing on my Uncle Harry's horse that killed him," and your farm call can get real interesting.

I was called out to see a nice Warmblood-type gelding named Willow at a local boarding facility. Holly had a lot of horse experience, and she was a practicing physician, so she commonly treated most of the minor horse ailments herself. A call from her usually meant our visit would be like fourth grade was for me: long and complicated.

"It started with a little scratch on the back of Willow's pastern," she began. "I didn't think too much of it at first, but after a few days it had spread to his other legs. I think we're dealing with something infectious."

"That's an accurate assessment," I began. "This is a classic case of something called 'scratches,' 'cuz that's what it looks like, and it can be real difficult to treat."

"That's what somebody here at the barn thought, but you know how things are. I'm getting lots of free advice from all the experts. I've heard everything from allergies to skin cancer!"

Holly knew the drill. Though her specialty practice did not involve skin, she understood how difficult some things can get. Diagnostic challenges come in many varieties, but few are more potentially confusing than those involving skin. The equine disease commonly called "scratches" is a classic example of this. I've also heard it called "mud fever "or "grease heel," and I'm sure there are other regional variations to keep things nice and complicated.

This malady commonly starts out looking like little scratches, hence the name, on the pasterns. It is often seen in wet environments, especially in horses whose ancestry involved plows (aka draft horses with long hair on the lower legs called "feather"—not "feathers," which is a common feature of chickens). It probably starts with some minor cut or abrasion—some disruption of normal skin structure—but it can escalate to something real ugly. It can cause moderate to severe swelling of the lower legs, resulting in altered gait or even lameness, thus adding to the confusion, as tendonitis will present with swelling and lameness, and the presence of a wound on the surface can suggest the inciting cause for a damaged tendon. It can also mimic skin cancer and an autoimmune disorder called "pemphigus"...simple, right?

All of us live in a veritable sea of micro-organisms. I've marveled before at the fact there are innumerable bacteria, fungi, and viruses—the varieties and vastness of normal populations are baffling. I'm sure there are many species we have not yet even identified that are living on, in, and around us. Most of these bugs are harmless; some are quite beneficial, living with us or our horses in what is called a "symbiotic relationship": both species benefit. For example, some species of bacteria live on food material in the bowel, but they aid in digestion of certain feeds and thus are a benefit to the "host" (the animal with the gut). The bacteria are readily available in food stores, and the host gets more efficient digestion—a classic "win-win" relationship. Some bacteria produce B vitamins that are essential for the life of the host. But a few are "pathogenic," or "parasitic," existing at the expense of a host animal, providing no benefit at all—kinda like the forty-year-old kid living in your basement that just can't seem to find suitable employment.

If we consider the life cycle of any parasite, there is a delicate balance for their survival. If the pathogen causes too much illness, the host animal dies and that really wrecks the parasite's plan for survival. The bacteria, viruses, and fungi don't really "care" about the host, but the longer the lunch wagon lives, the more the microbes can reproduce, thus insuring the survival of their species. Of course, there's whole list of things that thrive on dead stuff—just drive by roadkill some hot afternoon and you'll be acutely aware of the gaseous biproducts of "postmortem microbial degradation" (aka "rot"). The fact that we can survive at all in this potentially hostile environment is a wonder, but it is partially due to the "normal" non-pathogenic bacteria keeping the bad bugs in check, and the strength of our immune system.

A few years ago, it was discovered why some pathogenic bacteria are so successful at survival. There are several species of bacteria that have developed cooperative colonies to form something called a "biofilm." They stimulate the host tissue to secrete material that looks like slime or scabs that actually protects the bacteria from attack by the immune system of the host. Imagine that! Bacteria working together to make the host animal form something for *their* defense! In addition, the replicating bacteria can share information that allows their little baby bugs to develop resistance to antibiotics. It's like the mommy bacteria showing a class of baby bugs a picture of penicillin: "Stay away from drugs!" is her take home message. (Okay, it may not be that simple, but you get the drift.) Knowledge of the biofilm-forming bacteria has given us an advantage in treating some diseases, and disrupting this barrier is an important aspect of therapy.

Think of the biofilm as a shield, protecting the microbes. Once the biofilm shield is removed, many topical treatments will kill the offending microorganisms, but the scabs should be scraped off as soon as they form, the hair clipped from the surrounding region, and the horse housed in a dry area. The key to treatment is "clean and dry." Wrapping these lesions for extended periods tends to retain moisture, which, in turn, helps the microbes maintain the biofilm, defeating treatment efforts. Some stubborn cases can require long-term antibiotics, and a few have allergic or immune components that can take months to fully resolve. And a very few never do. However, many will respond to simple nursing care. Understanding the roll of biofilm can make treating this disease very rewarding.

Wound healing is a complex process. Horses are unique in many ways and their approach to wound healing is…interesting. Skin has remarkable regenerative capabilities, and superficial wounds can heal very quickly. Extensive wounds that involve 'subcutaneous tissue" (SQ or "sub-cutis"), the layers of tissue beneath the skin, skeletal muscle, or bone, can take more time to heal. Some of these deeper tissues will not regenerate, so the body forms a repairing scaffold called "granulation tissue." This fills in areas of sub-cutis and muscle that have been opened by an inconvenient T-post, wire, or tree branch. Skin wounds in most animals will stop "healing" when the granulation bed reaches skin. Once this restoration is achieved, the layers of skin migrate over the defect and *presto*—no more wound! Horse wounds also heal like this—*except* below the knee or hock. Just to be contrary, horses don't stop healing at the skin margin in wounds of the lower legs, they keep making something called "proud flesh." (That's the topic of a whole 'nuther discussion.)

While proud flesh, scratches, or even skin cancer may share appearances and location on lower legs, management can be quite different. Equine "scratches" usually looks like large, tenacious scabs slightly raised above the surrounding skin. In contrast, "proud flesh" is always pink, usually without much scab, and bleeds profusely when disrupted. Once a good scab is formed over a proud flesh wound, it is usually best to leave it alone. However, in a case of scratches, this is actually a biofilm that must be removed before treatment can be effective. Unfortunately, the "exudate," or secretions, found in this type of biofilm is so tenacious that removing it can be painful. Dishwashing liquid, corn oil, Avon Skin So Soft, or hydrogen peroxide can be used to pull off the scabs, but there's no magic concoction that makes this easy, and some horses resent the aggressive nature of this part of the treatment. Sedation may be required for thorough removal of these scabs in some of the more sensitive patients.

So I started treating this good horse by scraping off the scabs. This worked okay for about a minute, then Willow was apparently reminded of what every mom has said at least once in her career: "If you pick at it, it will never heal!" He didn't exactly kick me, he just sorta fanned my face a little with a front foot. It happened so fast, I couldn't react till it was over.

"Maybe you should sedate him a little," Holly said.

"Great minds think alike," I replied, wiping an aberrant bead of sweat generated by the near-death adrenalin on a cool fall morning. I sedated him a little and finished showing Holly how to keep the scabs somewhat controlled. It took a long time, as these things are typically tenacious. But we got his legs cleaned up pretty good using clippers, a soft brush, and a mixture of soap and mineral oil to help remove the crusts. I doctored the lesions with "silver sulfur sulfadiazine" under a soft, dry wrap. On some really stubborn cases, I include a topical steroid painted on the surface. This may sound a little backward, but some steroids are both anti-inflammatory and suppress the immune response. In some cases, subduing the immune system actually helps things heal. The plan was to leave the wraps on Willow for three days, then keep using the topical medication every couple of days unwrapped, scraping off the scabs if they recurred.

Willow healed up nicely after a few weeks of nursing care and resumed his career as a fairly high-level dressage horse. He has had a few flare-ups of scratches, but early intervention kept the infection to a minimum.

_ Milkmaids, Spoiled Wine, and Dead Chickens

I was vaccinating a horse one day, something I did on a real regular basis, but this particular patient was unique, and his reluctance to see the benefits of preventive medicine—also known as "needle shyness"—had distracted me. Vaccinating is not usually a dangerous procedure, but this horse was testing my nerve. I was artfully dodging teeth and front feet from my unwilling patient, Fluffy, while my client, Mrs. Tillis, was asking me what I was doing. Of course, my immediate response could have invoked a terse explanation about self-preservation, but that would be… unprofessional. It never pays to get mad at the horses; they are just trying to protect themselves, and who can blame them? After reminding myself of the necessity of the equine survival instinct, the scientist in me sort of took over. I wondered, *Yeah, what* was *I doing? There must be an easier way to make a living!* No, I wasn't thinking that—well, maybe, but just for a moment. Then my spring-loaded, well-caffeinated brain bounced to the history of the science of vaccination.

In this modern age we tend to take things for granted. We can buy medicine at the supermarket to cure diseases that were fatal a generation ago. (My grandfather died of a perforated gastric ulcer in 1939. Today, an occasional dose of a modern antacid would have saved his life!)

Although new medicines appear on the market on a daily basis, vaccines are not new technology. They were used clinically long before we understood how they worked (or there were people willing to sue if they didn't work!). But vaccines basically teach the immune system what a disease organism looks like—a sort of biological "facial recognition software" so our immune system knows the bad guys when it sees them. The use of vaccines has all but eradicated infections like polio and smallpox. But where did these vaccines come from? The vaccine fairy didn't just land at the local doctor's office or feed store. Somebody had to invent them. Somebody really smart, or, at least, lucky and observant.

Not all medical advances are the result of careful research, development, and clinical trials. Some of our greatest advances came from careful observation and a gamble or two. For example, Edward Jenner, a practicing physician in England, observed that milkmaids never got smallpox. Smallpox was the source of great concern because, in the 1700s, sixty percent of all Europeans came down with the dreaded disease and twenty percent of them died from it! Jenner noticed that the milkmaids would get scabs on their hands that looked a lot like smallpox, but they *never* died or even got sick. He had no way of knowing if there was a difference in the disease affecting just the milkmaids or there was something in these women that provided some sort of resistance. After all, the discovery of the immune system was centuries away. However, Jenner, armed with his observations, an abundance of intestinal fortitude, and some willing test subjects, took scabs from the hand of a milkmaid, and with a piece of broken glass, introduced this infected tissue into the skin of healthy subjects.

Imagine that! The village doctor comes up to you one day and says, "Hey, Nigel, I have an idea of how to prevent smallpox. Olga here, has a few scabs on her hands. I'd like to scratch your skin with this broken beer bottle and rub those scabs around on you. What do you think? You'll be okay, I think. I mean, I'm pretty sure. Come on, what's the worst thing that can happen?"

Apparently, his pitch was effective. Later, he "challenged" the vaccinated subjects with active smallpox lesions. This produced two astounding events: First, these people actually *let him try to give them small pox*! And even more amazing, they did not succumb to the deadly infection! The process of scratching the skin to introduce medicine, called "variolation," may have been invented by the Chinese a few centuries before Dr. Jenner, so it was not a new idea. How Jenner found out about it is a mystery, and it gets more confusing. The term "vaccination" comes from the same Latin derivative for "cow," like the Spanish *vaca*. So Jenner took a Chinese technique and gave it a Latin name using English people for guinea pigs. And the procedure has remained basically unchanged to this day. Go figure.

Although the term "science" commonly induces mental images of white coats and test tubes, some of the greatest scientific discoveries were glorious accidents. For example, about 1650 a Dutch "haberdasher" (cloth salesman) named Antonie van Leeuwenhoek wanted to see the quality of the threads in the cloth he was selling. Glass lenses had been used for eye glasses since the thirteenth century; it was probably Galileo that put two lenses together to invent the telescope, and he also used a variation on this theme to invent the microscope. Van Leeuwenhoek bettered Galileo's microscope by learning how to make higher quality lenses, thus greatly improving the ability to see the small fibers in the cloth. If he had stopped there, his name and his invention may have been nothing more than a historical footnote. But he didn't. He started using his improved invention to expose a microscopic universe that had been hidden in plain sight. He revealed the presence of single-celled life forms in pond water and coined the term "animalcules"—tiny animals—which launched the field of microbiology.

Let's fast forward two hundred and fifty years or so. A French chemist named Louis Pasteur was working at the University of Strasburg. Some local wine and beer makers were having quality control problems. They thought this was a problem with chemistry, as nobody really knew how "fermentation," the process that turns sugar from grapes or grain into alcohol, occurred. It was Pasteur's work that proved it was the activity of yeast, a mold growing on the sugar from the grapes that produced alcohol in a biological process, not just a chemical reaction. He was able to grow these organisms in the laboratory. Though other men really invented the science of microbiology, Pasteur made it medically—and clinically—relevant.

In Pasteur's day, the germ theory of disease transmission was just that: a theory. Nobody had proved it yet—most diseases were caused by bad air, divine retribution, evil spirits, or space aliens. Pasteur had lost three of his five children to "typhus," an infectious and often fatal gastrointestinal disease. At the same time, a similar disease called "fowl cholera" was causing major economic challenges for the European agricultural economy, killing chickens by the trainload. Pasteur applied the knowledge he gained from his studies in the microbiology of fermentation to address the pathology of a bacterial disease.

Within a few months, he was able to isolate the organism he thought might be causing the disease in chickens and grow it in culture plates. In order to prove that these cultures contained the offending bacteria, he was able to repeatedly transmit the same disease to healthy chickens. This work provided a profound leap in our understanding of biology. Imagine Pasteur working in his lab with no real guidelines, no textbook on techniques or even basic principles to direct his study of disease-causing organisms. Just because something grows on a culture plate, doesn't mean it causes a disease. The connections here are very difficult. But despite the limitations of this daunting task, he figured out the cause of the disease with nary an evil spirit or "ET" to be found.

But how to prevent it? That was the question he eventually answered. The answer came in yet another great scientific accident.

Pasteur was called away from his lab for a few days. When he returned, he resumed his experiments, infecting healthy chickens with fowl cholera cultures he had in progress before he left. To his surprise, the birds got sick, but they didn't die. He repeated the experiment, with the same results: The old cultures made some of the birds ill but would not transmit the fatal disease. He grew new cultures, inoculating the same birds he had given the old cultures to, and they did not develop symptoms of fowl cholera. It would appear to most of us that we had messed up the cultures somehow and would tend to throw out the whole thing in frustration. But our friend Louis was different. He was patient and observant. Something in the old cultures appeared to be *protecting* the birds from the infection that had previously proven fatal.

Thus, by accident, he discovered the process of "attenuation"—altering disease-causing organisms so they are harmless, and not only harmless, but actually protective! He didn't know how this happened—indeed, we still don't know exactly how the immune system is stimulated by vaccines to protect us from disease. Pasteur, the nineteenth-century chemist with nothing but a few test tubes and the power of observation, pioneered the sciences of microbiology and immunology. He developed vaccines for anthrax, fowl cholera, and rabies. Many of his processes (does "pasteurization" ring a bell) are still in use today.

So the next time someone asks you what you know about vaccines, just tell them, "milkmaids, spoiled wine, and dead chickens." That ought to clear it right up for them!

Judicious use of vaccines can be beneficial to most horses. However, not all vaccines are safe and effective. In fact, the immune system in some horses really does not like some vaccines. Adverse reactions like painful swelling at the injection site, fever, lethargy, or mild colic have been reported following vaccination. We should think long and hard before vaccinating horses with these reactions every year. Like people allergic to bee stings, some of these reactions can get worse with each exposure. Although many vaccines can be purchased online or at local retailers, this is one aspect of horse health that warrants the hands of a trained professional. Proper medical management in all aspects of equine health can help us maintain a good quality of life in these amazing animals.

_ "She's Really Not My Horse!"

Most of my writing is an attempt to provide information about horses: medicine, surgery, or behavior, flavored with a little common sense and a dash of my twisted sense of humor. Occasionally, however, the people connected to these magnificent beasts do something so baffling, I am compelled to write it down. The old adage, "Truth is stranger than fiction," could also read, "You can't make this stuff up!" Working with horses is difficult enough, but if there were no people involved, it would be downright easy. Here's just one reason why.

Jane was a former client. The reason for "former" will become obvious in a minute. She owned a public boarding facility in my practice area. While she tried to provide good care for all the horses on her place, accidents happen, and they provide fodder for my stories. And, if nobody dies, it will eventually be funny. (The key word here is "eventually.")

Although there is really nothing funny about an injured horse, the most interesting stories have multiple layers. So let's start with a moderately injured, not-too-halter-broke, fairly valuable, ten-year-old mare. The owner lived out of town, seldom saw the mare, but wanted the best of care for her "dressage prospect." The term "prospect" is often used by people trying to sell a horse that has no real apparent skills or that they just can't seem to get to a reasonable level of broke. So "prospect" may just be a euphemism for "I hope someone will buy him." (If the unbroke, middle-aged "dressage prospect" seems a little incongruous, hold on, it gets better.)

One spring afternoon, Jane called me out to see the injured horse. It turned out that a new stable hand had mixed up the population during a routine turnout and the social interaction in the new herd dynamic made things a little...interesting. Red got herself between a fence and a nasty old mare who resented the new visitor in *her* pasture. The result was a moderately severe laceration to Red's right hind limb that required some sutures to close. The doctoring part started out okay, though Red required more than a little pharmacologic assistance to encourage her cooperation. I was glad that I could still move pretty fast for an old guy.

I was just about finished with the bandage when Zelda, Red's owner, showed up. She had left work in a panic after Jane informed her of the accident.

I told Zelda that, though Red had required more than a little sedation for the procedure, I thought that she would recover uneventfully after a few bandage changes. I left some materials and instructions, and Zelda assured me that she could handle the aftercare.

"It's interesting that Red needed so much medicine," Zelda said. "I've noticed some attitude changes in her recently. She just doesn't seem like my horse anymore."

This observation would prove prophetic.

Zelda called me the next day. She was frustrated that she couldn't change Red's bandage and repeated the observation: "She just isn't my horse." So she brought the mare to my clinic so I could change wraps and watch her for a few days. It had long been my policy to ask for a deposit when horses are left in my care to cover my up-front expenses—they're not just some old cars I can park in the "back forty" until the clients "remember" to come get them. These guys continue to *eat*, and that ain't free.

Zelda questioned this by saying, "Why do you need money? You got my horse?"

I tactfully responded that the presence of her horse would not pay my bills. She got this and wrote me a check for way less than the bill was up to that point, which bothered me a little. But I *thought* she was good for the bill and glad for the help I was providing.

I was wrong.

The next day, things got complicated. The mare presented signs of colic. As I expected, the horse needed a fairly large dose of tranquilizer to get any treatment done. So, since I had her feet slowed down a bit with sedation, I changed her bandage and treated her for colic at the same time. I called Zelda to let her know about the added complexity of Red's case. Unfortunately, the pattern persisted for several days. The colic symptoms were not really bad, but the mare just wasn't right. The vet bill was expanding by the day, but her attitude was not improving, and mine wasn't getting much better, either. Finally, the discussion turned to referral for possible colic surgery.

"She's a young horse, and a great dressage prospect," Zelda lamented, "so I sure hate to lose her. I just can't afford the price of a colic surgery, even though her recent personality changes make it seem like she just isn't my horse anymore. Is there anything else you can do to help her at your place?"

"Zelda," I began less tactfully. "Red is at least twenty years old, so I don't know how much time a colic surgery will buy for her." During the course of any colic treatment, I look at the color and moisture of the patient's gums to assess hydration. You couldn't help but notice this mare had the mouth of a horse *at least* twenty years old.

Zelda was incredulous. "What?" she exclaimed, nearly shouting, "She's only nine or ten—I got her papers!"

"The horse you brought me has the mouth of a horse at least twenty years old," I began. "Although judging a horse's age by his teeth is an educated guess, this horse hasn't been ten years old for a long time."

"Can I call you back later?"

Well, I waited for a day. Then two…three. No call back. Repeated calls to Zelda went straight to voicemail. I had been doing a fair amount of veterinary work for her, and the phone *never* went to voicemail. This was not a good sign. At this point the mare was technically abandoned. Finally, I called the public boarding facility owner, Jane, and told her that Zelda had not returned my calls, so I was bringing the mare back to the barn, and they could change the bandages there…maybe. She had started eating with normal interest, so the colic part of the case was apparently resolved. The cut on her leg would heal without much treatment at this point, so I really wasn't worried about her recovery. This type of wound could result in some minor cosmetic defects but would not be expected to alter her movement or quality of life. Jane's reply was astounding.

"Don't bring her back here. I've locked the gate and you can't get in!"

It was becoming clear that the plain red Thoroughbred mare, of ambiguous age and unknown origin, might be a semi-permanent resident. Oh, boy!

I called the State Board of Veterinary Examiners, County Animal Control, the sheriff's office, and finally, my insurance carrier to ask what I could do about this apparently abandoned mare. The answer was succinct and consistent: "Nothing." I couldn't sell her, and I sure didn't want to keep her. She really didn't need much, if any further treatment, but she was sure on my feed bill, and though that wasn't very much, it kept growing. I had nightmarish visions of feeding this cranky old mare for another five years just trying to figure out what to do with her. She'd probably live to be forty! Zelda had left her trailer at my place, but I couldn't legally lock it up or keep it for ransom. I was stuck with a capital "S"… or something else that starts with the same letter.

A few hours later, the phone buzzed in my pocket.

"This is Billy Bob," an unfamiliar voice began. "I believe you have my horse at your clinic."

Billy Bob explained he was a new trainer at Jane's public boarding facility, and a green stable hand had mixed up his aged red mare with Zelda's not-so-aged one. This explained the sudden "behavioral change," but I was amazed that Zelda didn't realize the mare *really wasn't her mare*; not just figuratively! Billy Bob asked me what the bill was, and I gave him the bad news.

"About two thousand dollars," I replied, as the fee for Red's care had greatly eclipsed the level of routine bandage changes due to the complications of colic, repeated sedation, and almost two weeks' stay at my place.

"Well, she's really not my horse. She sort of belongs to my partner and me, but I can't believe the bill is that high for a simple cut. I *never* would have called *you*. I would have doctored her myself. I can't believe Jane didn't know this!" Billy Bob added he didn't have any money.

I asked him to just come get the mare.

"Well, my trailer is in the shop."

I volunteered to deliver the mare if he would like. This wreck was getting more complicated by the minute: the bill was getting larger, the cut and the mare's attitude weren't getting any better, and I didn't know exactly who to talk to about treatment or heaven forbid, euthanasia. At this point, I just wanted her off my place.

"I really don't have a place to put the mare to care for her right now, but I'll call you back in a few days."

A few days! It was beginning to look like I was the proud new owner of a twenty-year-old mare with some medical needs *and* an expanding dislike for me. I really empathized with this poor mare cuz when she needed a little treatment, *I* was the only advocate she had, and she wasn't real thrilled about *that*.

I called Zelda, the "original owner," and the phone went to voicemail. I called Jane at the boarding facility...more voicemail.

Finally, Billy Bob called me back. "Just put her down. She's old and I don't have the money. I'll bring you a check for the tallow truck, and I'll pay your bill... eventually...though she's really not my horse."

By now I was really confused about the ownership of this horse, and I was not about to euthanize her till I got it figured out. Of course, she was still at my clinic, still getting treated, still not getting any happier about being there, and the meter was running.

The phone buzzed in my pocket again.

"This is RJ Gotrocks," a new voice announced. "You are treating my horse for a cut and a colic." More of a statement than a question. Wow! Cue the music from *The Twilight Zone*.

I explained my concern and confusion, but Mr. Gotrocks assured me that Red had been quite a horse in her day, but he wanted to know if I was certain this was his mare. He said, "My mare is only seven years old, so I'm wondering exactly which horse you have." At this point I was only certain that *nobody* knew whose mare it was, and why was he asking me?

I told him the mare at my clinic was about twenty years old and had a lip tattoo that was not readable (a common problem with old tattoos) but was a clear indication she had been on a racetrack at some point in her life.

"Well, then she isn't Red," he began. "She was foaled in 1997."

I replied: "Well, this is 2017. Let's do the math," adding a chuckle so I wouldn't sound too sarcastic or condescending.

"You must be right," he admitted. "Time sure flies!"

He said he would eventually pay his bill, but *his* trailer was in for repairs—I guess there was an epidemic of disabled trailers that week. He really didn't have a place to keep her, but if I could deliver the horse to his house, his secretary would meet me there, and they'd figure out something.

At this point, I was just glad that Red would be living someplace else. I hooked up my trailer, loaded my patient, and rolled off to Mr. Gotrocks' place, almost an hour away. I pulled in the driveway and the place seemed deserted. Mr. Gotrocks was conspicuously absent. There was no truck or trailer to be seen, but behind the house there was a barn with five or six stalls and several paddocks. This facility was a reasonable place to house and treat Red, so the "I really don't have a place to put her" excuse was ringing a little hollow.

I walked back to the trailer door to unload Red, though I was not really sure what to do with her. I didn't want to just leave her there, because I wasn't altogether sure I was in the right place. But I certainly didn't want to take her back to my place—Red wasn't too keen on that prospect, either. Finally, a youngish looking man came out of the house. He introduced himself.

"Hi, Doc. I'm Billy Bob."

I was getting more confused, but not surprised. Was he a secretary or a trainer? At this point, I was just glad to have someone to hand the lead shank to, and I didn't care if he was a secretary of Gotrocks Inc. or the Secretary of State—I was fixin' to leave that place with an empty trailer.

Thankfully, Red survived her injury and got back with her rightful owner…I think. Mr. Gotrocks eventually paid his bill, less the very small deposit the mare's first "owner" had given me. At that point, I was glad to get anything out of the deal. I did not get paid for the two hours I spent delivering the mare, much less the time I spent calling half the country trying to figure out what to do with the case. In the end, I assumed this was a "cut my losses" proposition, at best, so I was thankful the mare turned out okay.

Thank God this ordeal is finally over, I thought.

Several months after I delivered Red, a familiar voice fairly purred through the speaker on my phone. "Did Mr. Gotrocks ever get hold of you?" It was Zelda (Owner Number One). I was shocked she had finally returned my calls, since she'd abandoned the mare weeks earlier, and her trailer had apparently vaporized one day while I was away from my clinic. I wondered what on earth had happened to renew her interest in the case.

"I worked really hard to try to get you paid on that deal," she continued. "It took a little time, but I think I have convinced him to pay your fee. After all, she really wasn't my horse." At this point, I was way passed caring whose horse Red was, just glad someone *finally* claimed her, and it wasn't *me*.

After I caught my breath, I was able to thank her for her concern, and yes, Mr. Gotrocks did finally pay his bill.

"Great. Can I get my deposit back?"

I paused for a minute, wondering just exactly how to respond. This lady had avoided my calls for weeks, abandoned a horse that was not hers, and didn't do a thing to take the mare back to her rightful owner. Now, *she* wanted money back?

"I think Mr. Gotrocks still has it. After all, it really wasn't *my* deposit!"

Sometimes I just crack myself up, though I'm not sure she really appreciated the humor...she hung up before she could hear me laughing.

_ Strangles, Stress, and Pigeon Fever Panic

"Looks like he almost swallowed a cantaloupe," was Smitty's assessment of the lump under the jaw of his horse who was also, as it turned out, named Smitty. Smitty the Man was an accountant and quick with his figures. Smitty the Horse was quick to turn a cow and had supplied the accountant with a few belt buckles and some cash for their efforts in local team pennings. They shared more than just a name: Their mutual affection was obvious.

I examined the lump near the throatlatch of the young gelding. Even a gentle touch to the area caused Smitty the Horse to shy away from my hand and roll his eyes at me as if to say, "Ouch, Doc!" Smitty the Man would flinch a little bit, too, out of empathy for his ailing partner. There was no drainage from this lesion, and the horse's temperature was a normal one hundred point six. He was eating with his usual gluttony, and other than the large lump under his jaw, was apparently normal.

"It can't be strangles, Doc. I had him vaccinated last year!" Smitty the Man was worried about all the gossip he had been hearing since his horse had developed this malady. The conventional barnyard wisdom had the gelding diagnosed, dead, and buried two hours before I got there. Therein lies the real problem with oozing, draining, yucky abscesses on horses in public stables: they are considerably more detrimental to the horse *people* than to the horses. Because of potential effects on stable politics, cases like this are best handled with the glib tactfulness for which I had become famous.

"This is an abscess," I said, "probably caused by a splinter from a fence board or something. It is *possible* that it is the result of an infectious process, like 'strangles' or 'pigeon fever'—it's hard to say. But, regardless of the cause, he'll be all right."

I was *sooo* smooth.

It took all of three seconds for half the people in the barn to stampede to their cell phones to warn the world of the impending doom. By the fourth second, the panic-laced rumor had escalated to the point where *both* Smittys were going to die and all the surviving horses would soon be sick with pigeon fever, strangles, and terminal acne. Nobody heard me say it was probably just a splinter and the Smittys would be fine.

Initially, it may appear easy to distinguish an infectious disease, like strangles, from something physical or traumatic, like a thorn or splinter. In order to understand the difficulties encountered in making such a diagnosis, it is important to think about how the immune system produces an abscess.

The word "immune" comes from the Middle English word for "exempt." So if we have "immunity" we are exempt from disease, but the process is just a bit more complicated than that. In order to understand intricate systems, I find it necessary to break things down into simple sections. In its most elementary form, immunity governs the ability to distinguish "self" from "non-self" and escorts the non-self particles from the body. For example, Smitty the Horse's immune system would reject the splinter, bacteria, or anything "not Smitty" as foreign, while it would recognize a normal skin cell as part of him. When the splinter pierces the skin, a complex set of reactions is initiated to incite an inflammatory response. This type of inflammation is non-specific and is stimulated by any foreign substance "invading" the body. At first, this will cause heat, redness, swelling, pain, and loss of function. Later, several types of "white blood cells" (WBCs) will be attracted to the inflamed area. The WBCs serve a variety of complex functions. In the case of a foreign body, like the fence board splinter, the primary mission of the WBCs is to destroy the alien particles.

Some of the WBCs contain small packages of enzymes that can be released when a foreign substance is encountered. These enzymes are not specific in their destructive power, so they blow up everything in sight. Like killing a fly with a cannon, it's effective, but messy. Therefore, the yellow goopy stuff commonly referred to as "pus" is actually liquid horse (or liquid dog, or liquid Agnes—you get the point). The effect of the inflammatory response is so efficient that sometimes the foreign body is completely expelled. This is why inflammation is our friend.

Most over-the-counter pain medications work because they impede inflammation. In fact, although aspirin has been used for well over a century as a pain reliever, its mechanism of action wasn't determined until a few years ago: It reduces inflammation. The folks that sell these drugs on TV probably will not agree, but the inflammatory response is beneficial. So, at least initially, it probably should not be suppressed! This may seem counterintuitive, but think about it. The heat and redness that are produced is caused by an increase in blood flow to the area. The blood brings more nutrients, growth factors, and other components we have not yet even identified to the region. The blood vessels become leaky so that these factors can be easily delivered, and the offending particles are flushed from the body. What a system! Why would we want to inhibit it? If an inflammatory process lasts for more than a few days, treatment may be warranted. Initially, it should be viewed as a normal, useful development of the healing process.

The course of events can take several days to complete. In Smitty the Horse's case, we were seeing the stage of inflammation where the area was quite swollen, but no drainage had occurred because the WBCs had not had time to do their work. Just like the great big pimple you get on your nose the day before a job interview or hot date, the thing was big and sore, but you couldn't squeeze anything out of it yet. As the process progressed, the center would soften and eventually burst and drain. Usually, the drainage will occur toward the outside and cause no further harm. Occasionally these things burst to the inside and produce fatal illness: peritonitis if they are over the abdomen, pneumonia if they burst over the chest or neck. It is always a good idea to look at large abscesses with the ultrasound. The use of this instrument allows us to see the inside of the abscess, and if the center has become liquefied, we can guide a long needle in to establish a draining tract toward the outside.

I explained that an examination with the ultrasound might be helpful. Sure enough, a pocket of liquid Smitty was visible in the lower part of the lump, and I was able to drain about five ccs of thick, tan fluid out with only minimal discomfort to either Smitty.

"This is looking more like pigeon fever," I confided when I was sure that nobody else was within earshot. "These large, thick, painful things usually are."

"We do have a lot of pigeons around the barn." Smitty the Man shrugged. "I didn't think they would cause any harm."

"I'm not sure why they call it 'pigeon fever,'" I confessed. "Horses that get it almost never run a fever, and they don't catch it from pigeons. The textbooks all say that it is caused by a specific bacterium called *Corynebacterium pseudotuberculosis.* (Don't look for that on "Final Jeopardy.") The actual bug doesn't seem to be important, because the treatment is the same. Establish drainage to the outside and flush with peroxide two or three times daily to keep it from healing over too fast. There is an antibiotic available that may help, but it's a little expensive," I said.

"Penicillin?" Smitty asked.

No, 'rifampin.' It's a drug that has been used to treat tuberculosis in people. I have had some success in treating abscesses in horses with it. Two weeks' worth of treatment is a couple of hundred dollars. Penicillin injections will make the horse good and mad at you, but it won't do a thing for the abscess," I replied.

"Will he get better without it?'

"Probably. The only real worry is if it bursts to the inside, and that would be a real good reason to put him on rifampin. Of course, like anything else," I added, "there's no guarantee."

"Then you're sure it's not strangles?"

"Pretty sure. 'Strangles', or 'distemper', is caused by another specific bacteria, *Streptococcus equi,* and the abscesses under the jaw are soft and not painful. Strangles tends to be contagious, and I've seen barns where about a third of the horses came down with it. Neither strangles nor pigeon fever is fatal, except for when the abscesses burst to the inside."

For economic reasons, Smitty declined the use of the antibiotic. Instead, he flushed the draining wound with cold water judiciously twice daily, and monitored his horse's attitude and appetite. Smitty the Horse never missed a meal and submitted to the flushing with just enough reluctance to let everyone know that he was still feeling all right.

Within two weeks, the lump had all but disappeared. There was some hair missing in the area due to the heat of inflammation, but it would return in time, and Smitty the Horse would be as handsome as ever. Despite the conventional wisdom of the barnyard, nobody died.

_ Happy Horse Van Lines

In these modern, fast-paced times one of the greatest dangers faced by horses is not some new, infectious disease. Nor is it some dreaded birth defect or horse-eating suburban predator. This threat is, ironically, the pride of almost every modern horseman: *The Horse Trailer*. I must confess that there is one parked in my yard right now, as it seems to be a necessary evil in this day of fences, pavement, and super highways. However, each year I see many injuries—cuts, lacerations, bruised bodies and egos—due to these contraptions.

Although it is dangerous enough to be incarcerated inside one of these things approaching warp speed on the freeway, most injuries occur when the horse is getting in or out. This can be due to a naturally belligerent, uncooperative personality, but many owners can grow out of this with counseling. The main reason that some horses are reluctant to load can be due to the way they perceive the world around them.

The central nervous system (CNS) of the horse, the brain and spinal cord, processes information in a way that has allowed the horse to avoid predators or other dangerous inhabitants of their environment. The CNS evaluates the surroundings of the horse by visual, auditory, and olfactory means (sight, sound, and smell) to locate food and avoid becoming it. The latter two senses are easy to observe. Just watch the behavior of a horse when he sees something for the first time...or even the sixteenth time (this was one of my Thoroughbred Buddy's more puzzling qualities). The ears go up like radar for obvious reasons. The horse may snort loudly through his nostrils to immediately clear any mucus that may interfere with his sense of smell (or make him sound like a lion or something—I'm not sure why they do that). You can almost hear the rusty little wheels turning in the walnut-sized brain as the information is being processed through pricked ears, flared nostrils, and a *very* good memory.

The sense of sight, however, is processed in a way that is not so obvious. The eyes of the horse stick out on the side of the head. This allows a greater field of vision than in, say for instance, man, whose eyes are placed in the front of his head. (My third-grade teacher, Mrs. Frankenstein, had eyes in the *back* of her head, but that's a whole 'nuther story.) The horse can see almost one hundred and eighty degrees on one side from a spot about four feet in front of the nose and past the point of the hip to the rear without turning his head. Because of the way the eyes are wired up to the brain, the horse perceives one "monocular" image from each eye and one "binocular" image from both eyes. That's a total of three images, folks. And you thought *one* image was confusing!

Although the field of vision is great in each monocular image for the horse, the binocular image is somewhat limited. The horse is completely blind in a narrow space from the middle of his face to a spot about four feet from the tip of his nose. The easiest way to visualize this concept is to walk around with a bale of hay about belt-buckle high. If the pain in your back doesn't cause you to squint too bad, you may be able to see to the left and right of it, but you will have a blind spot for about four feet in front of you. Now hold the bale up long ways in front of your face and think about just walking right into a phone booth. This is why it is usually easier to load a horse in a stock trailer, or one with a wide gate, instead of one of those skinny little two-horse boxes. (When I first discovered this about forty years ago, I remember hearing those rusty little wheels turning inside *my* little walnut-sized brain!)

To further complicate matters, the way the horse sees the world can add to his opinion about horse trailers. First, the equine "pupil," the hole in the middle of the iris, is not round like it is in man, but horizontal. This pupil shape gives the horse a good field of vision along the horizon, but it does not allow real sharp focus. This is because, from the horses' standpoint, it is more important to recognize a lion on the horizon than it is to read a newspaper. Second, though the horse has excellent vision in low light, the time it takes to adjust between bright and low light is longer than it is in man (up to twenty minutes!).

So there are at least four obstacles between the horse and the trailer: 1) The blind spot extending about four feet in front of his nose. 2) A longer adjustment time from bright to low lighting. 3) Me! If I am standing right in front of him. 4) Me again! If I am mad at him because he can't seem to get it through his head how important it is for him to submit to a dark, very confining area...that moves!

In addition to the somewhat unique way the horse "sees," the complexities of behavior must be considered in the often-frustrating task of trailer loading. The areas of the brain associated with vision are linked to memory centers. This is how we learn: We see the letter "c" and remember it is the symbol for a sound. We combine it with other letters, and soon it can produce a distinct mental image of something warm and furry: "c-a-t". While the alphabet is not usually a part of the horse's skill set, he does have an excellent memory. It is interesting how we can ride past a stack of fence posts every day for a year without incident. But move just one of the posts, and many horses will notice the difference.

Head posture can add an interesting aspect to vision, as well. When my head is down, I may be embarrassed, or thinking, or looking at a horse's foot. When a horse's head is down, he's eating...or thinking about eating. So the "head-down" posture is the "happy place" for a horse. In a pasture, he keeps it there about sixteen hours a day. When his head is down next to the end of the trailer, he is in the grazing position—his comfort zone. I have made the mistake of pulling his head up to get him thinking about the trailer. However, in the mind of the horse, a "head-down" posture is typically one of cooperation. When his head is down, *his mind is in the trailer,* so the last thing we want to do is jerk his head up!

Tranquilizing a horse for a trailer ride is almost never a good idea. First of all, it is dangerous enough for a horse to be in one of these portable phone booths when he has all of his faculties about him, nevermind when he is under sedation. Even a mild sedative can produce incoordination that may result in injury. Most of the modern tranquilizing drugs used on horses are quite safe. However, some of the older drugs, like "acepromazine," have a prolonged effect and can be quite dangerous. In male horses, one of the common side effects of this drug is penile prolapse. (This is why it can be used to aid us in cleaning a sheath.) Penile prolapse during a long trailer ride can result in permanent paralysis that may require *amputation*.

The most important aspect of medical management for shipped horses is the prevention of dehydration. Rest stops every four hours or so are recommended to let the horse stretch his legs, lower his head, get a drink of water, and pee outside the trailer. Oral electrolyte pastes are never a good idea, as they tend to *draw water out* of the bloodstream and add to dehydration.

If the horse will be traveling for more than four hours, a gallon of mineral oil given by a stomach tube the day of shipment is a safe and effective way to prevent impaction colic. A recent study showed that treatments with a "bronchodilator" (a drug to expand airways in the lung) the day before shipping was beneficial in preventing respiratory infections. The use of leg wraps is controversial. If the legs are not wrapped, the horse can "feel" where his feet are. If leg wraps are used, they may impair sensory information that prevents injury. If wraps are used, they should extend past the "coronet" (the line between the hair and the hoof wall). This will get your expensive wraps dirty, but they will provide better protection. If you *must* put bedding in the trailer, use straw instead of shavings or sawdust. I have ridden in trailers bedded both ways, and breathing sawdust is no fun.

Finally, it is important to know people that are transporting your horse. Get references and check them out. Not every transportation company has experienced horsemen for drivers.

When I think about horse haulers, I think about Oscar. As a small boy, Oscar used to sit outside his home in Little Rock, Arkansas, and watch the trucks roar down the interstate. It became his dream to one day become the master of one of those eighteen-wheeled giants.

His big break came shortly after his twenty-sixth birthday and the loss of his job as assistant night manager at the local Tastee Freeze. The want-ad section of the local paper proclaimed: *Truck Driver Needed*. The words leapt off the page like a neon sign. The second line sealed the deal: *No Experience Necessary*. That was as good as a divine mandate and sent Oscar on his quest for his Class A license and the freedom of the open road. Two months later, he was proudly wearing a uniform shirt that had *Oscar* embroidered over the left pocket and *Happy Horse Van Lines* over his right. Although he knew absolutely nothing about horses, he was elated by the prospect of being a professional truck driver. He was instructed to meet his partner at the "Eat Here and Get Gas" truck stop just off I-40, and the two of them were to drive the second leg of a cross-country trip that would end in Fresno, California.

Ominously, the first team of drivers was three hours late. Oscar and his new partner, Bill, were naturally nervous, as it was their first day on the job. The late arrival of their colleagues made them all the more anxious to be on the road to make up the lost time. The eighteen wheels had not completely stopped turning when the two rookie drivers climbed into the cab, quickly checked the paperwork, and eased the big rig toward the interstate on their quest for gear-jamming freedom.

Oscar shifted the truck through the gears in mostly the proper order with only an occasional grinding noise emanating from somewhere behind them. When the van reached highway speed, Oscar glanced at his partner who was attempting to sort through a stack of health papers, Coggins test reports, and other forms.

"Did you check the horses before we left?" Oscar asked.

"Yeah," Bill replied with a pencil in his mouth, trying to remember which form to fill out next. "All of 'em are fine; one of 'em is takin' a nap."

"Yeah, I like to sleep on a long trip, too. But none of that tonight!"

"Yeah! California, here we come!"

The highway was peaceful in the early morning. The headlights cut through the vast darkness. The roar of the engine and the whine of the wheels invaded the silence of the countryside. A cool, damp breeze flowed through the cab of the truck as country music from a distant radio station popped and fried through the speakers. For Oscar and Bill, life was good.

The driving part was easy, as long as Oscar did not have to shift gears too often. His clutch foot was a slow learner and seemed to lack communication with his accelerator foot, shifting hand, and coffee cup. He was thankful that the country was fairly flat, and by the time they got to the Rocky Mountains, he'd likely have this gear-shifting business down to an art.

The team decided to stop in Clovis, New Mexico, just over the Texas line, for breakfast. The bad food at the truck stop was only the beginning of their trouble there.

"Don't ever eat truck-stop chili for breakfast," Oscar moaned as he climbed up to the van window to inspect his passengers. His next words erupted as hot and sour as any bad breakfast heartburn he had ever experienced. The "napping horse" was *dead*.

"What are we gonna' do now!" Oscar screamed at his partner. "You can't tell a sleepin' horse from a dead one?"

"I ain't no vet'nary!" Bill defended his professionalism. "I thought he was sleepin'."

After a few minutes of shouts, threats, and impressive profanity, cooler heads prevailed and the two soon-to-be retired truckers returned to the coffee shop to formulate their plan. Several cups of coffee later, Bill had a revelation. "We'll get a replacement! How hard can it be to find a plain brown horse?"

Miraculously, it was not very hard at all. Clovis, New Mexico, was the home of one of the largest horse auctions in the world, and consequently, the home of more than a few horse traders. After a score of phone calls, our heroes reached "Honest Al Hardaway, Purveyor of Fine Horses."

"Honest Al," by his own description, was just the man to help these boys through this unfortunate situation. Al carefully examined the deceased passenger, noting her age, weight, color, and markings.

"I know where there is a little mare that is a pretty close match to this one," Al said, "but she won't come cheap."

"How un-cheap?" Oscar asked.

"Three thousand...and I can have her here tomorrow."

"For three grand, you can have her here tonight!" Oscar's chili was talking to him again, and he had little time for tact.

The two pooled their finances with maxed-out Visa cards, hocked their high school rings, and got four hundred dollars wired to them by good old Aunt Agnes. This Aunt had historically been a sucker for the old "swerved to miss a cat and smashed the radiator" story. Oscar said a prayer of thanks to the god of short memories.

Honest Al, as good as his word, produced the replacement mare, and for a slight additional fee, removed the body of the unfortunate traveler. Late afternoon found the Happy Horse Van Lines truck characteristically grinding its way west on I-40 with eight live horses and two broke drivers aboard. Twenty-six tedious hours later, Fresno, California, glittered in the summer twilight, giving the duo some hope that the failing light would aid them in their deceit.

However, Ms. Wilma Wiley, proud owner of a plain brown Morgan mare named Brownie, was nobody's fool. "This is not my mare," she asserted.

Oscar and Bill were incredulous. "The invoice we have says that this brown Morgan mare is to be delivered to Wilma Wiley of Fresno, California." Oscar wondered if she could see the lump in his throat.

"THIS IS NOT MY MARE!" She grew less patient.

"Why do you think that this is not your horse?"

"Because my mare IS DEAD!" she exclaimed. "She died at a show on the East Coast, and I arranged to have her body shipped back here to be buried!"

_ Horse Humor and Intelligence

I have started quite a few colts for myself and for others. I find it an interesting, if not sometimes dangerous, avocation. My years working with horses has taught me lots about equine behavior—in fact, you might say I have been continually in the steep part of the learning curve. This has taught me how to stay in the saddle...and how to land when I cannot.

A study in horse behavior gives us tools to use in specific cases, but in a larger sense, it gives us freedom to "think out of the box." If you get around enough of them, most young horses will give you a general impression about who they are by the seventh or eighth saddling. Buddy, that Thoroughbred of mine, for a lot of reasons, was different.

Our early rides (the Salinas River Beach episode aside) were uneventful. He never bucked and only rarely balked. As soon as he figured out what I wanted to do, he was as willing as a horse could be. He liked to move out on the trail. Actually, that was one of his many endearing qualities: He could really *walk*.

I can't remember ever riding a horse that could walk as fast as Buddy. It seemed as though I had stumbled on to a perfect riding horse.

Of course, I soon learned that Buddy had a sick sense of humor and was full of surprises.

My new friends Ed and Susan had invited me to go with them and some other friends on a camping trip in the redwoods a couple of hours away. There were miles of horse trails and good camping places. I left word with my answering service that I would be out of town for a few days. I didn't think my absence would hurt my practice much, because, in those early days, most of my clients would be on the trip anyway.

It is hard to describe the beauty of the place known to the locals as Jack Brooks' Horse Camp. It has become one of my favorite spots on earth. The trails wind through hills filled with stands of giant redwoods, tangles of manzanita, and grassy flats rimmed with ponderosa pine. Some of the trails are narrow, steep, and in places, almost dark at mid-day under a canopy of foliage that may reach over two hundred feet above the forest floor. The morning mist hangs in the narrow valleys as a cool, ghostly curtain, separating horses and riders from the modern world. The silence is only broken by the occasional cawing of a mountain raven or whispering leaves answering thudding hooves on well-packed earth. Red-tailed hawks rule the skies and only the rare intrusion of an airplane reminds the rider that a more complicated world might still exist somewhere in the distance.

We trailered the horses and gear in late one afternoon and set up camp. I awoke the next morning to the delicious aroma of wood smoke and Ed's coffee. The sound of horses munching breakfast hay bags and stamping contentedly was enough to make you think your bed roll had been transported, while you slept, to another time in a distant past.

I always teach a young horse patience by giving him the opportunity to stand tied to something unbreakable for extended periods, so Buddy had tolerated the night fairly well tied to the trailer with hay and water within easy reach. On several occasions, however, he had snorted and danced around like he fully expected Big Foot or something equally dangerous to jump out of the woods with the intention of adding a little horse meat to his diet. Much to his surprise, sunrise found Buddy with all his body parts intact, even if his mind was a little frazzled. I saddled him after we both had breakfast, and we were soon on our way.

The first mile or so was a little bouncy. Buddy was excited, and as a recently retired breeding stallion, he had very little platonic experience with other horses. He was a little confused and expended a lot of energy going sideways. In fact, I was beginning to think he might make a dressage horse, since he was obviously so adept at lateral work. Since the first part of the trail was on an open flat, I wasn't too worried.

We topped a ridge and were treated to a view of the beautiful, deep valley rimmed by the Brooks Trail Loop. Here, the trail narrowed considerably. Although it would not be considered dangerous for a normal horse, for one that insisted on showing off his ability for walking sideways, it presented a challenge.

On one side of the trail was the mountain. On the other side, there was nothing but air and the tops of redwood trees whose roots were in the valley floor two hundred feet below. Common sense would dictate that one's attention be divided between the trail directly in front and the airy precipice immediately to our right. However, Buddy's rear legs slipped off the trail repeatedly as he kept looking uphill to our left. I don't know if he was looking for monsters, bird watching, or just enjoying the feeling of my nervous "pucker," but it made for an *interesting* ride. As my blood pressure had risen to the point of delirium, I was beginning to think it was pretty funny. Here we were, about to fall over the side of a two-hundred-foot canyon, and Buddy was worried about what was *uphill*! The concept of gravity had not apparently been of much concern to this horse, and I was running out of ways to explain it to him.

This became a pattern that persisted most of the day, much to the delight of Ed and Susan. As the anti-suicide portion of my brain engaged, I considered stepping off this maniac on the uphill side and giving him a shove over the edge. Fortunately, or unfortunately, common sense got the better of me, and I refrained from such behavior because I really liked the saddle I had on him and couldn't stand the thought of scratching it up.

I returned to camp that evening somewhat rattled but physically intact with hopes for a more relaxing ride the following day. I unsaddled Buddy and tied him to the trailer with some doubts about our future together. I brushed some of the sweat off both of us and hung a hay bag for him before I walked over to where Ed and Susan had camped. We warmed ourselves over the fire and had a delightful supper. Conversation was light, but Ed couldn't resist a few digs about my trail horse.

"You told us that horse was a Thoroughbred, Doc, but I think he's part crab. I have never seen anything walk sideways for that long!"

The next morning, we headed out the same grassy flat toward the Brooks Trail Loop. The other horses were more subdued than they had been the previous morning, either from familiarity with the terrain or mild fatigue. Buddy, on the contrary, acted as if he planned to repeat the "horse imitates large crustacean" performance he had given the previous day. His back feet continued to slip over the edge of the trail while he focused on something just plain fascinating farther up the hill. Exactly *what* it was is unknown to this day. We again survived the day, and my heart eventually regained its natural rhythm, but I was less amused than I had been previously.

Although he lost his interest with the uphill part of the trail, Buddy never lost his sense of humor about other things. While saddling, I usually expect my horses to stand still without being tied to anything. This may seem a little inconsistent with my previous tying lessons, but it is the basis for "ground tying," a skill that needs to be established early. I let the lead rope or reins drag the ground while I brush the dirt off the horse's back, saddle up, and pick out the feet. If the horse starts to walk off, I put him back where we started, say "Whoa" once, and go back to what I was doing to him when he lost focus and walked off. Gradually, I can leave him "ground tied" this way for longer and longer periods until, eventually, I can walk away from him, and he will stay put. It takes practice, but many "normal" horses will retain good manners like this with only an occasional "Whoa" for correction.

Early in our relationship, Buddy taught me never to use his name and "normal" in the same sentence. Oh, he picked up the ground tying business all right, and he quickly learned *anything* I was smart enough to teach him. He did have some occasional, convenient lapses of memory, however.

By the second year we went to Jack Brooks' Horse Camp, Buddy had given up his crab-walking exercise. He'd had plenty of practice launching me into the spacious California skies, as you've heard in earlier stories, and he did manage to learn about ground tying, too. He was a reasonably green-broke horse for our second trip to the redwoods together.

We were on a particularly narrow and steep trail one cool, fall morning. We had been going for about four hours and were headed back to camp, about two miles out. Buddy had lulled me into a false security by acting uncharacteristically sane, and I was enjoying the sights. I had leaned my head way back to look up at the dizzying heights of the redwoods as we glided silently over the moist thatch on the forest floor. I was so engrossed in the sensation that my hat fell off. The trail was very narrow, but luckily, the hat fell directly over Buddy's substantial butt and landed on the trail behind us.

There was no place to tie a horse on this part of the trail, so, trusting Buddy to remember his ground tying manners, I got off on the uphill side and dropped the reins on the ground as I went back to retrieve my hat. I turned to get back into the saddle, and Buddy walked away two or three steps—just far enough away so I couldn't reach him. He didn't run away like he normally did after he bucked me off, he just stuck his chin out to one side so he wouldn't step on the reins, walked a few steps, and then stopped and looked at me. I'd tell him, "Whoa," and advance a few steps toward him, but every time I got almost close enough to touch him, he would walk away, stop, and *grin* at me. I know this sounds crazy, but Buddy, in a very devious and calculating way, could grin. He soon tired of this game, and sticking his chin out to one side, trotted down the trail toward camp as if he fully intended to return triumphantly riderless. I didn't mind the walk back to camp, but the thought of being mercilessly ridiculed by my so-called friends was too much to take. I began to holler "Whoa!" a little more emphatically. As this failed miserably, I launched a shameless tirade accusing Buddy of possessing canine ancestry and unnatural proclivities toward close relatives.

This got his attention, but I am uncertain as to whether the content or simply the volume of my speech was responsible for its effectiveness. About two hundred yards down the trail, he stopped, heaved a disgusted sigh, and waited for me to catch up and get on. I fully expected Buddy to walk away again, like Lucy predictably pulling the football away as Charlie Brown runs up to kick it. Ever the surprising one, Buddy stood there with that stupid grin on his face that fairly screamed, *GOTCHA!* and let me back into the saddle like absolutely nothing had happened.

Ever since there were only two horsemen on the face of the earth, they have argued about the relative intelligence, or lack thereof, in the beast they held in some affection. Is the dumb one easier to train, or is the smart one? (I still haven't figured out which category would contain Buddy.) Anyway, he *never* pulled that walk-away stunt again—that is, until about two years later.

It was a drizzly, early spring day, and I decided to take off for a ride and picnic up at Jack Brooks'. The fact that it was raining didn't slow me down any; I had good rain gear and was in no danger of melting. Buddy and I had the entire park to ourselves. The rain had just about stopped as we rounded the bend where the Brooks Trail Loop gave us a beautiful view of the canyon where silent treetops peeked through misty gray clouds. We headed down the trail, grateful for the view, and accompanied only by the softly squeaking sound of damp saddle leather and the clean smell of a freshly washed redwood forest.

The first two miles passed uneventfully. We came to a familiar, steep, narrow piece of trail where a sapling had blown over. I dismounted, dropped the reins and started to remove the obstacle. Having completed the task, I headed back toward Buddy. He waited until I was within about three feet of him, and then abruptly turned around and walked off about three steps, with his chin stuck out to one side so he wouldn't step on the reins, and looked at me with a knowing grin.

Since the *last* time he'd played this mind game, Buddy had spent many hours ground tied while he waited for me to get "one more thing" out of the back of the truck. He had not repeated the act once. Now, there we were, less than a hundred yards but two years away from the scene of his first mental victory, and he pulled it again! He finally stopped after about thirty feet. I guess he figured that was all he needed now to make his point.

_ Training, Tendonitis, and a Tree-Climbing Toyota

I was daydreaming when the phone rang. It was a steamy, early summer morning, and I was wondering how I was going to stand three more months of interminable heat. Though the temperature was really bothering me, it didn't seem to bother my patients very much. Well-meaning horse owners often thoughtfully put up shelters in pastures that lack much shade. This is apparently wasted on some horses, because I commonly see them standing out in the sun (or rain, sleet, hail…whatever) instead of inside. I guess the owners feel better for offering alternatives.

The phone broke my stream of consciousness and pulled me back into the perspiring present. A young lady had some minor concerns about swellings on the lower legs of her endurance horse.

"It's probably nothing," she started, "but I have a young Mustang that has the potential to be a world-class endurance horse, and I don't want to over-train him."

This was not the first time I'd heard concern about swollen legs, but "over-training" *was* a first. We made an appointment for the next day. She didn't seem too worried, so I didn't think another day would matter.

I pulled into Kerry's yard and saw Duster standing tied to a live oak just about ankle deep in mud—with shade from the tree offering little relief from the heat. I quickly learned of Duster's history. He was a BLM adoptee that Kerry had recently acquired at an "Adopt a Mustang" event nearby.

During the late 1980s, the Bureau of Land Management (BLM) was trying to solve the problems caused by the overpopulation of feral horses on public lands. The "Adopt a Mustang Program" was just one of many attempts to control an amazingly fertile group of horses. Cattle ranchers were leasing government land for grazing, and the feral horses severely limited the amount of grass available to ranchers' livestock. One solution was to round up the horses and take them to slaughter. This had become a major public relations nightmare, and the BLM was trying to appease the animal rights groups and the ranchers at the same time: no mean feat.

Many people think that adopting a Mustang is the way to get a horse cheap. In addition, the "wild Mustang, never been touched by human hands" label carries a romantic mystique that is irresistible to some people who have "always wanted a horse." Kerry was one of these folks.

I have met quite a few of these BLM horses, and they tend to be pretty reasonable to get along with. I think that some of the most contrary get "weeded out" by default—if they can't be caught and haltered, they aren't going to be standing tied to a live oak tree. However, these horses have been the subject of more than a few veterinary train wrecks, and little did I know, this was about to be another one.

I introduced myself to Kerry with a handshake and to Duster by gently scratching his withers. He responded by lowering his head and licking and chewing to indicate he was in his mental comfort zone. He had very swollen front legs from just beneath the knees extending all the way to the coronet. When they teach you about diagnostics in vet school, "signalment and history" are drilled into your head until you can recite them in your sleep.

The "signalment" is the age, sex, breed, and use of the horse. It is important in our diagnostic plan because it gives us an automatic "rule out" for lots of things. A four-year-old gelding is not likely to have "Cushing's disease" (found only in *old* horses) or testicular cancer (you get the drift—he's a *gelding*). The "history" is an outline of where he's been, what he's been doing recently, and any medical problems he may have had. For example, if I knew that Duster had just walked over a hornet's nest, I probably wouldn't use the ultrasound to see if he had tendonitis.

The signalment and history told me exactly what I needed to know. She had been riding the horse for about thirty days and had entered him in a twenty-five-mile endurance race the past Saturday. Kerry was as kind and compassionate as she could be, but she was pretty new with horses and really needed some help.

"So how long has he been in training?" I needed to be sure I heard her correctly, as most endurance trainers wouldn't even think of entering a race without months of training, covering hundreds of miles.

"Oh, we have been in very intense training for a month," she emphasized *month.* "So I know he is fit…I couldn't hold him back!" This was more a testimony of the athletic desire of the horse than anything else. (It was not good manners that stopped me from saying this, but rather years of reaping the unpleasant consequences of my too-quick tongue.)

I looked at Duster's swollen legs and suspected we were looking at some severe "tendonitis." The common term "bowed tendon" is what horse people call it. The tendon on the back of the leg below the knee or hock becomes very swollen or "bowed" due to trauma or prolonged stress. A single kick to a pipe panel can do as much damage to a tendon as a twenty-five-mile race can do to an unfit horse, but repeated bouts of moderate stress was likely the cause of the problem in this case.

When I untied Duster to walk him out of the mud, I realized a really bad situation just got worse. He was lame. Really lame. A quick exam of his feet revealed heat and a pounding pulse: Duster had laminitis. (I've discussed both tendonitis and laminitis in earlier chapters.)

I took a deep breath and said, "Well, Duster has some problems." The look on Kerry's face was hard to read. I continued, "He has tendonitis, or severely damaged tendons, and laminitis, which is severe inflammation in both front feet."

"I caused this," she said, but before I could say anything she added, "I was afraid of over-training. I guess I did."

I stood there looking at a good horse that was severely injured—maybe irreparably—and felt a little "righteous indignation" rising up in me. I sure wanted to holler and lecture a little. However, as bad as I felt for Duster, it was pretty hard to get mad at somebody who made an honest mistake. As a young boy, I had done the exact same thing to my very first horse. She wasn't the best horse who ever looked through a bridle by any stretch, but no horse deserves what I did to her. I wasn't cruel, just ignorant, and I got a sense that the same thing had happened here. It was a painful lesson for both of us, so I had some empathy with my young new client.

Kerry was green, and like me in my younger days, was learning some hard lessons. I explained to her the process causing both problems and as gently as

I could, told her that this was not from "over-training," but that this horse had not really been "trained" at all!

I outlined a treatment plan for Duster and explained to Kerry that the chances for him returning as an endurance horse were pretty slim. I explained the reason for training for fitness and just what a labor-intense process it was. This was not a commitment of weeks but one that would require months to *years* to achieve the level of fitness necessary to compete on any level of endurance riding. She was saddened by this news. I asked her if she would like a short description of fitness training, and she said yes, and that she was eager to learn.

I explained the training process to her like this: "The horse in motion is one of the most inspiring in all of God's creation. There are few things more exhilarating than seeing the world framed in a set of horse ears. We can sit on their backs and ask them to go places they would not normally go, and they comply. They carry us readily as they have throughout history into our fields, into our cities, and into our wars. From the standpoint of the horse, what we ask them to do is not 'natural,' yet they serve us willingly and usually without question. It is our duty to care for them—not like we change the oil in our pickup, but rather as stewards of a marvelous gift. The beauty of the horse is apparent to everyone, but to the true horseman, it is the horse's athletic ability that makes him so treasured. We can 'train' them to perform the tasks we desire, but without the proper physical conditioning, no horse can reach his genetic potential, and we are not providing the best care if we ask for performance beyond these boundaries.

"At the most basic level, 'training' is getting a desired response from the horse when we ask him to move his feet—or stop moving them. When you really think about it— stop, start, left, right, sideways, back up—there aren't a whole lot of other options. Once these are mastered, he can run barrels, perform 'dressage,' or leap tall buildings at a single bound—at our request! There are a lot of books and videos about just *exactly* how to do this, but the one thing that is missing from most of these is *training for fitness*. A fit horse is a sound horse. In my practice, I see quite a few lame horses. These are usually horses that are 'parked' most of the time. Conversely, properly conditioned endurance or polo horses are rarely presented to me for lameness. This is a classic 'use it or lose it' situation."

Many years ago, I knew a veterinarian who was also a polo player in Argentina. He was a four- or five-goal player, which means he was a good 'un. I asked him how he had the time to keep his ponies fit. He said most of his polo colleagues had "day jobs" and hired kids to keep their horses "legged up." He said it wasn't complicated. The kid would show up at his barn at daylight, saddle the first horse and tie the other nine head to tail and take off at a dead run. The kid would ride all ten horses that day, switching every hour or so and come back about dark. After three or four months of this seven-day-a-week regimen, all his horses were pretty fit and almost never broke down.

A horse is by no means a simple animal, he is not just a motorcycle with a brain. There is something unique about a horse, whether we are just watching him run across a field, or actually feeling him between our knees while he is nearly flying (if you haven't experienced it, I can't describe it to you). How the body systems of these amazing athletes work together is truly fascinating science.

About a year later, Kerry called me again. Again, it was Monday, and she had been pulled from an endurance ride on Saturday. As I drove through the gate of her place, I saw my buddy Brian's pickup parked along the road, leading up to the ranch house. This part of the country was pretty rugged with fairly deep ravines cut into the side of the hills. A little way up the road, I saw him standing on the edge of a deep cut where you could see into the treetops at about eye level. You could almost step into the top of the tree about thirty feet up from bottom of the little canyon. Then I saw what he was looking at: a late model Toyota was stuck in the top of the tree. I thought, *Now that's something you don't see every day.*

Apparently, Kerry had moved her Dad's car, the aforementioned late model Toyota, for some reason. She must have skipped some aspect of the proper parking procedure, and this break in protocol resulted in the unorthodox placement of the car in the tree. Although I was clearly out of my realm of expertise, I asked Brian if I could help (like *I* could help?). Brian just shrugged his shoulders, so I left him to his parking problem to see what Kerry had for me.

I got to the house and there was a horse tied to a tree—different horse, same tree I found Duster under a year before. This was another pretty stylish BLM gelding—I could tell by the freeze brand on his neck.

Kerry came out of the house, and we exchanged pleasantries that did not include the Toyota perched in the oak tree near the gate. She proceeded to tell me about the endurance ride two days ago and how the vets there pulled her horse from the race.

"I guess they thought he had a problem," she said, sounding a little frustrated, "but I think he just needed some more time for his 'P&R' to adjust."

During endurance rides, there are periodic vet checks to ensure the health and safety of the horses. If the "P&R" (pulse and respiration) rates do not come down to normal limits in a certain time, the horse cannot continue. A fit horse will have normal P&Rs within the allotted time.

I listened to the new horse's heart and lungs with a stethoscope. I was astounded. This was two days after the race, and he was still in something called a "metabolic inversion." As you learned earlier in this book, normally, the resting heart rate of a horse is about forty beats per minute and the respiration is about twelve breaths per minute. This horse had a pulse of sixty and a respiration of eighty: a metabolic inversion. This meant his metabolism was so stressed that he was literally trying to "blow" carbon dioxide out of his bloodstream. It is a complicated situation, and not one that should last for two hours, much less two days.

I initiated treatment for the obvious acid/base imbalance, pain, and dehydration. In the field, without lab support, it's a guess as to just how "acidotic" a horse may be—how much acid is in his blood. Apparently, I guessed right, because the horse lived.

Treating the horse was relatively simple. Treating Kerry proved to be something altogether different. I was trying to figure out what to say. I thought I had explained the basics about fitness when we were trying to help Duster, but here we were, a year later, and though I wouldn't have thought it was possible, things were worse! This poor horse wasn't any more ready to compete in a twenty-five-mile race than Duster had been.

I was just about to start my lecture when she solved my problem.

"I have read a lot about endurance horses since the last time you were here. I should have followed my instincts, because I know this is all due to over-training, and I'm just sick about it!"

This time it was my turn to shrug my shoulders. I packed up my equipment and went back to the tree-climbing, over-trained Toyota thinking maybe I should have stayed to help Brian after all.

Buyer Beware

*The term "horse trader" conjures up characters
that are often associated with some of God's
less-than-noble children. While most people are basically
honest, some horse traders are a little bipolar
in the integrity department. And, amazingly,
some buyers sorta fall into the mindset, "
A lie is not a lie if the truth is not expected."
So "buyer beware" applies to the purchase
of just about anything with four feet—especially horses.*

CHAPTER

9

_ "He's Just a Yearling"

When I was a bright, young veterinarian just starting practice back in the eighties, I got a phone call from a man named Bob Gray who lived out of state. He asked me if I was available for a pre-purchase exam on a real good colt that he was thinking about buying. In those early days of my practice, this was like asking my cat if he was available for a can of tuna and a nap! I was so eager to practice medicine, I would have vaccinated his goldfish.

"When would you like me to look at this colt," I asked while I thumbed through my nearly-empty appointment book. "I'll try to work you into my schedule." I took a deep breath and hoped that I had not violated some part of the veterinary oath.

"Any time would be okay with me," he said. "I won't be able to be there when you look at him, so just do it when it is convenient for you." The voice came over the phone like a ray of hope, saving me from having to enroll in the Ace Truck Driving School to keep from starving. "The colt has some great bloodlines, and I am planning on using him as a foundation sire in my breeding program. If you find anything wrong with him, I need to know about it. This is a real expensive horse, and I don't want any surprises. He's just a yearling now, but I have a lot of hope for him." Mr. Gray paused, then repeated: "He has great bloodlines."

I had no idea that this last phrase would come to haunt me for years.

Bob gave me the name and phone number of the lady who owned the colt in question. I called Carla, and we made an appointment for later in the week. She was friendly enough but let me know clearly that there was nothing wrong with the colt. If Mr. Gray considered a prepurchase exam necessary, that was "all right with her."

I have never considered myself a distrusting fellow, but I have been involved in enough horse trades over the years to realize their potential to bring out the scariest parts of human nature. In addition, I have purchased enough lame, crazy, crippled and just overall *bad* horses to become, well, "cautious" when dealing with the buying and selling of horses.

For example, when I was still a student, way back in the early seventies, one of the ways that I supported my college habit was by riding colts for people and trading a few horses myself. One time I bought a big, stout, red, *four-year-old* gelding that I called Red Man. I rode him for quite a while as he had about every bad habit a horse could have. When I finally sold him, he was about *fifteen* years old. I didn't ride him that long, he just wasn't that young! I took quite a beating physically and economically, as this old snide had crippled a couple of local cowboys before I got him, and he hadn't seen his fourth birthday since LBJ was president.

Some of life's best lessons are also its toughest, and I was lucky to have survived that one. It did motivate me to learn how to tell the age of a horse by looking at his teeth, and I got pretty good at it out of economic necessity.

A horse has three pairs of incisor teeth that are easily seen in the front of his mouth. These are named from the center of his mouth outward. The central pair are, of course, in the middle, the intermediate pair are next, to the left and right of the centrals, and the corners are on the extreme outside. They are the same for both upper and lower jaws. A foal is born before any incisor teeth are erupted, but they appear fairly predictably, though variations occur.

Any broodmare will tell you that the central pair of incisors will erupt in a foal about the seventh day of life. (Readers that have nursed a child know the sensation!) Most lactating mares agree that this is way too soon for their own comfort, but it is part of the foal's natural growth process, and the mares seem to survive in spite of it. The intermediate pairs erupt at about seven weeks, and the corners at about seven months. These are all "deciduous," or "baby," teeth. Adult teeth replace their deciduous predecessors in an equally predictable fashion at two and a half, three and a half, and four and a half years in the same order, from central to intermediate to corner pairs, respectively.

Baby teeth are smaller, whiter and more "pinched" at the gum line than adult teeth. So with practice, it's not difficult to learn how to age a horse with a fair degree of accuracy. After a horse has reached the age of ten, there is more guess work involved, but, up to that time, it would be unusual for an experienced hand to be more than a year off in estimating the age of a horse by his teeth.

I arrived at Carla's ranch at the appointed time to examine a big, stout, clean-legged colt. It was easy to see why Mr. Gray was interested in this colt as a stallion prospect because he sure was nice. He moved around the lot like his feet just barely touched the ground, and his long, flowing mane and tail gave me the impression that he was on the verge of flying. He was a little snorty, and I had to rope him in a small pipe corral to catch him. Carla said that they had weaned him late, and they hadn't taken the time to handle him much.

Not only was he hard to catch, he was pretty narrow-minded about any kind of veterinary examination. He would not let me pick up his feet, or listen to his heart and lungs, or even look in his mouth.

"Maybe we could watch him move around in the round ring," I suggested, "and let him blow off a little steam so we can examine him."

I watched the colt run around and over the ranch hand on the way to the round pen, and I admired the athletic ability of both of them. After about forty-five minutes of watching this colt circle the man at nothing less than a dead run, he slowed down a little, and I thought that maybe I could complete some kind of exam on him. We steered him back into that little bitty pipe pen, with the hired hand leading and me driving him from behind by waving my hat and clucking at him when he balked. It looked to me like this was the colt's first lesson in leading, and it wasn't much easier to approach this time than it had been earlier.

I had handled a few salty colts, so I was used to the certain lack of enthusiasm that some horses have for human contact. I was beginning to wonder just how old this colt was, because he sure seemed big for a yearling, and he had that beautiful long, flowing mane and tail. Anyone that has ever had a tail chewed off a show mare by a colt or a bored stablemate can tell you that it takes a *long time* to grow much tail. (That is the reason that so many show horses go around with their tails braided and in protective wraps or bags.) Anyway, this colt was not about to tell me how old he was, and he was in no mood for a dental exam.

With the help of the hired hand, I got a "twitch" on the upper lip of this good-but-reluctant colt. A twitch is a rather barbaric-looking, clamping or twisting apparatus that is sometimes placed on the upper lip of an uncooperative horse. I almost never use these things because I believe that patience and finesse are superior to brute force, but I was running out of both of those virtues, and I couldn't think of another way to look in this colt's mouth. The twitch calmed him down considerably. He bit at me a few times, but I did get a good look just before he struck at me with both front feet.

Just as I had suspected, he had *adult* central incisors and was in the process of shedding his intermediates. With all the diplomacy I could muster, I suggested to Carla that there must be some mistake because the horse Mr. Gray was interested in was a yearling, and *this colt* was about to turn four years old.

"No he's not," she said coolly. "He's a yearling. He has excellent bloodlines, and I have the papers to prove it." And she did, too—she showed them to me like she fully expected that it would change my mind. Butter wouldn't have melted in her mouth for a couple of days. This lady was *unflappable.*

"I can't argue that you have the papers for *some* yearling colt, but this ain't him!" I exclaimed, with some of my diplomacy waning. This lady's attitude was making me more suspicious by the minute. She was just too complacent about the whole thing. If somebody had pointed out such a discrepancy about one of my horses, I would have become a little agitated, at least. But she just looked at me.

All the way back home, I wondered about what had just happened. I could be six months or a year off in my estimation of the colt's age, but not *two and a half years*!

I called Bob Gray later that evening.

"Well, what did you think about the colt?" he asked.

"He's not a bad horse," I said. "In fact, I was rather impressed by the colt I looked at, but he may not be what you think he is. Have you ever seen him?" I asked.

"Well, no, not in person," he said. "I've seen pictures of him, and he has outstanding bloodlines," he added that line again. Then, "What do you mean, 'He's not what I think he is'?" he asked after a long pause.

"The horse Carla showed me today is coming four this spring. He's not a yearling."

"That can't be!" He was shocked. "He has such good bloodlines. There must be some mistake."

By now, the genetics of the situation was becoming rather amusing. I was beginning to wonder what happened to the horse that matched the papers they were trying to pass off with this colt. After all, an unregistered four-year-old is worth a lot less than a yearling "with such good bloodlines" and all the papers to prove it.

"Well," he said, "thanks for all your help, Doc. Go ahead and write up the health papers for him, please. I'd like to ship him out here right away."

I did and he did. I don't know how this horse did at stud, but I wonder if his papers really improved his popularity.

_ Mules for Sale

It was midsummer and my friend and client, Alex, was looking for a pair of saddle mules. He had recently retired and was comfortable enough to enjoy some time in the high-country a-horseback. He had tried several horses, but he and his wife had not found a good match—Alex suffered from back pain and was looking for some kind of horse that wouldn't jar him so much to make the pain of riding outweigh the pleasure of it. Someone told him he should try a mule.

So he called me one Friday afternoon.

"Hey, Doc," he began. "You told me I should contact you before I bought a horse, so I'm hoping you can help me now." He had been searching for just the right mounts for him and his wife for a few months, and I had offered my assistance in the past.

"I'm always glad to help," I replied. "Where is he?"

"He's down near Salt Lake City, and I was hoping you had some vet contacts who could help me there."

He gave me the name of the town. I didn't know any vets there, but I had an old buddy who lived nearby, so I thought I could find someone.

"When are you going?"

"I'm on my way now. Should be there in about five hours."

"Well...THANKS FOR THE ADVANCED NOTICE!" I didn't exactly yell into the phone, but I'm pretty sure he felt my good-natured chastisement.

"I figured that such an influential member of the veterinary community could just wave his magic wand and make this happen!" he quipped. "We're planning on staying a few days, so maybe someone can work us into a schedule."

"Well, I appreciate your inflated view of my professional status, but my magic wand is in the shop—along with my crystal ball. And, if I had a magic wand, I'd just stir up a couple of mules here in Idaho and save you the trip! I'll see what I can do and call you back in a while."

So I called my old buddy in the Salt-Lake-City area, and he gave me the name of the local vet who did *some* equine work. He didn't know her personally, but said he'd heard good things about her. I called both the numbers he gave me, but they went directly to voicemail. This is a common thing for vets, as most of us are pretty busy. So I left my name and phone number, explained what Alex needed in the way of a pre-purchase exam, and the name of the guy with the mules.

After a few hours...crickets. I was a little dismayed that the Utah vet had not returned my calls. Calls to her from Alex went unanswered, as well. This was fairly unusual. I have never been too busy that I didn't respond to the call of another vet, especially one out of state with a request similar to the one I made, unless there was a reason not to. Maybe she didn't especially care for mules, or maybe, just maybe there was a "history" with the seller.

I didn't hear anything from Alex for a few days. Then the phone buzzed in my pocket.

"Hey Doc, I wonder if you could stop by sometime soon, I got some questions on the mules I bought."

"What did the Utah vet say?" I asked, already knowing that if Alex had questions at this early date, either the Utah vet never saw these mules, or we were about to experience some unpleasant surprises.

I pulled into the barnyard on that bright, hot day to find two mules tied to the fence. One was real quiet, the other one was pretty unhappy about her new association with a fence post, as she pawed, danced, and raised a small plume of dust to indicate her opinion of her new accommodations.

"Howdy, Doc. Meet 'Molly' and 'John.'" This was a clever appellation, as the generic name for a mule is not "mare" and "gelding," but rather, "molly" and "john." "I never could get a vet out," he began explaining, "but the seller guaranteed 'em for a month, so we got time for you to look 'em over."

This "money back guarantee" was a fairly common ruse employed by horse traders when the buyer is out of state. They figure that if something turns out wrong, or the new "owner" discovers the horses' secrets, the buyer won't bother with the time and expense of hauling 'em back. This was cleverly termed a "tail light guarantee"—meaning the warrantee expired as soon as the tail lights of your trailer disappeared from the seller's barn. It is neither fair nor honest, but it happens with predictable regularity.

"Molly is twelve," Alex began, "and we told 'em we didn't want anything younger than nine, so the trader said that John was nine. Molly is real broke— the guy said she was a champion reining mule, second in the world." I hadn't known there was such a thing as a "reining mule." Alex continued, "but John is a little green. What do you think?"

Molly was a medium-sized, plain red mule with *no* white markings. (The absence of any white markings would become significant.) The most striking thing about her, other than her apparent hatred for Alex's fence posts, is that she had real small feet. Real small. She looked like a full-grown man still wearing the boots he had in the third grade. The heels were collapsed and under-run. This was not a good sign.

When seen from the side, the angle the toe of the hoof strikes the ground should be parallel to that of the heel. When seen from the bottom, the heel should be just about as wide as the foot is at the tip of the frog. Molly's feet did not have this conformation. "Collapsed, under-run heels" means the "digital cushion," the soft tissue structure under the frog, is failing, and it is the beginning of lots of problems. In the beginning, it may not present as severe lameness, but it will often be the source of problems later on. Buying a horse (or mule) with this type of foot poses a new set of risks in a transaction with enough risks already.

It gets better.

I was a little surprised when I checked Molly's teeth, as she had the mouth of a seven- or eight-year-old mule, not twelve. Aging an equine by their teeth can get a little "iffy," but you ain't gonna miss five years on many younger animals. She was apparently registered with the American Mule Association. This increased her value and was used as her proof of age.

The AMA is kind of an interesting "breed association," since mules are sterile. Mules are the hybrid cross of a male donkey and female horse. I often wondered who the first person was that decided this was a good idea, but it apparently worked out okay. In an interesting twist of nature, the cross between a stallion and a female donkey is not the same as a mule. This hybrid is called a "hinny." Hinnies are quite rare; they look more horse than a donkey, with a more horse-like head and shorter ears. But, like a mule, the hinny is also sterile.

The fact that Alex's molly mule had absolutely no distinguishing or identifying markings made it relatively easy to switch the papers. I didn't accuse the seller of doing anything unscrupulous (he may have bought the molly under similar circumstances—thinking she had papers), but a "registered" twelve-year-old is generally worth more than and "unregistered" eight-year-old so there was some incentive to get careless with the documentation.

Molly also had some abnormal fat deposits along her top line. This was more than just a fat mule. The lumpy deposits were an indication of something called "metabolic syndrome." These equines have a tendency to become insulin-resistant—it is sort of a "horse diabetes." This, in turn, can result in damage to blood vessels, immune suppression, and laminitis. When I observed Molly trotting on the longe line in a fairly soft footing, she was a little short-strided. This could have been an indication of lameness, or it could have been just the way she moved.

The three problems I detected so quickly were some big red flags. And....most "real broke" horses will stand quietly without a lot of fuss. I mentioned this to Alex. This made him unhappy. The remainder of the exam didn't do much to improve his mood.

After an uncomfortably long silence, he said, "What? You mean Molly will need special shoes, special diet, and we still might have problems later? And why would they tell us she was older than she is? Wouldn't most horse traders want to take years *off* the horse, rather than *add* to 'em?"

"Good point," I began, "but a couple of things to consider here. First, a twelve-year-old, registered plain red mule is worth more than a seven-year-old, un-registered one. I don't know why registration adds value to a mule, you sure ain't gonna breed her, but this is the way it goes in most cases. With no white markings, it is not inconceivable that someone *mistakenly* thought Molly was registered." (I wrinkled my face to emphasize the sarcasm of "mistakenly" as I wink-wink-nudge-nudged that the papers did not *exactly* belong to the molly.)

"We paid a lot of money for these mules," he replied, and he told me exactly what he paid—the price of a fairly nice car. I was...impressed.

"Well, it looks like there was some confusion about exactly which molly this was," I responded tactfully. In reality, bad horse trader tricks don't happen very often. Most people are pretty honest when selling horses, especially traders or breeders, as they depend on repeat business. You don't have to cheat someone very often to spoil their desire to do business with you. But I've been around long enough to have seen about every bad trick there is, so I was suspicious.

My suspicion was not diminished when I looked at John. He was small, about thirteen hands tall, and the dark gray "steel dust" color we wish all gray horses would retain. Gray horses are born black or dark red. The gray hairs take over as they age, so by about ten years or so, most are completely white. The steel dust color usually appears between four and nine years, and this mule was a little more "steel" than "dust." So it was no real shock when I looked in his mouth and found baby teeth in his corners. (Remember: Baby teeth are smaller, whiter, and more pinched at the gum line than adult incisors.) This meant he had the mouth of a four-year-old. I told Alex that determining the age of a horse by looking at teeth is part art and part science, but baby teeth are never seen in a nine-year-old mule. Ever.

It got better.

If the mouth of this young mule wasn't enough to make me "prick my ears," there was something else. It was subtle, almost imperceptible. But after a few minutes, it came through loud and clear: *This young mule was awful quiet.*

In reality, most mules are pretty quiet, at least when they are just standing tied. When they are expressing their opinion on something they deem controversial, like receiving veterinary care, for instance, their placid nature can quickly evolve to the "fight-or-flight" mode for which they are famous. A horse will "kick at you" occasionally, but a mule will "kick you" with uncanny accuracy and live forty years just to get even once. So this particular horse trade was not passing the smell test on many levels, and my "BS meter" was being severely tickled. I rarely saw horses that were drugged prior to a sale, but it happened. I was seriously wondering if John had been the recipient of some pharmacologic assistance prior to his presentation to Alex. The good thing about a prospective buyer having possession of the animal in question for a few days is that most drugs wear off in a day or two. Knowing this helps allay fears that there is something in the horse (or, in this case, mule) that may help him "keep his secrets"—like lameness, for instance. But there is one sedating drug, "fluphenazine," that lasts a long, long time—about a month, in some equines. It is used by veterinarians for horses that need help coping with long-term convalescence from an injury, or those who are not real cooperative about bandage changes or other forms of treatment they think unreasonable. Although it is not legal for a non-vet to have the stuff, it ain't impossible to get. If you know the "right people"—I guess they really are the "wrong people" (let's just call them "undocumented pharmaceutical reps" to be politically correct)—you can buy anything.

Although I almost never even broach the subject of a horse being drugged, this alligator in the bathtub was starting to nibble on my toes. I sure didn't want to accuse anyone of sedating a sale horse, as it would hurt some feelings—to the point of legal ramifications in some cases—but I needed to act on behalf of my client. In view of everything else I had seen thus far in Molly and John, it wasn't much of stretch to assume chemical assistance was part of this trade.

Cautiously, I mentioned this to Alex.

"You really think they may have drugged him?" he asked. "I guess I want to send Molly back to the guy, but I would like to proceed with the exam on John."

"Everything I have seen about these two makes me real suspicious," I replied. "And we need to consider the presence of drugs here. They may affect the exam. A horse on heavy-duty pain meds or tranquilizers will not respond to a lameness workup the way he would in his natural state. I'd be real cautious about this now. We might consider some blood tests for drugs before we get into this any further."

I pulled a blood sample from John, hoping I was wrong, and that he really was just a real quiet four-year-old. Then Alex said, "You know, Doc, I think we better wait on this. We still have a month to decide. I have this in writing." He paused. "I don't want to buy more problems, but I guess I need to talk to this guy before we do much more."

I called Alex the next day to find out what the trader said. He said he had not heard from him, so he guessed he was out of town, or just busy. He told me he had two farriers look at Molly and both said that corrective shoeing and possible lameness was definitely in her future. I was glad Alex had a bit more ammunition for the next encounter with the mule man.

I said, "Not to be too negative about this, Alex, but you know he didn't think you were calling to tell him you got home safely! I'm thinking he's wondering just what to do next! Have you thought about stopping payment on the check?"

"I gave him cash."

"Well, you can't stop payment on cash," I exclaimed, "even in Idaho." It was a lame attempt to add a little levity to a serious situation. It failed. We were talking about a lot of money.

The guy did finally call back. According to Alex, the trader exploded his phone—calling him everything but Christian—accusing him of being stupid, ugly, and Republican!

"They told us not to sell our mules to the likes of you!" the seller screamed at Alex over the phone. I don't know who "they" were, or how "they" would know Alex—he was not part of the mule community and lived about six hours away.

This was where it got interesting, and educational.

I do a lot of "pre"-purchase exams to help people make the right decisions about buying or *not* buying a horse. I also do a fair number of "post"-purchase exams for people who chose not to spend the money before they bought somebody else's problem. I'll let that sink in a minute. This is usually painfully expensive for the new owner, and not the kind of job security I like!

In performing the pre-purchase exams, I try to have both buyer and seller present so both parties know what I'm seeing and my comments about any potential problems that arise in the process. (For most post-purchase events, the seller has apparently left the country, 'cuz in, many cases, you sure can't find 'em!) When I find a problem, sellers will predictably provide one of two types of responses. If they are surprised, they almost certainly didn't know "Ol' Rusty" was pigeon-toed, parrot-mouthed, and paralyzed. If they get mad, well it is an absolute, dead solid, perfect indication that the news—whatever it is—was really not "news" to them. They knew it all along, they are mad that the buyer knows it now, and they are more than willing to shoot the messenger—namely me!

So this guy's reaction on the phone was an absolute confession of his guilt in this mule trade. He confirmed it by his next statement. "I'm gonna come down there tomorrow and give you all your money back for Molly," he screamed so loud he really didn't need a telephone. I didn't really expect this guy to show up, but if he did, I was fully expecting him to "discount" his refund for the twelve-hour trip it took to reclaim the mule.

What happened next surprised even a skeptical old codger like me.

While I was talking with Alex, the mule trader was talking with Alex's wife on another cell phone. I could overhear her saying, "The vet's on the other phone with Alex. Would you like to talk with him?" Then, with both their phones on speaker mode, I was able to talk with the mule trader. I introduced myself and told him I had been in practice for thirty-five years with some fairly extensive experience with mules. He told me about his stellar reputation in the mule business and that Molly was the Number Two reining mule in the world. The pitch and volume of his voice was changing rapidly, and I could tell he was just about to explode at me for wrecking his mule trade.

I really hate to argue, and I am not good at any confrontation. In the Bible, in the book of Proverbs, King Solomon says, "A soft answer turns away wrath..." I have used this concept many times, and it almost never fails.

So I tried to avert the coming apocalypse. "I am so proud of you for stepping up and doing the right thing by giving Alex his money back. This is an honorable way to conduct business, and not common in this day and age. I know this is not easy for you, but doing the right thing is often difficult, so thank you."

There wasn't a whole lot the guy could say after that, but I sensed he was struggling real hard to say *something*. All he could muster was, "Goodbye."

I didn't call Alex the next day, but I was surely wishing I was a mouse in the haystack so I could see and hear what happened. On day two, my curiosity conquered what little sense of good manners remained, so I called Alex to find out what happened.

"I was just gonna call you," he exclaimed as he answered the phone. "The horse trader showed up yesterday afternoon and said he was gonna take Molly to *his* vet, who is a lameness EXPERT!"

I couldn't help mentioning that most vets specializing in horses do a lot of foot and leg work, but I was glad his was an "expert."

Alex went on, "When he got here, he said he was taking John, too! He did say he'd still sell me the tack that was part of the trade, but I told him, no, I'd take all my money, and he'd take all his possessions. This did not make him happy, but he gave me all my money back."

"What does that tell you about the true nature of John?" I asked.

"I think he figured we knew a few of his secrets," he replied, "and didn't want us to share 'em with somebody else. That's why they're secrets."

"I think you're right," I confirmed. "Why would you sacrifice a sale—even part of a sale—for that much money if you didn't have something to hide? I'm sorry you had to go through all of this. But I think this was the best possible outcome."

A few days later I got another call from Alex.

"I just heard from the mule man. He took Molly to 'his' vet, the lameness expert, and he said she was perfectly fine! So he says he's gonna put her back in the show ring."

I took this as more of a "neener, neener, neener" from the mule man, rather than a critique of my work from another veterinarian. After all, two farriers agreed with me. But the rebuke from the trader with the "stellar" reputation who couldn't tell a nine-year-old from a four-year-old was an interesting twist.

_ Saddle Horse for Sale

I must really love the horse business if the past forty-five years is any indication. Apparently, this is not just a passing fancy with me, because try as I will, I just can't quit. It's sorta like the guy who keeps hitting himself in the head with a large hammer because it feels so good when he stops. The fun part of the horse business is horse *people*, because in the words of no less a philosopher than Forrest Gump, "...you never know what you're gonna get!" I apparently get along well with other horse people because we share a common ailment. Since my phone keeps ringing, I must be doing okay.

One of the most challenging parts of being a horse doctor is the legendary "pre-purchase exam." Of the three things that can happen in the aftermath of examining a horse prior to purchase, two of them are bad.

Situation 1: The horse is perfect in every way, everybody is happy. (This is quite rare, but it does happen, I just can't remember when.)

Situation 2: The horse has a problem. This is much more common, and it often makes the seller unhappy. I am convinced that people are basically honest, and that most of the time the discovery of a problem is news to the seller. However, this usually puts a major dent in the deal. I am not there to add misery to the seller's life; I'm trying to protect the interest of my client, the potential buyer, by noticing possible problems. My goal is to facilitate the purchase by educating both parties to the presence *or absence* of problems.

Situation 3: The horse has a problem that doesn't get noticed until the buyer's check clears the bank and the seller has apparently been abducted by space aliens, because he is nowhere to be found. This is not common, but the scenario usually starts with a phone call that goes something like: "I don't know what's wrong with my new horse, Doc. He was gentle as puppy when they delivered him yesterday, but today he's run me out of the stall, kicking and biting at me like he's turned carnivorous all of a sudden!"

One day I had arrived at a barn for another fun-filled adventure in the wonderful world of pre-purchase evaluations. I wasn't looking forward to a visit to this particular barn because my previous visits had been unpleasant. Not excruciating, just unpleasant. I had a bad feeling about the barn manager/trainer the first time I met him, and unfortunately, he had repeatedly proved me right. He was from the Deep South—Georgia or Tennessee, I can't remember which—but he had that wonderful accent indigenous to that part of the world. Folks from that region have a unique way of speaking that lifts the last words in a sentence in such a way that it sounds like they are almost singing a question. Anyway, this trainer's name was Bubba, only, to hear him say it, it was more like "Bubber." (I guess anybody with a name like "Madison Seamans" doesn't have a lot of room to make fun of names.)

I could have listened to Bubba's delightful southern drawl all day long. He was quite a charmer, with his easy manner and a dialog that was seasoned with unique, down-home phrases that made me want to like him.

The horse in question was a big, stout, pretty, gray, gaited gelding that was an "honest ten years old," which is horse-trading lingo meaning that he had the teeth of a horse that *really was* about ten years old. Many horse traders will call an older horse "ten" because it sounds better than "twenty," and it can be a little tricky for most folks to tell the age of one older than ten even if they have looked in the mouths of a lot of horses. The gray horse had a lot of style and balance about him, but there were a couple of things that bothered me right off.

"Bubba," I said, "it looks like the hair on the backs of both front legs was shaved off about three months ago. Can you tell us about that?"

Old Gray, as the gelding was called, had the hair over the flexor tendons on both front legs just short enough to suggest that it had been shaved pretty close about sixty to ninety days previously. The troubling part was that the legs had been shaved from just above the fetlocks to just below the knees, which is exactly where clipping would be needed before an ultrasound exam could be performed to look for tendon damage.

"Oh, ah always do thayat," Bubba drawled, "this time of yare. That old long hair makes 'em look like plow hosses, ya' know." He gave an easy chuckle. The first red flag started to flutter, if not wave. Cosmetic clipping usually involves most of the lower leg, not just the back side.

Mary, my client and the potential buyer in this deal, had been silent until now. "Why didn't you clip the back legs?" she asked.

"Oh, ah guess we just got busy, and didn't get 'round to it," Bubba drawled. "He's really not a show hoss, anyway."

I reached down to feel and get a better look at the tendons in question, and I noticed a piece of suture material in the skin over one of the flexor tendons. I asked him, "Why is this stitch in his skin?"

"What?" Bubba replied.

"There's a little piece of suture material in the skin over the flexor tendon. Did he have some surgery there?" I asked.

"That ain't no stitch," he replied quickly. "It's just a piece of dirt or somethin'!"

"Look," I said, holding the neatly knotted loop of nylon monofilament suture material between my thumb and forefinger. It had been placed in the skin like a tendon splitting procedure had been performed on this horse for acute tendonitis.

Bubba took the cigar from his mouth and leaned over for a closer look. "Well, ah'll be. Ah don't know what in tha' wu'ld that could be," he said. "Maybe he cut hisse'f, or somethin'. Ah'll have to look in the medical records," he said as he walked away from us. He returned in a few minutes. "Ah just called my vet's office. Thaya' gonna' look up in thaya' records and find out what that stitch is. I'm sho' it's nothin' to wuh 'bout," he assured us.

Although I was beginning to have my doubts about the whole situation, I continued the exam. On both of his front feet, Gray was quite sensitive to hoof testers around the edge of the coffin bone, the solar margin, as well as in the area over the navicular bursa, located just under the middle of the frog. Red flag number two was now fluttering.

His back feet seemed okay. We took Gray out of the barn to watch him trot on the longe line. I prefer to watch a horse trot when I am looking for a lameness. The trot is a two-beat gait, a fact that makes it easier to detect imbalances and abnormalities than at the canter or walk, which are more complex three- and four-beat gaits, respectively. With a gaited horse, however, things can get complicated. They don't trot "square," so sometimes the location of the lameness can be difficult to determine—unless they're real lame.

The day that *I* looked at him, Gray was lame when we observed him on the longe line in both directions. The lameness was consistent and obvious. All three of us agreed that Gray was "a little off" that day.

Next, I performed "flexion tests." This is done by holding a leg up so that all of the joints of one limb are flexed for sixty to ninety seconds. After this time, the horse is led away at the trot in a straight line. Although this test is not specific for any one problem, lameness after flexion is an indication of pain in a joint, tendon, or ligament. Gray was lame in the left rear after flexion. He stayed lame on the left, even after flexion of the other hind limb three or four minutes later. This was not good. The other bad news was that the *more* things I found wrong with Old Gray, the *less* happy Bubba got. I really didn't want to make anybody mad at me, but it sure was turning out that way, and Bubba's attitude made all the red flags wave—vigorously.

Mary asked me, "Do you think an X-ray would tell us anything, Doc?"

"It might," I replied, "but radiology alone may not locate the exact cause of the lameness. To do this, we would need a full diagnostic workup. This would include nerve blocks, more flexion tests and probably an ultrasound." I turned diplomatically towards Bubba. "You understand that, don't you, sir?"

He just stood there, stewing silently, and nodded as a small jet of steam erupted from his collar.

"But if the X-ray was clean," Mary ventured hopefully, "that would mean that he was okay, right?"

"Not exactly," I said. "The radiographs may give us a diagnosis, but the horse is *lame* today, and that poses some very real potential problems."

"What do you *think* is so *wrong* with him, Doctuh," Bubba said, emphasizing the "think" and the "wrong" with unveiled contempt.

"That could only be determined with a more thorough exam," I said.

"Well," Bubba started, then paused, and after clearing his throat pointedly said, "what would be yo'ah *educated* guess?" No effort was made to hide his growing disdain for me.

"Well, my *educated* guess would be that it could be a lot of things, but I'll bet he has arthritis in his left hock, at *least*, and maybe some problems in both front coffin bones and the tendons of his lower front legs, as well," I replied, trying to maintain professional decorum.

"I'd be willing to split the cost of the X-rays with you," Mary volunteered to Bubba. "What do you think about that?"

"Oh, ah *will* have mah vet X-ray this hoss today, but ah wouldn't have *him* do it. He's *yo'ah* vet," Bubba replied as he pointed at me with his chin. I could hear alarms and sirens synchronized with the waving red flags. This was getting worse by the minute.

I walked back outside toward my truck and Mary followed me. She still did not seem to understand that this horse had some real problems, and she really shouldn't buy him unless she was prepared to deal with the expense of diagnosing and treating them, not only *possibly* in the future, but right now. The horse was lame, *right now.* I collected my fee and left the barn thinking I had explained the situation adequately, and she was going to continue looking for a horse *elsewhere.*

Three or four days later, I received a phone call from another lady who was interested in a horse at Bubba's barn. She wanted me to recommend a veterinarian who could perform a thorough pre-purchase exam for her. She had mentioned to Bubba that she was going to have me look at the horse, but he told her that I was not allowed on his place!

Oh, well. As a good Baptist preacher told me one time, the truth shall set you free, but first it's gonna' make you real disappointed!

The next day, I was in for another surprise. Mary called and related further details in the ongoing saga of our Southern Gentleman horse trader. Apparently *his* vet was not interested in getting involved in this case and suggested that, if another opinion was requested, another veterinarian should be contacted. I considered this highly irregular, but I kept that opinion to myself (which is also highly irregular).

This was where the plot thickened. A third vet was called in, and his examination revealed absolutely no lameness and only a very slight response to the flexion tests. Mary pressed for radiographs of the hocks, and a *fourth* vet was called in for his ideas. The fourth one concurred with Dr. Number Three and told Mary that, although she was foolish to want X-rays because the horse was perfectly sound, he would be glad to provide the service.

According to Dr. Number Four, Old Gray did have "degenerative joint disease," "arthritis, in his hocks," but it was "no big deal," and he didn't think it was going to cause any problems. Of course, Mary was real confused, now. She wanted to know what she should do.

"I can't tell you why Gray was not lame when the other two vets looked at him," I said. "As far as the arthritis in his hocks," I continued, "it's not surprising that the radiographs showed some of that, because that's what he looked like after the flexion tests."

"Yes, I remember you said that after your exam," she agreed, "but why would the other vet say that it was no big deal?"

"If he didn't see the horse when he was lame, he might think that it was an incidental finding on a radiograph. Arthritis of the hock, or 'spavin' is a common problem. It usually causes lameness in horses between the ages of about seven and fifteen years. It can look worse on a radiograph than it really is, clinically, for a couple of reasons."

I paused before continuing, "Although it looks like just one joint, the 'tarsus,' or hock, is really four joints. The top joint is the one that moves the most. The bottom three only move a little bit—not enough to noticeably move the lower leg, but just enough to cause pain if there is arthritis present. As the irritation continues over time, the body deposits calcium in these bottom joints. They will become cemented together and, eventually, stop moving at all. This usually won't happen until the horse is about fifteen years old, so up to that age, he may experience a little, or a lot of pain because of the arthritis.

"That's why we see spavin as a clinical problem in the age range I mentioned earlier. Before the age of about six or seven, there usually hasn't been enough damage to the joint to cause problems. After the age of about fifteen or so, the body has locked those lower joints down solid so they don't move around enough to cause pain. We can treat active cases of spavin with injections of joint fluid preparations, like 'cortisone,' or 'hyaluronic acid' (HA) placed right in the joint. This often cuts the pain so that the horse can resume exercise, but the process of fusion can still take years to be completed and multiple treatments are almost always required. There are also surgical or chemical methods of 'sclerosis,' or speeding the deposition of calcium to fuse the lower joints, which, in turn, stops the pain, but any of these treatments are far from foolproof, and produce variable results.

"In other words, what I'm trying to tell you is that, if you already owned this horse, I wouldn't tell you to put him the sleep or anything like that, but we would have to start some type of treatment. This can get fairly expensive when you consider the amount of time that he could possibly be laid up, and like everything else, there is no guarantee that the treatment will help him."

"What should I do?" Mary asked, apparently still not clearly following my lengthy explanation.

"Look for another horse," I said immediately. "It costs just as much to feed a lame one as it does to feed a sound one."

I almost never council clients to buy or not to buy a horse. All I *should* do is tell the client what the problems are and the potential for successful management over the foreseeable future. I felt sorry for Mary, since I knew that she liked the horse and had been given differing opinions. This, added to an intense sales pitch, was not helping her make a decision. It is times like these that we need to trust *one* person and base our decision on that.

_ Yella

"I'm looking at a mare for my daughter," Mrs. Collins said, "and I was wondering if you think you should look at the horse before we buy her."

"It's always a good idea to have a complete physical exam performed on a horse prior to purchase," I said. "There can be some subtle symptoms that even an experienced horseman may not notice that could indicate potentially serious problems."

"Well, our budget is a little tight, so we wouldn't want to spend too much on an exam. How much do you think something like that would cost?"

We discussed my fee, which was quite nominal, for a thorough exam without X-rays or ultrasound studies. I explained that the price of the horse was usually not the largest part of the economic picture. "If you buy a horse without a prepurchase exam and the horse turns out to have a problem later, it may end up costing you quite a bit to diagnose and treat it. Of course, if we can fix it, then you may be okay. On the other hand, some of the lameness problems I see in practice tend to get worse over time. When this is the case, you may not be able to sell the horse to somebody else, especially if *they* get their vet to look at him first," I explained.

Pre-purchase exams are tricky. Everybody wants a sound, sane, pretty horse. Unfortunately, this type of horse can be fairly hard to find. But problem horses are never in short supply. My attitude on this may seem a little callused, but about sixty percent of the horses I see for pre-purchase exams have significant problems. Some of these problems we can manage pretty well; others, we cannot.

We made an appointment for later in the week. I arrived with my usual punctuality and was introduced to Kim, the seller, and her lovely buckskin mare.

"She sure is a nice mare," I said. "What do you call her?" She gave me her long, official, registered name which, like most, was an attempt to include lots of her pedigree. "I'm A Little Poco Pepe Pine Doc Bars O Lena San" just doesn't exactly roll off your tongue.

"Oh," I said. "What do you *call* her?"

Kim grinned sheepishly and said, "Yella," with a delightful drawl that reminded me of home.

"You don't sound like you're from around here," I said. "In fact, you sound a lot like me. What part of Texas are you from?"

I had been teased about my accent from the minute I arrived in California. Of course, I always thought that *I* sounded normal and everybody else had an accent!

"Dallas," she replied. "We moved out here three years ago. I'm a nurse and the job market was better here." She paused and patted Yella on the neck. "I hate to sell her, you know. I just love her, but I've just been too busy to ride her much, and it doesn't seem fair to her."

I usually begin the examination with a few questions about the medical history of the horse. Have there been any illness since she has been here? Any signs of lameness? What is the vaccination and deworming history?

"Is this mare on any medication?" I asked. Of course, the answer to this question is almost always, "No." As I said earlier, it is rare that anyone would drug a horse prior to a potential sale, and they sure wouldn't admit it if they had.

We started the physical exam, as usual, with hoof testers. Although they can apply lots of pressure, they usually don't elicit a painful response in a normal horse. Yella, on the other hand, was very sensitive in both her front feet. Her back feet were not sensitive at all.

"See this?" I said as Yella flinched significantly each time I applied a slight pressure with the hoof tester. "That means she is a little sore along the sole and around the edge of her coffin bone, the large bone in her foot."

"What could that mean?" Mrs. Collins asked.

"Well, it could just mean that she simply has some stone bruises, or been recently trimmed," I explained, "but, looking at the shoes and the nail holes, I'm guessing that it's been at least a couple of weeks since she's been shod. Whoever did it is doing a good job for you," I added. "The mare is sure properly shod. How long has it been since you rode her?" I asked Kim.

"I rode her over at Miller's arena two weeks ago, but she's been in her stall ever since. Like I said, I haven't had much time, with work and all. She's never been lame before."

We took Yella outside and watched her move on the longe line. She was very short-strided and had a little downward head bob when the left foot was on the ground at the trot, indicating lameness in the right foreleg, probably the foot.

We continued watching her move for a few minutes, and she consistently showed us a fairly significant lameness. I stopped the exam right then. The mare was obviously lame, and I wasn't going to suggest that anybody buy her that day, at any price.

"What does that mean, exactly?" Mrs. Collins asked. "Is she really lame?"

"Yes, I'm afraid she's a little off today," I replied. "It's hard to say exactly what her problem is, but I sure can't tell you to buy her like she is now."

"I'm sure she's all right," Kim interjected. "She's probably just got a bruise from the hard arena."

"What do we do now?" Mrs. Collins asked. "I really like this mare."

"Well, just on the chance that she had a minor bruise or something like that," I said. "We could come back in a couple of weeks and check her again, but I wouldn't want her to be on any medication or have new shoes, or anything that might confuse us about her condition."

Everybody agreed to the plan and two weeks later I was back to examine Yella again. This time, she was perfect.

"She looks okay now, right, Doc?" Mrs. Collins said in a way that was more of a statement than a question.

"Yeah," I agreed. "She looks pretty good today." My old suspicious nature was whispering to me that something wasn't right.

We brought Yella back into the barn, and I repeated application of the hoof testers to all four feet. This time, she showed no painful response at all. I continued the exam by listening to her heart and lungs with my stethoscope. I also examined her eyes with my ophthalmoscope. There was no evidence of cataracts or any retinal degeneration. A thorough dental exam revealed the presence of some sharp points on her jaw teeth, which would need to be filed off or "floated" in the near future. There were no abnormalities found during the reproductive evaluation, and despite the cold lubricant on my shoulder-length plastic sleeve, Yella was as cooperative as could be for the entire ordeal.

After I had completed the hour-long exam, I asked Kim if the mare had been on any medication since we'd last seen her.

"No," she said.

"Well, in that case," I began tactfully, "with your permission, I'd like to take a blood sample and keep it for *your* protection, Kim. That way, if somebody should accuse you of doing something wrong, we'll have the proof that she is clean today. Does that sound reasonable?" Kim agreed that it did.

This was my sneaky way of really putting her feet to the fire about whether or not she had given this mare something to mask the lameness we had all seen two weeks earlier. Usually, if somebody is guilty of drugging a horse, this will help to clarify a foggy memory. I have heard responses like, "Oh, well, I just remembered, Doc, the shoer was just out and he trimmed her a little close. I think my boy may have given her a little bute a couple of days ago." Or, "Yeah, Doc, I seem to remember that we did have a little trouble getting her in a trailer the other day, so we did give her a little 'ace' to calm her down a bit."

Kim never batted an eye at this suggestion. So I figured that everything was okay. I never had any intention of actually testing the blood; I just wanted to see her reaction.

About thirty minutes later I was pulling up to the barn for my next call when my truck phone rang. It was Mrs. Collins. She was not happy.

"Kim called me up earlier and told me that the deal was off," she almost screamed into the phone. "She was *humiliated* at your insensitivity about her horse and how you wanted a blood sample! What if you decided to run the drug test six months from now?"

"What?" I said, trying to grasp the logic that still evades me to this very day.

"She's insulted about the drug test, and she won't sell me the mare."

"Well," I started, trying to keep my composure, "if she has nothing to hide, she shouldn't be mad at either one of us, now, should she? Think about it for a minute. You were standing there with a check for five thousand dollars in your hand. That was the price she had asked and you were willing, no, *trying* to pay it. Do you think she would refuse your money if she wasn't worried about *something* in this deal?"

Click!

"Thanks for your understanding," I said to the dial tone. The whole thing seemed so obvious to me; I couldn't believe how badly I had failed to explain it to these folks.

My client at the next barn overheard part of the conversation. It was apparently *real* obvious to him. He said, "Somebody drugging horses?"

That was the first and only time I ever made anybody mad at me for trying to help them avoid a five-thousand-dollar mistake.

_ Never Trust a Sneaky Pony

Dentistry is one aspect of horse health care that is often neglected. The first sign of dental problems is usually weight loss, but many folks don't think of dental problems because the horse almost never complains of a toothache. If the horse is losing weight, many people complain that the stable manager isn't feeding enough, or that the feed is not good enough, or "that mean old mare keeps chasing my horse away from the hay pile." Of course, group feeding situations can present nutritional problems because the dominant horses always eat first. Nevertheless, I always examine the teeth of a horse that is "a little off his weight."

One afternoon a new client called me about a one such weight-loss problem.

"This is William Andrews. I bought a pony from a guy over in Watsonville that told me you said all we needed to do was to float his teeth and get some medicine for his eye and he'd be fine. I got this pony as a birthday present for my granddaughter, an' I'd like to get 'im fixed up in time for the party next month. Can you come out an' see 'im sometime soon?"

I was impressed that my fame had spread over to Watsonville, as I really didn't do much work over there. I told William that I could come see his pony later in the week.

When I arrived I had to admit that although the unknown seller's referral and confidence in my medical ability was flattering, I had never seen this cute little gray pony before.

"What do you call him?" I asked.

"Sneaky."

"How old is he?"

"The guy said he figured he was about twelve, but he wasn't sure 'cause he didn't have any papers," William said. "Can you check his teeth and also look at his eye? I think he might have a little infection in it."

I looked in Sneaky's mouth and guessed that, if he was a Republican kind of pony, he was about old enough to have voted for Nixon in just about any of the elections he ran in. He was missing most of his jaw teeth and those that remained were so out of alignment that they could not be filed or "floated" enough to help him grind his feed properly. One look at this poor pony's left eye told me that he had been blind on that side for many years, and nothing short of a whole new head was going to help him.

I told my new client about my findings, and he was mildly skeptical.

"You can at least float his teeth, can't ya'?" he asked. "I can see that he has 'em all when he opens his mouth." Then he added, "And be careful. He'll bite you when you aren't looking."

As a brilliant diagnostician, I quickly deduced this connection with the pony's name.

I explained that while this pony did indeed have all his "incisors," or his front teeth, he was missing several of the grinding teeth, or "molars," that are normally farther back in his jaw.

"The molars actually start just behind the corner of his mouth and go back in his head to a spot just below his eye," I explained. "These are necessary for the horse to be able to grind his feed. Normally, these teeth are arranged in two long rows called 'arcades' that grind together in a circular motion. His teeth will continue to 'erupt,' or grow out of his jaw throughout life to keep up with the wear that the grinding causes. When one or more teeth are missing, the opposite tooth grows down into the space where the missing one was. After a while, the teeth start to mesh together like the teeth in a gear and hang up on each other instead of grinding the feed smoothly. This is called 'wave mouth.'" I ended my soliloquy eloquently: "In this case, it ain't fixable."

"Well, can you give me some medicine for his eye?" Mr. Andrews was undaunted.

"I'm afraid that pony's eye has been that way for a long time, and there's not much we can do to help him there, either."

"What can we do to help 'im to gain some weight, he's awful skinny."

"You can try one of the pelleted feeds and soften it with a little water or corn oil," I said. "Some older horses do fairly well on that type of feed. His blindness may cause some problems," I added. "Some one-eyed horses seem to get by just fine; others may not be for anybody, especially not a small child. I'd sure be careful."

Although he was disappointed, William accepted the situation and told me that he would try to find a good home for him as a pet for somebody.

About two weeks later, I received a call from a lady regarding an eye problem in a horse. I arrived at her barn one morning and saw the very same pony tied to a fence in the yard.

"I bought him from a guy that said you said all we had to do was put some salve in his eye and he would be okay," she said confidently. "My neighbor said that we might have to float his teeth. Can you do that?"

Where had I heard this before?

I told her the same thing that I had told the previous owner. She was equally disappointed but said that she would try to find him a good home as a pet for somebody.

Another month went by. With so many patients in my busy practice, I had all but forgotten about that cute, little, skinny, one-eyed, gray pony until early one Saturday morning. My long-time friend and client Mrs. Wiggins (you may remember the story of her colt Willie) had me on the phone with a question or two about weight loss in horses.

"I want you to come out and see this pony, Doc," she said. "I can't seem to get any weight on him."

I arrived at the Wiggins' place at the appointed time and saw a familiar pony tied to the hitching post.

"Howdy, old partner," I said as I scratched Sneaky under his jaw. "You really get around, don't you?" He rolled his one good eye at me as if to say, *Here we go again!*

I examined the pony for the third time for as many owners and told Mrs. Wiggins the same thing I had told the first two—it was getting a little redundant. She shrugged and said that she would try to find him a home as a pet for somebody. I knew Mrs. Wiggins would trade a horse, now and then, and I couldn't help but wonder where I would see Sneaky the Pony next.

I didn't have to wait long. A couple of days later, I got another wakeup call from Mrs. Wiggins.

"What do you know about this 'Impressive Syndrome,'" she asked, slightly on edge.

"Why do you ask?" I questioned, "Do you have a horse with the problem?" I knew this was going to get interesting.

"Yeah, well, sorta'..."

I told her what I told you about HYPP earlier in these pages, and that because it is a genetic condition, there is no "cure," and the horse will never "grow out" of it.

"That's what all the other vets have told me," she said without trying to hide her frustration.

"Did the vet who did the prepurchase exam tell you about the gene test that is available to identify carriers of this problem?" Of course, I already knew the answer to this question.

"I didn't get 'im vetted,'" she replied predictably. I knew she was always looking for the bargain horse, only to find out too late why he was such a bargain.

"How much did you have to pay for him?" (My curiosity just gets the best of me sometimes...)

After a long pause, she said, "I didn't *pay* anything for him." And after another, long pause: "I traded that gray pony for him last week, and this new horse has had three 'spells' with this paralysis-thing in the last three days!"

I wished that I had been a fly on the wall of the barn when that trade was going on. I can only imagine, but I strongly suspect that *both* parties walked away thinking, *So long, sucker!*

"This may sting a little"

~Madison Seamans DVM '22

Index of Illustrations

ACKNOWLEDGMENTS

(Don't Skip This Part—It Ain't Too Bad)

Lots of successful people "pulled themselves up by their own bootstraps." As a professional horseman for over half a century (stings a little to write that "out loud"), I have achieved some small measure of success, so I think is it's important to thank the folks that help me get that first pair of rhetorical boots to pull on, if you get my drift. The list is long.

First is my lovely bride, Annette, who has been my partner, editor, riding buddy, and chief critic. She puts lots of red pencil marks on my manuscripts, lets me eat in her kitchen with mud on my boots and blood on my shirt (or worse), and puts up with my late hours and more character flaws than I care to share.

Jim Sorenson of Palo Duro Canyon, Texas, owned the first big horse outfit I ever worked for and taught me that learning to ride was relatively easy: keep at least one leg on either side and your mind in the middle. Learning how to be a horseman will take the rest of your life.

Dr. Leon Scrutchfield and Dr. Mike Martin of the College of Veterinary Medicine, Texas A&M University, who told me: "Don't come up with a treatment plan till you know what you got in your truck"; "Diagnostics is not what you don't know, it's what you don't look for"; and "If you hear hoof beats, don't look for zebras." I heard these so many times from both of 'em, I can't remember the original source.

And who could forget Dr. Joe Joyce, whose encouraging words still ring in my ears: "Don't worry, Seamans, no matter what you do, you can't kill 'em all!"

There were many other instructors at Texas A&M who gave of themselves to push us to be the best we could be. It is because of them that I learned how to think—in the box and out of it—and received a good start on the best education possible from almost forty years of "practice." I am forever grateful.

Thanks to the acceptance committee of the aforementioned university who made the questionable decision to let me in their vet school in the first place. AND to a few people who unwittingly provided enough adversity, pain, and aggravation to drive me to succeed (you probably don't even know who you are, but you have been a true inspiration).

Almighty God, for giving me the work ethic and dogged persistence to keep applying to Texas A&M for seven years. *Seven*.

To my agent, Lisa Hagan, and the great folks at Trafalgar Square Books for taking a chance on me. I hope I don't embarrass you too much.

And finally, to the many clients, characters, and curmudgeons that have provided me with the material for this book. Their humor, compassion, and sometimes stubborn humanness is why *you can't make this stuff up!*